ARCHITECTURE IN FREDONIA, NEW YORK, 1811-1997

FROM LOG CABIN TO I. M. PEI

Daniel D. Reiff

Published for
The Fredonia Preservation Society, Inc.
by
White Pine Press
Fredonia, New York
1997

Published for
The Fredonia Preservation Society
by
White Pine Press, 10 Village Square, Fredonia, New York 14063

ISBN 1-877727-86-5

Printed and bound in the United States of America.

First Edition

1   3   5   7   9   10   8   6   4   2

Title page illustration: *View of Barker Common, showing the Baptist Church, Fredonia Academy, and Presbyterian Church (Episcopal Church at far right), from Johnson House Hotel; painted in 1862 by Mrs. Julia Wilcox Clark (Collection of Barker Library).*

TABLE OF CONTENTS

PREFACE

As an art historian with a specialization in American architecture, one of the factors that impressed me the most positively when I came to Fredonia in 1970 was the range and quality of its houses and public buildings—to say nothing of its striking new campus. One of my colleagues in the Art Department of the State University of New York College at Fredonia was Jesse G. Wright, Jr. (the director of the Michael C. Rockefeller Arts Center gallery), who also enjoyed historic buildings. During that first academic year he suggested I prepare a "photo exhibit" of notable local architecture—since he saw that I was an avid photographer—with a brief text to go along with it, for one of his gallery exhibitions. I had just prepared, a year or so before, a brief stylistic review of the architecture of Georgetown, D. C., written around 62 photographs of buildings between 1765 and 1911 for an architectural survey I had co-authored and edited.[1] An exhibit with some photos and text on Fredonia's buildings seemed like a great idea.

What transpired was the large scale exhibition which opened October 14, 1972, with 234 photographs, as well as paintings, books, furniture, plans, a repeating slide show, and the 124 page illustrated catalog *Architecture in Fredonia, 1811–1972: Sources, Context, Development*. It was thanks to Jay Wright's vision, and his assistants Barbara Lewis Thompson and Norman L. Funicello, that this all came about—to say nothing of the support of President Dallas K. Beal and Dean Robert W. Marvel, and the help of a host of local community volunteers mustered by Mr. Wright, a group which founded The Lakeshore Association for the Arts. (Full acknowledgments for this project, and the current revision, will be found at the end of the book.) The show was immensely popular, and revealed that local architecture had a strong following.

1. Architecture in Fredonia Exhibit, November, 1972.

The purpose of the exhibit, and the catalog, was three-fold. First, I wanted to present a "guide to the styles," similar to Marcus Whiffen's *American Architecture since 1780: A Guide to the Styles* (1969) which had recently appeared, only using *local* structures as the models, to help residents better understand their buildings. I hoped to make clear that each period, whether it was vernacular Federal of the 1820s or Neo-Colonial of the 1920s, had a distinctive design, and details, of real architectural interest. It must be remembered too that in 1970 Victorian architecture was still considered ugly and bad by a great many, suitable only for remodeling out of existence or the wrecking ball. And contemporary architecture, such as the splendid new campus designed by I. M. Pei and Partners, was far less well understood or appreciated than today. As an architectural historian and an educator, this was my first aim.

My second was to demonstrate the wider links of our local buildings with national movements, with the grand pageant of architectural history through the centuries, and also put the buildings in an *urban* context of siting and planning. From my field work and research in Georgetown, D. C. during three summers, and the year 1969–70, as an architectural historian for the U. S. Commission of Fine Arts, I had also been introduced to the importance of "street furniture" and other details—such as fountains, paving, sidewalk treatments, plantings, carriage blocks, and the like, which added to the "urban delight" of a place. I introduced that too into the exhibit and catalog.

But my third concern was for architectural preservation, an outgrowth, naturally, of architectural understanding and appreciation. While teaching at Baylor University in the early 1960s I had started the campaign—which later came to fruition and signal success—to preserve the University's two oldest buildings, and had come to realize the vital part historic architecture, and the preservation effort, play in a healthy and forward-looking community. Thus a theme throughout the catalog, and the final section "A Future for the Past," focused on this movement, which in 1970 was actually a rather new one.

The success of the book, both locally, and further afield, in awakening interest in architecture and even preservation, was very gratifying, but was equally a testament to the superior local architecture bodied forth in the volume. By 1986 all copies had been exhausted, yet the book was seen as a "permanent resource" and still in demand. The fact that by 1996 six out of the seven copies held by Fredonia's Darwin R. Barker Library had been stolen is a real testament of its value to local residents! Now, thanks to the Fredonia Preservation Society, a new edition can be published.

This current edition is a thorough revision of the original text, bringing it up to date after 25 years of looking, recording, studying, and learning—expanding it too with buildings and topics omitted in the first edition. I have largely kept the original "guide to the styles" format as it seems to have worked well over the years. I have been aided in this gathering of new material by both Ann Fahnestock and Donna Carlson, former curators of the Barker Historical Museum, and especially by Douglas H. Shepard. His archival research, since 1985, into the history and dating of Fredonia buildings—and his reading, issue by issue, of all the *Fredonia Censor* newspapers, from 1821 onward—has been of incalculable assistance. Much of the improvement to this volume is due to his generosity in sharing this research with me, and ferreting out data I have requested.

Just as the text has been thoroughly revised, corrected, and up-dated, so have the photographs. Most of these are from my own negatives or copy work. Of the original edition's 236 illustrations, almost all printed by the late Ronald Warren, I have kept 106 prints, and re-printed from the original negatives 41. Thirty-six of the illustrations from 1972 have been replaced by later, improved, views of the same subject. Other photos have been omitted, but with their replacements, and the new material added, the book now has 110 new photos for a current total of 293 illustrations. I have occasionally included the year when some of my photographs were taken when, because of additions, changes, or some other reason, the date might be useful for archival purposes.

I have also added several features to this edition which I think will make it much more useful as a resource for education and research. Following the architectural entries I have included a listing of a few key books on local history which are of continuing value, and some other useful sources. Then I have added citations for a selection of newspaper and other articles which have appeared during the period 1972–1997 and deal with the local architectural scene. They contain a wealth of additional illustrations and information. I have also added footnotes. This has permitted expanding sections which have already taken up their allotted space, and including data and references of more tangential interest throughout. Many people still treasure their original 1972 editions of this book, so when an illustration in that edition, but omitted in this one, still has relevance, I have provided a citation for it.

There is also now an index, skillfully prepared by Douglas H. Shepard, so that one can locate a house address or person's name with ease. The two-page map will permit finding most of the illustrated buildings in Fredonia, and seeing their geographic relationship to each other.

My hope is that *Architecture in Fredonia* in its "new and improved" form will thus continue to be a valued resource in the appreciation and understanding of Fredonia's splendid architecture and other distinctive features, and that it will help inform and enrich all of our lives for many years —and another generation—to come.

— *Daniel D. Reiff*

Besides providing a foundation for the understanding and appreciation of Fredonia's remarkably varied—and high quality—buildings over the years, the 1972 exhibit and book focused also on architectural preservation. The idea of adapting older buildings for modern uses, thus saving most of its original design character—and its place in the historic urban fabric—developed as an important architectural, and cultural, movement in the 1960s, largely in response to the disasters wrought by Urban Renewal during that decade. The redevelopment of Ghirardelli Square in San Francisco, a grouping of 19th and early 20th century commercial buildings, into a vibrant modern shopping and office complex during 1962–64 (second phase 1964–68), and its nearby emulator The Cannery (completed by 1967) is usually heralded as the first major effort in adaptive reuse to receive national attention. My contact with it was while working in Georgetown, D. C. where old warehouses by the C & O Canal were transformed similarly in 1969–70. The passage of the Historic Preservation Act in 1966 (establishing, among other things, the National Register) demonstrated the importance on a national level of this approach.

It was clear, in 1970, that Fredonia was indeed a very well-cared for village, and that there was a general sense of the importance of its historic architecture to its overall quality of life. But I soon found that there were few people really interested in a concerted effort to help raise local consciousness as to the values a well-maintained, and appreciated, historic fabric conveyed. County Historian (and Town of Pomfret Historian) Elizabeth L. Crocker was my only professional ally for many years. Today, however, with a village full of beautifully restored and renovated houses and public buildings, major adaptive reuse projects completed, and a nearly universal understanding of the real benefits—both material and cultural—that the preservation movement has brought, we can sketch out some of the stages in this success following the 1972 exhibition.

After the exhibit closed I frequently gave talks and lectures to any local group who would have me—service clubs, libraries, historical groups, garden clubs, and public meetings in Dunkirk and Fredonia—on the topic of adaptive reuse and historic preservation, in part spurred on by what I considered the disastrous course of the Urban Renewal program in neighboring Dunkirk.[2] I also on occasion wrote preservation-oriented articles for the Dunkirk-Fredonia *Evening Observer*, which always evinced a strong, and civic-minded, interest in architectural matters.

Even nowadays, when the positive values of historic architecture and adaptive reuse are widely understood, it might be useful to list some of the main reasons we value older buildings. First, naturally, is the visual delight they provide us, in overall designs or in intricate details, even if we do not recognize all their historic sources—they're just interesting to look at. When one has studied historic architecture a bit, their interest increases; we can trace the evolution of style, design, and planning for each era, and what was considered significant to the owner and architect. Their varied architectural associations give additional depth to our appreciation. A third factor is that such buildings are vehicles of history. They are the settings where people worked, lived, worshiped, *did* things, and reflect history and life in a very direct way.

Buildings are also cultural expression: they body forth in a direct way artistic, societal, and even personal interests and aims; the "extra expense" of making a building a "high style" rather than ordinary design was often unrelated to functional concerns, but was personal or cultural. Fifth, buildings are vivid testaments to craftsmanship, to the evolving interests and skills of carpenters, masons, woodworkers, stone carvers, plasterers, painters, and others who actually brought the structure into being. And buildings too are records of our technological advances, both as to structure and materials, and as to the mechanical systems (heating, lighting, sanitation, ventilating, etc.) we now take for granted. But perhaps the most significant appeal of older buildings is that they provide us, in a community, a "sense of place," a feeling of roots, often considered an important desideratum for psychological well-being.

Adaptive reuse of older buildings helps keep them around, but also makes good economic sense. Usually it is cheaper to renovate an existing building than start from scratch, and one retains features not easily duplicated today. Many also recognize the tourist appeal of renovated downtowns, preserving the best of the past for the benefit, and enjoyment, of the present.

One of the first salutary developments in Fredonia was Mayor Charles St. George's decision, in 1974, based on a presentation at a New York State Council of Mayors meeting, that having a Historic District for downtown Fredonia would be a good idea, and could possibly help in getting outside funding. In 1974–75 Miss Crocker and I, with the help of one of my advanced students, the late Ronald Wooden, completed this work (finally entered into the National Register in 1978). A broad overview of the values of adaptive reuse and architectural preservation reached a wider public audience in 1975 when I gave the Kasling Memorial Lecture at the college on that topic. I also began, in 1977, to focus two of my courses in American architectural history (19th century and 20th century) so that ample sections included Fredonia architecture, with the 1972 book as one of the texts. The Mayor also established in 1977 a Village Downtown Renovation Committee, aimed at sign and facade improvement, but there was only lukewarm response to being given free advice on what they should do in these matters.

2. "Old Main" after conversion to Senior Citizen housing (photo 1984).

The first major triumph of adaptive reuse was the conversion of Fredonia State's former Old Main building, a key landmark—both visually and historically[3]—in the center of the village, into Senior Citizen housing, during the period 1977-79. Only the vision and tenacity of developer Henry F. Sysol, Jr. prevented Old Main from being demolished; it continues today an important local landmark.

Although this was a first glimpse at proper cleaning and adaptive reuse of a historic structure, it was, really, unique. More "typical" was the careful exterior cleaning (by chemical washes, not the destructive sandblasting heretofore common) and adaptive development into offices of the old Fredonia Fire Hall, in 1979–80. This was a near thing. The dowdy building, though structurally sound, was considered an eyesore by many. When put up for sale by the village one developer's plans were (as he later told me) to cut it down to one story "and throw some siding around it." Fortunately a pair of local businessmen, David Palmer and David Bryant, had other ideas. Mr. Palmer had heard one of my preservation talks (at a Rotary Club meeting) and thought the building had a lot of potential—especially since, being in a Historic District, it could now receive important federal tax credits if renovated according to Department of Interior guidelines. It was a stunning success, and set the tone for all future projects: careful cleaning of the brickwork, in-fill work to match exactly, and interior renovation which kept much of the original wood trim and pressed metal ceilings (even where not fireproofed and reinstalled, they are still preserved *above* the later dropped ceilings).

3. *Fredonia Fire Hall (37 Church St.), fall 1979.*

4. *Fredonia Fire Hall after renovations, summer 1980.*

The success of this venture alerted a local bank, owners of the White Inn property, to a new possibility, and Palmer and Bryant were approached about taking over that as their next venture. They did, and beginning in 1980, the historic renovation of the building, and its wonderful interiors (largely due to the expertise of Nancy S. Palmer, a former art historian) have made the White Inn a major highpoint in Renovated Fredonia.

The next concrete example of successful rehabilitation of exteriors of local buildings was the removal of massive signs which blocked the ground floor arcades of the Odd Fellows building, and

5. *The White Inn in 1980, prior to renovation.*

6. *The White Inn, after renovation.*

the painting of details in striking "Victorian" colors, in 1983. The now revealed arches alerted many to the values of really looking at and studying older buildings for the architectural qualities —designed with such skill generations ago—which give them their architectural meaning.

The addition to the north end of Darwin R. Barker Library erected in 1983–84 (by architect Carol Case Siracuse) was another significant lesson. This wing not only incorporated an old gas station—years before remodeled into the Town of Pomfret Offices—but skillfully blended it all with the brick buildings around it by using a vernacular modern colonial style. It finished off the east side of the Barker Common Historic District with sensitivity. In 1983–84 was also when the college, thanks to the determination and persuasiveness of President and Mrs. Dallas K. Beal,

7. Odd Fellows building and signs, 1975.

8. Odd Fellows building after sign removal and renovation.

restored Fenner House (badly damaged by fire in 1979) for the college Admissions office—when the state bureaucracy had claimed it was too far gone to save without massive expense. Dallas and Kris Beal proved them wrong.

The late 1970s and early '80s saw a renaissance in domestic architecture. More and more local residents began painting their homes in multi-color schemes rather than just pure white, which

9. Town of Pomfret Offices and Barker Library, May 1983.

had been the custom for decades. One of the first was 193 Central Ave., which in various campaigns beginning in 1979, was back to its original color contrast—highlighting all its architectural details—by 1985. Using "Victorian" style colors also gradually appeared more frequently. An early example was 233 Temple Street (tan body with cream trim) of 1977; two of the most influential were 29 Newton St. of 1982, and 134 Temple St., a highly visible location, in 1989. This was also the period when I began (in 1983) a decade-long research project, based heavily on local

10. The same site after construction of new wing.

houses, on mail-order and pattern book designs, some of which information has found its way into this revision.

Probably our greatest local preservation success was the saving and renovation of the Village Hall and the Opera House. This long and complex campaign (an outline of the saga can be gleaned from the article listings in "For Further Reference" at the end of this book) began in 1982. It was the subject of much public debate, the active support of hundreds of local citizens, and numerous articles in the *Observer*, during 1983–84. Finally, after careful deliberation on all the factors—economic, cultural, even political—Mayor Louis Mancuso and the Village Board voted to renovate the existing Village Hall (rather than move out to another site, or demolish it and build a smaller replacement). It was in 1984 during this vigorous campaign that the Fredonia Preservation Society was formed, an organization which has remained a vital force for preservation to this day. The Village Hall was carefully restored and renovated between 1985 and 1989.

11. Fredonia Village Hall and Opera House after renovation.

12. The "1891 Opera House" after renovation.

Having an even greater impact on our community, however, was the restoration and renovation of the Opera House attached at the north of the 1891 Village Hall. This million-dollar project was taken on by the Preservation Society and, with the financial support of local individuals, countless hours of volunteer labor, a major grant of $262,000 from New York State through its

Environmental Quality Bond Act, the work was carried to a triumphant conclusion between 1986 and 1994, when it reopened. It remains an important cultural force—and a beautiful space—today.[4]

Downtown Fredonia also transformed itself during these years. The first prominent facade renovation was at 2 W. Main St., a brick building by Enoch Curtis but painted white long ago. With the paint chemically stripped in 1985, the elaborate brick cornice was more readily visible, and the polychromatic window voussoirs finally revealed. In 1986 the adjacent buildings, the Victorian Gothic Day Building, and the "Murphy Block," (two Italianate buildings plus the east portion of the 1852–53 Centre Block) were revitalized—the former by cleaning of brickwork and repainting the cornice; the latter by painting the three buildings in attractive colors to highlight the architectural details, another project of David Palmer and David Bryant. Thereafter, building after building, year by year, we have seen many of Fredonia's downtown structures revived by facade renovation and repainting.

13. *West Main Street buildings prior to facade improvements, Feb. 1986.*

14. *The same buildings after renovation and repainting, Aug. 1986.*

The thorough restoration and repair in 1991 of the two beautiful Mark Fountains (1901) in the Barker Common was another preservation triumph. Their revitalization, which restored portions missing for decades, carried out by sculptor Robert Booth, with student assistants, was a meticulous achievement. In part due to this success, renewed attention was focused on our historic Common, and a Barker Common Renovation Committee was started in 1992, which ultimately came up with a renovation plan for the whole Common. The attractive Victorian-style information booth, Victorian-style benches gradually superseding the functional models of the 1970s, and improvements in the planting and lighting, are due to this renewed interest. Soon thereafter the Downtown Revitalization Committee was formed, which aided local merchants, via free consultations from myself and theater set designer Gary Eckhart, in improving their facade designs, signs, and color schemes.

One of the most recent adaptive reuse successes was the transformation in 1996 of the old, and long-vacant Freshmart store on Center Street by its refacing in brick, addition of a corner tower (echoing the Village Hall tower in its form, and calling attention to the building on axis with Church St.) now transformed into doctors offices (John Haas, architect). The building opened for use in early 1997.

Finally, the Department of Transportation reconstruction in 1996–97 of Route 20, running through the center of Fredonia, resulted in the introduction of many attractive traditional features. The downtown now has early 20th century style light standards, and trees planted in cast iron grates along the sidewalk (which also has insets of brick paving along most portions), all adding to the appeal of the historic downtown.

This quarter-century of preservation progress, thanks to the dedication, hard work, and persuasion of many, was not without failures too. In fact, in the glow of these important successes it is easy to forget all the setbacks during this same period. A review of some of the major ones will remind us of what has been lost in this same 25 years, and how vital a continued diligence in making the most of our architectural heritage is to the unique character and appeal of Fredonia.

One of the best examples of Second Empire domestic design, a mansarded house at 161 E. Main St. was demolished between my first visit to Fredonia in January, 1970, and my moving here that summer—ignominiously (and ominously, as it was in a neighborhood of houses, and only two doors from St. Joseph's Church) to be replaced by a burger stand. But the most profound architectural loss was the destruction by fire on Feb. 28, 1973 of the Masonic Building, which was a key centerpiece of downtown Fredonia, facing the Common. The space still vacant, its loss is felt even today. Only four years later, 1977, lower Main Street was transformed by the destruction of a whole range of early buildings, swept away for the site of the new fire hall.

15. *Mansarded Villa, formerly at 161 East Main St.*

This architectural and cultural loss was, in a way, fore-ordained, since the master plan for the development of the downtown was prepared in 1969 by an out-of-town consulting firm with utterly no feeling for or interest in our historic buildings. The 1969 plan chose this site for a new municipal complex (presuming the destruction of the old village hall) as it was a "blighted" area. This sort of clean-sweep plan was spawned by the Urban Renewal programs of the 1960s which, however, by 1970 had been challenged, and in places (such as Newburyport, Mass.) discarded for adaptive reuse programs which made the most of the historic fabric, while adding new construction.

This site was thus chosen for the fire hall; no matter that it was (contrary to official guidelines) on a busy state highway, on a known floodplain, and at the base of a steep hill! Something of the struggle to preserve some of these old structures is outlined in the *Observer* clippings, between 1975 and 1977. Lost were the old Henry Hotel, a vernacular dwelling with Italianate wing; the brick Lester House (1834–35); the stone Hamilton House (from 1829), an utterly unique building for Fredonia; and finally the Sackett Building (c. 1903) with behind it, the old McCleur Mill (c. 1840?). Nowadays the visual and architectural possibilities for adaptive reuse, to highlight "Historic Fredonia," would be evident to most, but in 1975 they were just "blighted buildings" that had to go in the name of progress. The view from the creek shows that though recast in similar style, c. 1903, the Sackett and McCleur buildings were of different ages—and in fact a vintage photograph from the late 19th century depicts the mill (after having been remodeled and increased a half-story in height) closer to its original form. Inside, the massive side trusses, though hidden by the inserted floor, could still be seen on the upper level, and (though cut through here and there) discerned below as well. All of this—and all of its potential for delighting and enriching future generations—was swept away in 1977.

Fredonia's historic downtown suffered another blow in 1978 when three businesses, housed in well-maintained Italianate structures, were damaged by fire. Though repaired, the architectural character was lost (though with today's savvy and experience, could easily be re-constituted) to be

16. View of 72, 76, 80, and 90 West Main St. in 1975.

17. Sackett Building and McCleur Mill from creek (photo 1976).

18. McCleur Mill and Hamilton House in the late 19th century.

19. Interior of McCleur Mill (photo 1977).

replaced by bland facades which visually dilute the historic character of the area, though recent repainting has mitigated some of this.

A less dramatic nibbling away of the historic fabric of the village was the inexorable paving over of brick streets. These gave a distinctive charm to much of Fredonia, and were generally in excellent condition—to an engineer's mind, the perfect base for a modern, smooth (though hardly maintenance free ...) macadam road. I do not have a complete record of this, but those I chronicled include Church and Day Streets, paved over in 1978; Risley St. macadamed in 1980; and Summer, White, Gillis Streets, and Porter Ave., in 1993. In 1997, the southern half of Lambert Ave., the last of two more-or-less surviving brick streets (Curtis Place is the other), was blacktopped.

The demolition of interesting old buildings in Fredonia's downtown renewed in 1981 when the newly created office for Erie Savings Bank (later Key Bank) took over the D. F. Straight Building (1916) on W. Main St., and needed to have convenient parking next door—and eradicated the three 19th century buildings at the corner of W. Main and stretching down Center St. All these had some real character, especially the corner one (which, due to the bend in Main St., formed a visual terminus when looking from east to west). I always found its combination of tawny brick, quarry-faced stone lintels, inset decorative facade tiles, and bold galvanized metal cornice, a striking pivot for Main Street. Behind it, the other two structures also had visual appeal, especially the third structure with its fancy metal cornice.

These were the major losses in downtown Fredonia, but other notable buildings further afield should also be recorded: Enoch Curtis's Gymnasium (1898–99) formerly behind Old Main, was removed in 1979, and Harry Beebe's old Fredonia High School demolished in 1992.

Some interesting Fredonia homes disappeared during this period too. A Queen Anne style house at 14 White St. (with an elaborate oak staircase inside) was torn down in 1973; a Greek Revival home at 150 Newton St., with side entrance wing, was demolished in 1977; a square Italianate house with fine late 19th century porch was cleared from 18 White St. in 1988; an attractive Greek Revival house at 157 E. Main St., with good facade doorway and a side wing with distinctive classical window surrounds, was demolished in 1992; and a Queen Anne-style Radford Home (from their 1903 catalog, p. 57) at 232 W. Main St., was bulldozed in 1997.[5]

Another way in which Fredonia's historic housing stock has been lost has been through remodeling. Later in this book I explore remodeling in the 19th century, where we find that most of those cases replaced the earlier mode with a later stylistic variant of real architectural interest. But most remodeling in the 20th century strips off the distinctive architectural features—often just those that give a plain house its stylistic cachet—and gives us nothing in return. One well-

20. *Commercial buildings on East Main St., 1972.*

21. *The same group repaired after 1978 fire.*

known local example is the transformation in 1974 of a two story Queen Anne-style house at 156 E. Main St., which had some Stick Style detailing, into a one-story wing for the American Legion next to it—though it should be noted that by about 1920 the original house had been considerably altered already. The old Baptist Parsonage at 78 E. Main St., a gabled Italianate house with paired brackets, arched windows, and fine (somewhat later) porch, was stripped of these

22. *West Main St. at Center St., March 1981.*

23. *Center St. buildings, looking toward W. Main, March 1981.*

24. *Cornice detail, 10 Center St.*

"Victorian excesses" probably in the 1920s, and was given a shingled upper portion and clapboarded lower story—vaguely Craftsman in feel. It has since been remodeled again. Actually there are quite a number of older houses which, over the years, have had their Gothic Revival trim, Italianate brackets, or Queen Anne porches removed, leaving little of visual interest. Before the understanding of the inherent values of varied architectural styles, which in Fredonia grew slowly during the 1970s and into the '80s, such remodelings were not uncommon.

Fredonia has had, over the years, some remarkable cases of massive remodeling of houses which have utterly destroyed their original character, style, and even scale. *Politesse* prevents me from singling out any of these for brickbats, but anyone wishing to see examples of egregious architectural remodeling need only consult the editorial "Remuddling" page of the *Old-House Journal*, a national hands-on preservation magazine founded in 1974 (and now with a "readership" of over 300,000). Some of the most astonishing examples of insensitive—or willfully vicious—remodeling in the United States are illustrated there.

One local concern which can be highlighted, however, is the use of aluminum or vinyl siding on older homes. During the 1960s and '70s the standard approach was to strip off all historic detail—which was a bit harder to side around, and would need painting anyway—and "modernize" the building in that manner. Details, such as window frames, frieze bands, and corner strips, which help give scale and definition to carefully-thought out 19th century designs, were swept away. Sometimes the loss of detail is mitigated by using properly scaled narrow siding, reinstating corner strips, and even a polychromatic treatment—which does maintain the general outlines of the historic design. But there is still much of visual delight, and historic interest, that is lost, as the example depicts.

25. *Queen Anne style house gable detail prior to siding.*   26. *The same detail after siding.*

But siding historic houses with aluminum or rigid vinyl ("regular" vinyl siding has a slightly dished, or concave, appearance, which ironically is the shape worn-out weathered clapboards take) can often be done effectively. Several good examples are found in Fredonia, notably at 233 Temple St. (aluminum), and 30 Central Ave. (rigid vinyl).[6] It is interesting to note that some Fredonia houses, formerly sided, have had their "modernizing" cladding removed, and the original clapboards repaired and repainted—as at 29 Newton St. and 73 Eagle St. At 40 Newton St. a late 19th century house, long covered with artificial siding, has recently been released from this cocoon and is in the process of restoration; ghost images of lost window trim permit replacing lost architectural features which give visual richness to the historic fabric. And this is not unique: the number of Fredonia residents who now see their homes as "historic artifacts" worthy of sensitive care to bring out their best is, for an architectural historian, very gratifying.

It should be pointed out, however, that alterations in architectural scale can significantly change the character of a neighborhood. A recent remodeling on Central Avenue has brought this issue forcefully to bear for many residents. The original dwelling was a small Greek Revival house containing a recessed porch and delicate porch supports (similar to those at 171 Eagle St.). With its neighbor 172 Central, they evoked "early Fredonia" with its small houses spaced out widely away from the center of town—a rare survivor of an early urban pattern. In the spring of 1996 this house was swallowed up in an elephantine "addition"—the original dwelling technically still exists behind the two ground floor windows at the far right. Clearly, the character of the street has been dramatically changed.

While we can be very proud indeed of the progress, during this past quarter-century, in recognizing and appreciating our architectural heritage, and acting intelligently to safeguard the best of the past for the enrichment of all in the present and the future, it is progress which has had its ups and downs. But I believe that most Fredonians now recognize the advantages and delights in treating our historic buildings with understanding and respect. They are, really, a legacy, built perhaps years ago for generations long gone, for *their* aims and ideals. Although we may currently "own" a building, it really belongs to the village's broader cultural heritage; we are merely its current custodians. In art, if you possessed a fine 19th century marble statue and decided you didn't

27. Houses on Central Ave. (photo 1993).

28. The same view in 1997.

really like it, why you would sell it, and get something else—not try to "improve" it by lopping off its nose and ears, or filing down the drapery! Buildings are, after all, art too—the arts of design and planning and craftsmanship.

Architectural preservation saves more than just remnants of our artistic heritage. Notable buildings are the settings for, and visual evocation of, our cultural aspirations and achievements. They are, perhaps, even more potent documents of life and society than are the written records of libraries and archives. As such I believe they deserve our unceasing efforts to keep them, and nurture them, as vital parts of our daily lives.

In order to put Fredonia's buildings into the proper architectural context, and see some of the basic trends and theories which underlie them, it is helpful to briefly review some of the essential factors in the development of 19th and 20th century architecture. To do that we must first, however, glance at the bases in the preceding centuries as well.

Most people are familiar with at least the broad outlines of the development of western architecture, from the Romanesque and Gothic forms of the Middle Ages to the classically based structures of the Renaissance and Baroque—and thereafter, the proliferation of styles in the late 18th and the 19th centuries. By looking at some key concepts in the development, we can help put the rapid changes of the 19th and 20th centuries in perspective.

The most striking feature in the Italian Renaissance's revival of classical architecture was that the early 15th century architects, especially Brunelleschi and Bramante, studied Roman ruins not just to learn the ancient forms of capitals, moldings, vaults and detailing, but to rediscover the ancient *principles* of building—the proportional relationship of spaces, facades, columns, interior divisions, and so on. This they adapted, using the classical vocabulary of columns, pilasters and arches in their buildings (churches, palaces, hospitals, etc., of a sort unknown in ancient times), so that while the results might bear only a slight resemblance to actual Roman structures, the *principles* of design were felt to be much the same. The preceding Gothic architecture had, of course, also been based on elaborately conceived proportions, and design principles, but also on a structural system which gave rise to distinctive forms.

The new Renaissance discoveries of classical principles—just as the scholars were rediscovering Roman literature, philosophy, poetry and science—were codified by Leon Battista Alberti in his *On Architecture* (1452, 1485) which set out systematically much that had been learned of Roman proportions, modular relationships, correct use of orders, and the like.

The architectural innovations in Renaissance Italy were spread far, both by architects invited to other countries in the 16th and 17th centuries, and by architectural publications. Sebastiano Serlio's treatise, full of useful information and illustrations, appeared in six "books" between 1537 and 1551 and was popular in England as well as France. Andrea Palladio's *Four Books of Architecture* (1570) was even more influential. He discussed the classical theories of proportion (based ultimately on harmonic ratios derived from Pythagoras), and showed their application in the many villas and palaces he built or projected in northern Italy. He also provided careful engravings of classical orders, as well as a few complete ancient buildings.

But when the Italian late Renaissance style was adapted outside of Italy—where, after all, the classical past in the form of ruins had been a ubiquitous presence—it was seen more as a type of *decoration*, often grafted to older, Gothic-based architecture, rather than as a new mode of *design*. Whimsical hybrids were sometimes the result.

In early 17th century England a remarkably pure form of Palladian architecture was introduced by Inigo Jones, a court stage designer turned architect, who had traveled in Italy, knew Palladio's actual buildings, and owned a copy of the *Four Books of Architecture*. Jones' two major structures (1616 and 1619) are remarkably close to Palladio's sense of design for palace facades, and were immensely impressive in a country still building in a late medieval mode.

The popularity in England of the new style grew steadily in the 17th century, both for its inherent beauty, and its associations with a newly recovered body of classical knowledge. Palladian forms received a second, more academic, impetus in the early 18th century when the architectural amateur and patron Lord Burlington designed his country villa, Chiswick House (c. 1725), in conscious emulation of Palladio's Villa Rotunda (c. 1550); he also sponsored a major publication of Palladio drawings. While not the only source of classical style in the early 18th century (Wren's classical mode of Baroque architecture is the other major current), Burlington's Palladianism was especially influential. Throughout the 18th century, architects such as the Adam brothers adapted and refined this classical style of building to changing tastes.

For minor building (not palaces or major churches) the classical form was equally important. Vernacular building (which is not architect designed, but is more of a local and traditional builder's solution, often remaining constant for generations) grew more regular and less Gothic in the later 17th century. It could now be given greater sophistication by the use of some classical details, not, of course, provided by major architects, or drawn directly from Palladio's treatise, but rather as interpreted by country builders using popular manuals (which became very popular in the 18th century) based on the great folios. These handbooks provided engravings of appropriate classical door casings, cornices, mantels, and examples of the classical orders which the builder could use to embellish his otherwise plain structure.

These manuals were the source of much sophisticated design and decoration in 18th century Georgian America, just as in other outlying regions of England. They were the last vestige of this English adaptation of Italian Renaissance art.

In 18th century Europe there was however, a reaction setting in to the Baroque (and Palladian) architecture, a reaction which took the form of a return to simpler and more pure architectural design. This return was made possible by the rediscovery and publishing of engravings of the ruins of actual *Greek* buildings both from Southern Italy and from Greece proper. The first volume of a key work, Stuart and Revett's *Antiquities of Athens* appeared in 1762. Here were more pure, geometric, "primitive" forms, the massive Doric order, the simple, self-contained Greek temple shape, the stolid post and lintel system rather than arches and vaults. Soon these more "basic" architectural elements were being used, first for minor garden pavilions (1758), later for major buildings. The movement was aided by parallel, and interconnected, trends of a few architects in England and France for a more simplified and geometrical architecture. But it will be noticed that Greek features (and original Roman forms rediscovered) were used largely as a new formal and decorative vocabulary of architecture; no radical change, as that of the Renaissance, had occurred, though a sharp stylistic break had indeed been made.

The first major Greek Revival building in the U.S. was the Bank of Pennsylvania, in Philadelphia, of 1798 by Benjamin Henry Latrobe, an English architect who settled in America in 1793. This style, especially popular in the United States, also was combined, in most major Greek Revival public buildings of the next 50 years, with advances in fireproof vaulting, giving the monumental structures an equally impressive and geometrically simple interior space.

But it is immediately apparent that the Greek Revival (to be discussed more fully below), a break from the Baroque—which had been, after all, a chain back to the Renaissance, and from there directly back to Rome and Greece—was the beginning of many other "revivals." Almost any revival style, as deemed appropriate for associational, stylistic, or formal reasons could be employed. Furthermore, an esthetic concept which was developed in literature, as well as painting, in the 18th century—the concept of the Picturesque—gave further purchase to the whole idea of stylistic revivals. Very briefly, the esthetic of the Picturesque admired and advocated asymmetrical, irregular forms, with light and dark contrasts, and approved of the association (often literary, pictorial, or historical) that they would call up. In a way, this provided a sort of *theoretical* basis for the development of architecture in the 19th century. Furthermore, it suited a society that was rapidly changing, largely due to the industrial revolution, and a clientele less knowledgeable in the traditional (classical) literature. The first major stylistic revival, essentially parallel with that of the Greek, was the Gothic Revival. And more followed rapidly.

Thus we now have some basis to examine the apparent (and sometimes actual) confusion of 19th century architecture. One thread is, of course, the sequence of revival styles. This was linked to the development of the Picturesque esthetic, but also to *association*, an essentially literary (and pictorial) factor. In America, the Greek Revival, visually evoking the democracies of Greece, by its architectural formality and monumentality was perfect for major public buildings. The Gothic Revival, because of the medieval tradition, was most appropriate for churches and chapels; the castellated, associated with fortresses, for prisons, or even baronial estates; vernacular Italian forms, for informal yet imposing country villas; Egyptian, for funeral or medical structures; and so on. Naturally, popular adaptations for more modest houses, especially after 1840, gave the many revival styles an even greater remove from their original conceptions.

A second thread, as mentioned, was the Picturesque esthetic. We can trace much of the 19th century architecture as a fulfillment of the tenets of the Picturesque. In major architecture, as the century progressed, there is indeed an increasing restlessness of silhouette and roof line, of in and out projections and porches, which cause spatial, as well as light and dark, variety. The compactness or intricacy of the buildings as three dimensional form shows this clearly, from Greek Revival to Gothic Revival and Italianate, to Second Empire and High Victorian Gothic. So that while the vehicle (or style) for the forms changed, there were certain general underlying principles.

Thirdly, just as exterior form changed during the century, so did interior space, seen most clearly in the generally greater and greater freedom of plan throughout the century, taking the domestic dwelling as example. The standard plan for the smaller house of the 18th century in America was either the side hallway or central hallway plan—a wide passage, usually containing the stairs, having usually two rooms off one (or both) sides and running from the front of the house to the back. A variation of this formal arrangement can be found in many 19th century houses as late as mid-century (Figs. 29 and 30). But, with greater informality in external composition of masses (especially possible with Italianate forms), the interior could also become less symmetrical or rigid. In the villa plan illustrated (Fig. 31) not only is the asymmetry clear, but the sequences and nature of spaces is more complex. The hallway is entered from an enclosed vestibule, which is entered from a semi-enclosed porch; one side of the house has a light trellis veranda of semi-permanent construction; the drawing room and library are joined together by a wide doorway (not unknown, however, 40 years earlier) and are both extended by bay windows poking outward at each end. This great spatial freedom and complexity can be seen especially well in more elaborate houses, such as Fig. 32. It will also be noticed that now the hallway (passage) has become more of a hall (room), with the stairs in a separate, but connecting chamber. The number of space-expanding bays and double doors is also increased. And the rooms, almost pinwheel fashion, are grouped compactly around the central hall. Toward the end of the century this hall often is expanded into a useable living space, and contains a fireplace as well as the end of the stairs. In the example chosen (Fig. 33) the parlor flows freely from this entrance hall through a wide arched opening. Since reference will be made to the plan of most major buildings shown in this study, this sketch of development may be found useful.

A final thread which helps give perspective to the architecture of the 19th century is the development of new technology. While the art of building had not really changed much from the Renaissance up to the later 18th century, one development—that of wrought, but especially cast iron—began to make a distinct difference. While at first cast iron was used mainly to replace stone or wood pillars, it found more and more uses (especially in engineering, for bridges and train sheds) in the 19th century. With the construction of the famed Crystal Palace for the exposition of 1851 in London, gigantic structures of iron and glass, with interchangeable parts, and a largely non-historical style, were shown to be feasible. Many critics hailed this innovation as the architecture of the future, using new 19th century technology; but others were horrified by the non-allusive (non-historically based) styles that called up only themselves—materials and forms. But cast iron *did* become more common for commercial buildings especially from the 1840s onward in the United States. To be accepted however, they were generally designed in the full regalia of classical arches and columns, often like a Renaissance Venetian palace. But though clothed in his-

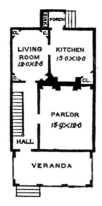

29. Plan of "A Simple Suburban Cottage" (by Withers and Vaux) from Calvert Vaux, **Villas and Cottages** (New York, 1857), p. 108.

30. Plan of "A Suburban Cottage in the Italian Style" from A. J. Downing, **The Architecture of Country Houses** (New York, 1850), fig. 34.

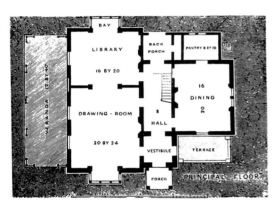

31. Plan of "A Villa in the Italian Style, Bracketed" from A. J. Downing, **Cottage Residences** (New York, 1842), design 6.

32. Plan of "A Wooden Villa, with Tower," from Vaux, **Villas and Cottages**, p. 181.

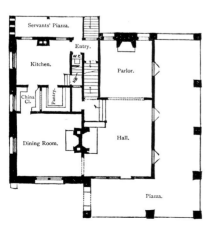

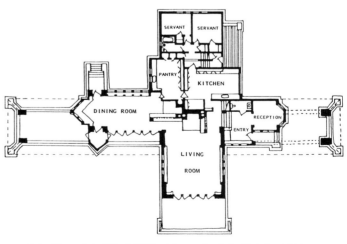

33. Plan of a Shingle Style House by John Calvin Stevens, 1885.

34. Plan of the Ward Willits House, by F. L. Wright, 1902.

torical garb, and thus disguised, the fact that this new technology *was* being exploited was a major step.

Clearly then, much was happening in 19th century architecture; and some of it provided the springboard for the development of modernist architecture of the 20th century. By examining briefly several important late 19th century architects, we can see the sources of many key features of 20th century modernism.

In the architecture of H. H. Richardson, during the 1870s and '80s—though his style was vaguely Romanesque in its forms—we find a mode of conceiving of, and organizing, his buildings *not* primarily as stylistic features, but as masses, solids and voids. The buildings were conceived of first (in tiny sketches) in terms of overall bulk and form, and then were more fully elaborated. Thus it went further than the apparently similar massing of Italianate designs, since they often owed as much, or more, to their plan as to any primary concept of the exterior as sculptural form. Richardson also used his materials—granite and sandstone, shingles, timbering and brick —in a way to bring out fully their natural texture or quality—an ideal of "honesty" in the use of materials, and the preference for "natural" materials and colors (in contrast, say, to stuccoed brick or to wood painted white), already extensively used by A. J. Downing and others 30 years before. In this use of natural materials and textures for their own esthetic ends, and conceiving of a building as mass and form, and not essentially "stylistically" or allusively, we have an attitude common in much 20th century architecture.

The idea of rejecting no longer viable historical style, and of rethinking traditional solutions of both the structure as well as the form of a building, was also put forth by Louis Sullivan in the 1890s in his skyscrapers (such as the Guaranty Building in Buffalo), and in the early 20th century in his small banks. The style he evolved is clearly distinctive, but it is his *own*, and owes very little to historical precedent. This trend, of a non-historical style—treating the building as form and material, as solution to interior spatial needs—was carried out fullest in the early 20th century by Frank Lloyd Wright, who had worked for Sullivan. In his houses of 90 years ago we have some of the first full statements of this new architecture, one that is conceived with form and materials, and what they can be made to do in an essentially abstract way—in themselves—rather than as allusions to past styles or orders. The plan of one of his early houses (Fig. 34) shows how even the interior, continuing a trend toward freer and more abstract space, breaks with the heretofore common idea of individual rooms, and is conceived rather as one living space flowing into another, around a central core, the fireplace.

In Europe during the 'teens and '20s an abstract modernist architecture developed as well. Their new mode of design was influenced in part by the Art Nouveau "revolution" of around 1900, but also by rapid industrialization. By the 1930s European modernist design began to be enthusiastically propagated in America. It soon became the dominant thread for commercial and public architecture, and remained so into the 1980s. In a way, therefore, much architecture in the 20th century developed a new *principle* of design, involving spatial and formal concerns above, and often excluding, anything stylistically historical.

Yet we must not forget that architects working in traditional styles (and updated variants of them) continued to have their advocates throughout this whole period. The popularity of Henry Bacon's Lincoln Memorial (1915–22), or John Russell Pope's National Gallery (1936–41), should remind us of this. Thus a duality—modernism and traditionalism—have existed side by side in most of 20th century American architecture, and can be seen in Fredonia's buildings as well.

This sketch of some of the currents in past architecture should help put the buildings of Fredonia in a more meaningful context, and tie together some of the points which will be made when discussing the individual structures.

During the 18th and 19th centuries, even professional architects had recourse to publications on building which provided them with whole facade designs, and all manner of details for inspiration. To make scholarly tomes (like Palladio) accessible to builders and master-carpenters, manuals based on these expensive works were produced—and also included practical details of framing and construction. Such architectural books, in one form or another, were used to the end of the 19th century.

The second half of that century also saw the growth of books of house designs for which you could order (for a fee) a set of plans—and by 1900, one could sometimes order all the materials to build it too! In the early 20th century this process was refined further by some companies precutting the lumber at their factory for the plans chosen. Such catalogs permitted up-to-date house designs to be erected by carpenters in even the remotest areas.

Below are listed and described a sampling of such books, some of which have specific Fredonia links (as noted in the individual building entries).

Andrea Palladio, *The Four Books of Architecture*, trans. by Isaac Ware (London, 1738). After Alberti's treatise, Palladio's (1570) was the first major theoretical as well as practical volume on the new developments in Renaissance architecture. He includes the various classical orders of columns (and proportions), plans and elevations of his own villas and palaces, bridges, structural and construction data, and engravings and plans of many ancient edifices. The proper proportional relationships in rooms, facades, etc. are discussed throughout.

William Pain, *The Carpenter's and Joiner's Repository; or, a New System of Lines and Proportions for Doors, Windows, Chimnies, Cornices, and Mouldings, for Finishing Rooms, &c. &c.* (London, 1792). This is an example of one of the many carpenters manuals which were common in the 18th c., which included much technical data on framing staircases, and other complicated carpentry. It also provided details for emulation: cornices, mantels, door casings, etc. The forms of the various orders are also carefully shown.

Asher Benjamin, *The American Builder's Companion, or, A System of Architecture Particularly Adapted to the Present Style of Building* (Boston, 1827). Benjamin, a Boston architect, published the first carpenters manuals specifically adapted to American tastes and needs. The first edition of this work appeared in 1806; in addition to the orders, interior details and framing instructions are included. A few house facades and plans (Federal in style) are also shown.

Minard Lafever, *The Modern Builder's Guide* (New York, 1833). One of the many publications of this New York architect, this contains many Greek Revival designs for interior and exterior trim, designs and plans for houses and churches, and the usual detailed plates on carpentry techniques, and the classical orders.

A. J. Downing, *The Architecture of Country Houses; Containing Designs for Cottages, Farm Houses, and Villas* (New York, 1850). The second of Downing's influential books on architecture (the first in 1842), Downing discusses at great length his ideas on what a villa (or cottage) should be, as well as some technical information, but which is not nearly as detailed as the previous carpenters manuals. The body of the book is the series of designs of completed and projected buildings (by himself and others) which are shown in perspective views and plans.

Calvert Vaux, *Villas and Cottages. A Series of Designs Prepared for Execution in the United States* (New York, 1857). Vaux, an English-trained architect, was Downing's partner for two years (1850-52) and this book includes many buildings they designed together. It follows the same format as Downing's books.

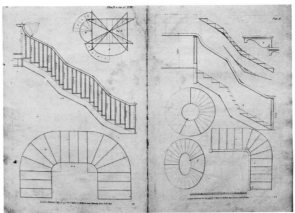

35. William Pain, *The Carpenter's and Joiner's Repository; or, a New System of Lines and Proportions for Doors, Windows, Chimnies, Cornices, and Mouldings, for Finishing Rooms, &c. &c.* (London, 1792), Plates D and 46.

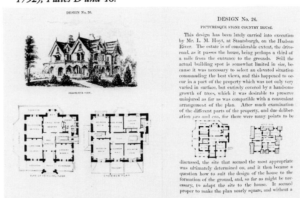

36. Calvert Vaux, *Villas and Cottages. A Series of Designs Prepared for Execution in the United States* (New York, 1857), pp. 282-83.

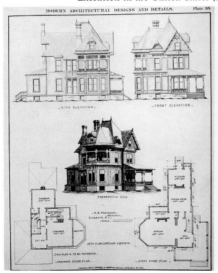

37. A. J.Bicknell and William T. Comstock, *Modern Architectural Designs and Details ... showing New and Original Designs in the Queen Anne, Eastlake, Elizabethan, and other Modernized Styles ...*(New York, 1881), Plate 38.

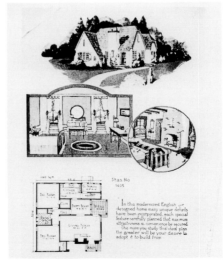

38. Floyd A. Dernier, *Distinctive Homes, 22nd ed.* (Los Angeles: Lumbermen's Service Bureau, n. d. [1920s]), p. 22.

Illustrated Catalogue of Ornamental Iron Work, Manufactured by Janes, Kirtland, & Co. (New York, 1870). This trade catalog has a full variety of fountains, lawn statuary and animals, urns, gazebos, pedestals, benches, fences, etc. in cast iron; some designs are remarkably close to items to be found in Fredonia. This sort of concern supplied vast quantities of such ironwork throughout the country.

Amos J. Bicknell, *Detail, Cottage and Constructive Architecture,...showing a Great Variety of Designs for Cornices, Brackets, Windows, Caps, Doors, Piazzas...* (New York, 1873). This is a return to true carpenters manuals, for while plans and perspectives of houses are given, most emphasis is on framing information, exterior and interior details, etc., aimed at the carpenter and builder. He published a great number of such books.

E. C. Hussey, *Home Building* (New York, 1875). A curious volume which lists all manner of building information as the subtitle indicates: "A Reliable book of facts, relative to building, living, materials, costs, at about 400 places from New York to San Francisco." Plates depict 45 designs for houses consisting of a perspective view, and floor plans. It was a popular builders book. Dunkirk and Jamestown (but not Fredonia) are included, pp. 250–51.

A. J. Bicknell and William T. Comstock, *Modern Architectural Designs and Details...showing New and Original Designs in the Queen Anne, Eastlake, Elizabethan, and other Modernized Styles...*(New York, 1881). It contains a wealth of useful data for the builder or architect. The designs are provided by lesser architects of New York and New Jersey.

James W. Shepp, Daniel B. Shepp, *Shepp's World's Fair Photographed. Being a Collection of Original Copyrighted Photographs...of the...Buildings...All Described in Crisp and Beautiful Language.* (Chicago, 1893). Although trade journals and publications were the major disseminators of new architectural developments, picture books of this sort certainly aided in spreading the popularity of the Academic Revival of the 1890s. Both exteriors and interiors of the fair's buildings are shown (as well as their contents).

Number 500 General Catalogue of E. L. Roberts & Co. (Chicago, 1903). This firm of "wholesale manufacturers of doors, glazed sash, blinds, mouldings, fine stairwork, art and window glass, mantels, grilles," and other such items represents the sort of "mail-order details" that local builders or architects could avail themselves of. In 441 pages thousands of designs are depicted, with measurements and prices.

Aladdin Homes, Catalog No. 31, 4th ed. (Bay City, Michigan, 1918). Aladdin was the originator in 1906 of the pre-cut "package" house, taken up soon by many others (Sears, Wards, Sterling Homes, etc.). Attractive perspectives, plans, and details and even interior views, of 57 houses large and small are presented, as well as a selection of summer cottages, garages, and barns.

Home Builders Catalog, Second Edition. (Chicago, 1927). A vast compendium (over 1,200 pp. long) of house designs of all sizes and styles, blueprints for which could be ordered by mail. Included also were essays on interior design, and a large section on building materials and equipment (furnaces, lighting, plumbing, windows, interior woodwork, roofing materials, bricks, plaster, etc.), oriented to both the architect and builder, and the prospective homeowner.

In a small town one usually has the feeling that somehow the buildings just "got built." One seldom thinks of the many craftsmen, contractors and builders, as well as architects, who were active in their construction. By briefly examining the careers of a few of the local builders and architects, and also the role and work of the architect in general, some of this sense of anonymity can be dispelled.

The early settlers clearly had no architects: in the rude wilderness log houses, built by common sense and an ax, were the first constructions. But once cut lumber was available, more weather-tight frame houses could be erected. But again, these were usually the plainest vernacular structures, their form and shape determined by the spanning capacity of beams, need to keep out the cold, the roof pitch calculated to shed snow, and the desire for the cheapest possible structure, rather than any stylistic aim. Of course the builder or carpenter might well be recalling the plan and structural form of other simple buildings he knew, but generally there was no sophisticated embellishment.

Most settlers in those days needed to have varied abilities—including building. An individual for whom documentary evidence survives who well represents the varied skills of early settlers is Aaron L. Putnam.[7] With his wife Dolly and small daughter Jane, he came to Fredonia from Massachusetts in 1834. Putnam's main skills were farming and carpentry. In 1835 he wrote to his brother Nathan: "I think I shall stay here in the village this summer and work at carpenter and joiner work if nothing happens about scythe, snath, sash and pail business." Although he inspected farms he thought of buying, he also bought and sold land (and made a profit on each transaction).

In these early years he worked some as a hired craftsman. In an 1836 letter his wife mentions that "Aaron has been to work on the meeting house most of the time. It is now finished..." [He] is [now] gone to work a finishing off a hatters shop." But Putnam also built for himself, as he writes in a letter of 1837: "I am now buisy refraiming one of my old houses whitch I have moved on to one of my back lots, to rent."

There were undoubtedly a great many Fredonia settlers who, like Putnam, could turn their hand to building when needed, but who were not full-time carpenters.

But by the second settled generation, with increased prosperity, professional carpenters could find ample use for their skills. The first Fredonia carpenter/architect was John Jones.

Jones came from a family of Welsh carpenters; his father, Thomas Jones, styled himself "Joiner," and had another, older, son, Thomas Jones, Jr. who was also a carpenter. An account slip of October, 1820 lists father and eldest son paid at 3/6 and 3/- per day while John Jones, probably still a very young man, received only 1/6 per day. The same account slip lists yet another Jones (David) who may have been a third son in this profession.[8]

John Jones, who came to America from Wales in 1824, settled in Westfield, New York in 1830. His first work in Fredonia seems to have been Trinity Episcopal Church, built 1834–35 in an early form of Gothic Revival. But his real design skill seems to have been in the new Greek Revival mode, and the Fredonia Presbyterian Church of 1835 was a good expression of this style. In 1836 he built 20 Central Ave. (a transitional Federal Style/Greek Revival house) for Thomas G. Abell, and the Abell Hotel on W. Main St. for him in 1837, the year Jones moved to Fredonia. In 1839 he bought a house on W. Main St. and rebuilt it with a majestic five-columned Doric portico a full two stories tall. With such an impressive advertisement of his skills in domestic design it is not surprising that soon he was building grand houses: the William and Elijah Risley mansions in about 1843, and the Levi Risley home about 1845. He was probably the designer and builder of most of the mature Greek Revival structures in Fredonia. Jones would have learned this new style from the study of carpenters manuals such as those by Minard Lafever (which provided a wealth of details and designs, and a few model facades), and also from inspecting the work of other carpenter-architects in Chautauqua County.

But the dividing line between carpenter and architect was rather hazy: in the remodeling of the Episcopal Church in 1849, he provided the estimates for the work, but was also employed as

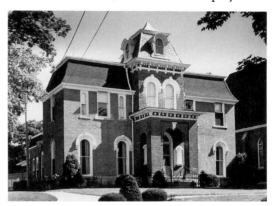

39. *Levi Risley House (c. 1845) by John Jones.*   40. *145 E. Main St. (1868-69) by Enoch H. Curtis.*

a carpenter. John Jones was killed in 1852 by falling scaffolding while working on the tower of the Baptist Church, which he had designed.

The next major carpenter—who became a full-time architect—was Enoch A. Curtis. He began his career just after the Civil War, and thus filled the gap left at the death of Jones. A good deal is known of Curtis since biographical sketches were published about him during his lifetime.

Born in Busti, New York on July 19, 1831, Curtis was from an old New England family; his father had come to Jamestown, N.Y. in 1829, soon buying land for a farm in Busti. Enoch Curtis went to school locally. In 1852, finding "building operations…occupation more attractive than farming," he was apprenticed to a local carpenter and joiner. He thereafter practiced this craft until 1862 when he joined the army. Curtis became a Captain in Company D, 112th Regiment Volunteers, and was seriously wounded in the battle of Cold Harbor in June, 1864.

After the war, Curtis moved to Fredonia. He gave up his former work as a skilled carpenter, presumably because of his injuries, and established a hardware business. Although as a carpenter he undoubtedly had had recourse to builders manuals (though the technical data in them were largely what craftsmen would learn in their apprenticeships) he now set himself to studying design books and other volumes on architecture to train himself to be an architect. One of his first designs was a very up-to-date Second Empire dwelling he built for himself in 1868-69 at 145 E. Main St., with interior woodwork by Robert Wolfers.

Curtis designed a great many impressive houses and public buildings in Fredonia during the next 35 years. These include the Presbyterian Church (1875), the A. O. Putnam House (1878), the N. A. Putnam House (1880), the remodeled Johnson House Hotel (1892), Forest Hill Cemetery Gate Houses (1895), and his own residence at 50 Central Ave. (1901). His published biographical sketch notes that he designed "many of the finest residences, churches and public buildings of Western New York and Northwestern Pennsylvania." His buildings have been located in Dunkirk, Brocton, Olean, and Panama, New York; but he also had an extensive business during the 1870s and '80s in Bradford, Emlenton, Erie, Greensburg, Oil City, and Titusville, Pennsylvania. References to at least 28 Pennsylvania buildings—churches, houses, schools, city halls, an opera house, and commercial blocks—have come to light. Since his style was quite varied—including Richardsonian Romanesque, Second Empire, Victorian Gothic, and variations of the Stick Style, Shingle Style, and Colonial Revival—he clearly kept up most capably with the latest stylistic developments. These would have been available in books, monographs and trade journals (such as *The American Architect and Building News*). Curtis died October 4, 1907.

The name of a third Fredonia architect of the early 20th century should be mentioned here, Harry P. Beebe (1865–1929). Not a lot is known about his career or buildings. His father, Milton E. Beebe, was a "well-known Buffalo architect" (according to the *Fredonia Censor* in 1889) who studied architecture during the period 1865–73 in Buffalo, Chicago, New York City, and Worcester, Mass. He set up as an architect in Buffalo in 1873, and his son undoubtedly trained under him; Harry was later associated with him in Buffalo. But Milton seems to have retired from active work in 1884 when he moved to Fredonia and purchased the Elijah Risley House, which he remodeled somewhat.

Harry Beebe is listed in Fredonia directories from 1906 onward as an architect. A few of his buildings have been identified. A design by him for the Stapf Building (Dunkirk) was published in *The Grape Belt* March 5, 1907: "H. P. Bebee [sic] of Fredonia, architect of the Graf Building,

41. Fredonia Grange (1915) by Harry Beebe.

and for the Independent congregation's new church, drew the plans and will be in charge of the construction." In Fredonia it is known that he built the old Fire Hall (1902–03), the addition to 108 Central Ave. (1913), The Fredonia Grange (1915), the house at 266 Central Ave. (about 1917), the White Inn (1919), and the old Fredonia High School. Many other local buildings by him undoubtedly await discovery.

In the later 20th century, the three architects who are illustrated in this book—Nelson J. Palmer (Dunkirk), I. M. Pei & Partners (New York) and Carol Case Siracuse (Fredonia/Dunkirk) —represent the professionalism which evolved more fully in the late 19th century; they prepare designs after studying the requirements, and supervise construction, but are not contractors also (as some 19th century carpenter/architects were).

A glance around Fredonia shows at once that there are scores of smaller dwellings, from the late 19th through the mid-20th century, with a distinctive architectural style at once historically recognizable: English cottages of various types, American Colonial, "reform" types of the early 20th century—Foursquares and bungalows—which have well-thought-out design. Where did these come from? Many were based on "mail-order plans," that is, their blueprints were ordered from firms specializing in up-to-date designs for the middle-class (such as Radford Architectural Co. or Home Builders Catalog Co.). A few were "mail-order houses," from companies (like Aladdin, Sears, or Bennett Homes) which provided all the materials precisely cut and fitted for a local carpenter (or even the home-owner!) to construct. And local carpenters and contractors themselves, informed by such catalogs (and by what architects throughout the region were building) were adept at drawing up plans and designs for houses that also reflected the popular historic modes, to be discussed in more detail later in this book.

In a way, the progress of the building art in Fredonia is a microcosm of the progress of the field over the centuries in America. It too began, in the 17th century, with the simplest crude shelters, followed soon by substantial vernacular houses (often late medieval in form). Throughout the 18th century much greater sophistication was achieved by builders using manuals which provided cornices, door casings, and other details to improve their houses. Some men of learning, such as Thomas Jefferson, who were amateur architects, had access to the folios of major architects in Europe and could erect buildings which began to approach those of professional architects in Europe in originality. But the profession of "Architect"—a person paid to work out the needs of the specific project, provide plans and elevations, and supervise the construction—was not really established until Latrobe began his work in the late 1790s. Charles Bulfinch, for example, working largely in Boston in the late 18th and early 19th centuries, was indeed close to being a "professional," but he was also employed most of his life as a city official, and, as was common with "gentlemen architects," would often give away, gratis, plans for worthy causes, or for friends. Latrobe, trained in the European professional manner (and also a fine engineer), began the field on a more stable course.

Architectural training at this time, even among the most well-known architects, was largely by apprenticeship. Robert Mills and William Strickland, in the early 19th century, learned architectural theory and practice by working under Latrobe; and this system was common into the late 19th century. Other architects—like Minard Lafever, John Jones or Enoch Curtis—entered the profession via the craft itself, learning to be carpenters and joiners first, and then studying the many books on architectural theory, design, and history available.

The numbers of such books is quite amazing. For example, during the 1840s, at least 48 such books were published in America; in the 1850s, 88; and after a down-turn during the 1860s because of the Civil War, in the 1870s 126 were issued! Perhaps the establishing of schools of architecture in America—the first, MIT, in 1865, followed by Cornell in 1871, Illinois and Syracuse in 1873, Columbia in 1881, Pennsylvania in 1890—even stimulated architectural publication. During the 1880s 192 new books appeared! And since the professional press also had thorough coverage of theory, design, and all manner of practical matters (as could be found in *The American Architect and Building News*, Boston, founded in 1876) local carpenters or architects wanting to keep up with the latest developments had almost a glut of resources to assist them. Today, the many trade journals keep architects informed as to latest stylistic and structural trends (the basics having been learned in architecture school), with the more involved technical matters available through industrial catalogs and suppliers.

This brief glance at the nature of the architectural profession in the 19th and 20th centuries will help us to see Fredonia's buildings in proper perspective.

Very often, knowledge of how a town was settled—and why—can help to elucidate the present plan and the pattern of architectural growth. Equally, the buildings themselves can contribute to a better understanding of the way, and direction, the town grew. By examining first some of the facts of the early history and settling of Fredonia, and then analyzing some of the results achieved by the late 19th century, we can get a better idea of how the present plan of the town was arrived at.

The history of the region in which Fredonia is situated is probably familiar to most. Indian occupation apparently began with the early Mound Builders, followed from the 13th to mid 17th centuries by the Eries, who were exterminated by the Iroquois in 1656. The Senecas, in league with the Iroquois, were the tribe that occupied this area in the 18th century when Robert Morris bought the land from the state of Massachusetts in 1791. He soon sold the tract to the Holland Land Co. (a group of Dutch banking houses) who, after the Indian claims were bought in 1797, surveyed the land between 1798 and 1800 and began selling parcels to pioneers.

The first three settlers at the present site of Fredonia came in 1803, built log houses on the east and west banks of Canadaway Creek, and began clearing the heavy woods for farms. The site was chosen because the only east-west trail forded Canadaway Creek here where the first settler, Thomas McClintock, had located his cabin. But these early settlers soon left, selling their land in 1807 to Zattu Cushing (who had come in 1805) and Hezekiah Barker. By now several other families had arrived and the nucleus of a village begun.

Although many of the first settlers chose the higher land on the west side of Canadaway Creek, others soon began to build their log, and presently frame, houses on the east side, where the current center of town is located. The first commercial structure, a tavern in the home of Hezekiah Barker (who had arrived in 1806) was located here, on the west side of what is now

42. View of Fredonia from the hill at Day Street and Central Avenue, probably late 1860s.

Barker Common. Soon other commercial establishments and improvements sprang up; Barker and another settler built a grist mill on the creek in 1807, and right after it, a saw mill. Elijah Risley, Sr. arrived that same year, and built a bridge across the creek in 1809. His son soon opened a grocery store (west side of the creek), but thereafter, settlement and businesses, such as the Leverett Barker tannery, tended to cluster along the length of Main Street, the principal road running across the creek and through the center of the settlement.

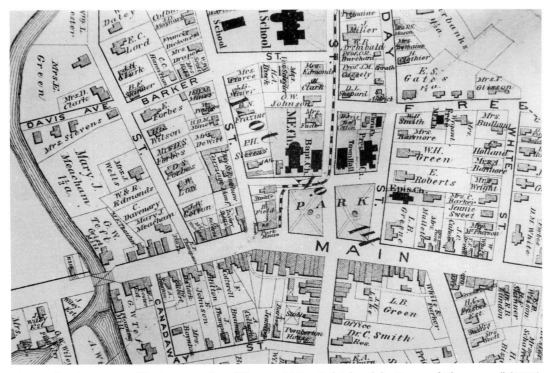

43. Barker Common, and business area, from "Illustrated Historical Atlas of the County of Chautauqua" (1881).

Fredonia rapidly prospered. By 1807 there were perhaps twenty-five families in the area. In 1809 Fredonia got its own Post Office, named Pomfret Post Office, after the township. Main Street was more regularly laid out, and Squire White, the town's first doctor, arrived. By about 1820 a stagecoach route passed through town; several streets generally parallel to the creek (and perpendicular to Main Street) were developed. Frame houses were rapidly replacing log dwellings. Soon the town had its own newspaper (1817), and in 1818 even a development next to the creek (Cascade Hamlet) for a number of trades—several smithies, leather workers, and wagon builders and soon a stone cutter, and a cabinet maker.

As can be seen, the basic form of the town was established only a dozen years after the first settlements. The creek, running roughly north and south, was crossed by Main Street; more or less parallel to the creek, several streets ran off of Main Street, north and south. Some, as Eagle Street, were roads to other towns; Temple Street was the other north-south route east of the creek. To the west, Chestnut Street, and Seymour (then Ridge) Street were the main routes. There were a few side streets which still survive today, such as Water Street. Central Avenue was then a mere trail northward to property owned by Squire Morton (108 Central) and Daniel Pier (316 Central); then it petered out in the dense woods. By the fortunate gift of Hezekiah Barker in 1825, a large plot of ground, later divided in two, became the center of the village. Thus the framework for the settlement's growth was established.

Although Fredonia had not been consciously planned or laid out (as some frontier towns were), but rather had grown up as the creek, original trails and roads, farms, and settlement patterns dictated, the growing village soon clearly established logical urban divisions. Commercial structures were erected around the creek, and on Main Street (primarily the south side). Around the Common were the major public buildings: the Mosley W. Abell Hotel to the west, on the

44. Methodist Church, Baptist Church, Village Hall, and Presbyterian Church, about 1900.

45. The same view, 1997.

Main Street corner purchased from Barker in 1814; at the north side the Baptist Church (built 1823), the Fredonia Academy (1822—though the two gothic towers at front were added only in 1850), and the Presbyterian Church (1835); and, on the east side, the Episcopal Church (1834–35). On the periphery of the Common, and on the streets running off from it (and off Main Street) were many early residences, especially on Eagle Street, though of course some houses (as those of the Risley brothers of the early 1840s), like country estates, were a little further from the center of the new village.

This logical basic pattern, in spite of rapidly proliferating streets and side streets, was maintained throughout the 19th century, and to the present day. In an early view of the village, looking southwest toward Barker Common, one can clearly see that the major public structures (the Presbyterian Church, Fredonia Academy, and Baptist Church, most prominent) form a focal point by the Common, with small, mainly vernacular houses gradually filling the space around. The shade trees, planted in regular rows after the land was cleared, are still rather small. Twenty-five years later, this central area (Fig. 43) was almost fully built up. The north side of the Common had an imposing row of churches, with the Village Hall, by 1890-91 replacing the Academy building; and even today, in spite of the visual hole left by the demolition of the Presbyterian Church, the effect is maintained.

The same is true of Main Street and its commercial buildings. A view on East Main of about 1875 shows the wide range of commercial buildings lined along the street, from handsome little Greek Revival shops near the center of the photograph to, further down, imposing Second Empire structures. The same view almost a century later shows that subsequent building simply filled in the spaces, or replaced a few earlier structures.

West Main, containing the oldest three-story brick commercial block, had changed even less (by 1972) since the view of about 1885 was taken. Except for small Greek Revival shops being

46. South side of East Main Street, c. 1875.

47. The same view, 1972.

replaced by nondescript 20th century structures, the original late 19th century fabric was astonishingly well preserved, maintaining the variety and richness of architectural styles which give a visual history of the urban growth. Alas, the loss of the Masonic building to fire in 1973 has "broken open" the urban block, and deprived West Main of one of its key, sophisticated, architectural focal points.

One of the finest early residential streets was Eagle Street, as well as parallel Cushing Street, where many Greek Revival structures are still found. But Greek Revival houses were also built on Temple Street, Forest Place, and Center Street, off of Main Street to the north, and also dotted

48. South side of West Main Street, c. 1885.

49. The same view, 1972.

along East and West Main Street. While mid-century houses helped fill in these and newer streets near the center of town—and also provide an attractive residential enclave along Canadaway Street, one of the oldest—by that time grander houses were also being constructed on the outer ends of old streets, as East Main, or on new streets such as Central Avenue, extended to Dunkirk by mid-century. Thus Central Avenue—especially wide, and with houses set well back (up to 50 and 75 feet!) from the sidewalks—became one of the major areas for late 19th century homes that showed clearly the wealth and prosperity of the growing village.

As can be seen, the "natural zoning" that this pattern of growth provided (and the nature of the original settlement fostered) has been maintained quite successfully to this day. Public buildings still surround the Common; the commercial structures are still concentrated largely along the central section of Main Street; attractive residences are still conveniently located only a block or two from the village center; and residential development still grows (and fills in lots) in the more outlying areas. Appropriately, the College Campus as developed in the late 1960s provided a transitional zone with the residential community around it with buildings at the periphery of the campus of brick, and of domestic scale (see Fig. 251); those at the center, less visible from the outside, are more formal, being of poured concrete and of considerably larger scale.

Thus, by happy chance and good planning, a felicitous urban scheme, which worked well in the 19th century, continues to provide a pleasant and enriching environment for Fredonia's inhabitants—and a congenial setting for its notable buildings.

50. South side of West Main Street, and edge of Barker Common, 1997.

31

Squire White House
Seth Cole House

formerly 52 E. Main St.
formerly Dunkirk

Although neither of these buildings is standing today, they represent the two earliest types of houses of Fredonia. Plain vernacular houses, such as the Squire White House, were once very common prior to, and overlapping with, the Greek Revival of the 1840s. But less well documented are its antecedents—log houses or cabins.

The Seth Cole House (1805) represents the type of log house that must have been common in Fredonia in its first few years. With the land being cleared of trees, logs of all sizes would be freely available, and fashioning them into simple but sturdy dwellings would have required few other tools than an ax. The dimensions of one such log house (a Williams family) built about 1805 are recorded as being 12 x 16 feet. Houses, barns, the first school (1808), all were of logs; they were obviously dark, somewhat drafty, and not very comfortable.

When sawed timber became available in 1808, more convenient frame houses could be erected. The Squire White House, formerly at White and East Main Sts., was built in 1812, three years after the doctor came to Fredonia. His financial success was due to his dealing in land, not his medical skills.[9] Such plain, almost styleless houses are called vernacular because they are essentially traditional buildings whose mode of construction is centuries old, and whose design is due more to purely functional, and structural, needs than any stylistic aims. (In Europe, true vernacular houses remain almost constant in design for centuries; their distinctive style and character are provided by the kind of stone or wood, thatch or tile, common to the area).

This lack of any exterior embellishments is seen in the Squire White House. The narrow clapboards overlap snugly to keep out the weather; corner strips seal and hold down the ends of the clapboards; the doors and windows have simple functional framing. The window panes are very small, twelve in each sash, a form which died out in most major buildings by around the mid-18th century.

Structurally, the house would have had a traditional heavy wood frame of 8" square timbers (lower sill, top plate, and corner posts), with 4" square studs all the way around. But many early Fredonia houses dispensed with the studding and covered the exterior with vertical boards—which economically replaced the studs and also provided an underlayment for clapboards or shingles at the same time. Quite a number of local houses have this treatment, discovered in remodeling or demolition. The view in the attic of 18 Canadaway Street depicts this method. The boards, 1½" thick, are 15 to 16" wide.

The interior finish of the Squire White House was probably as plain as the exterior, the rooms rather small, with, in each of the four corners of the house, the heavy framing timbers boxed in, and projecting somewhat into the room. The wing to the left, with a door at its right side, is probably his original log dwelling of 1809, which was kept, improved with larger windows and siding to match the main house built in 1812. Keeping the original dwelling in this manner was not uncommon. This little wing apparently had a small entrance alcove (lighted by the transom of four panes over the door) which might have had a stair to the space under the eaves; if so, it emulated a common 17th century form. Dr. White's house was moved off the property in 1868 (he had died in 1857) and was demolished in 1903.

The Squire White House represents the type of vernacular building which was common for the first frame houses of Fredonia. Others still exist, but because of the common practice of improving them, when money permitted, by remodeling them in the latest style, it is not easy to pick them out.

51. House of Dr. Squire White, 1812 (demolished; photograph c. 1855).

52. Remains of Seth Cole House, 1805, near mouth of Canadaway Creek (demolished; photo c. 1915).

53. Vertical boarding in 18 Canadaway St.

William Hamilton House, and
Ebenezer Lester House

formerly 76–80 W. Main St.

Two of the oldest masonry structures in Fredonia for years escaped much notice. The building to the right was built in 1829. An old plaque, formerly next to the front door, later inserted in a modern fireplace against the west wall, read: "Hoc aedifisium/Erectum/Aera Architectonica/A.M. 5829./Being the 4 Febry's [?]/of antimasonry A.D. 1829." The building was constructed of stone (hidden by the stuccoed facade) with dressed stone lintels over the doors and windows; this could be seen on the rear wall of the building. It is here also, on a lintel over a second story door (originally a window) that the builder's name is given: "Wm. Hamilton, 1829." From the plaque's rather curious Latin it appears that the builder belonged to the Masonic Order, which had been established in Fredonia in 1816.

The structure is vernacular in form, with smallish windows and thick walls, the color and texture of the stone formerly providing the major esthetic aspect. The stepped gable ends, a simple and less complicated form of finishing the end walls than sloped gables, are reasonably common in the early 19th century. Though used at times for fire protection from adjacent structures, it was essentially a treatment people simply liked, since one finds it on plain wood structures as well, even when free-standing.[10] There may be some slight influence, in the regularity of the forms (and the shape of the gables), from the more sophisticated Federal style, popular up to about 1825 in more settled areas (see next entry). The interior, changed years ago, was one large open space in 1972. E. A. Lester is listed on published maps as owner in 1854 and 1867, and his estate in 1881. Later frame extensions were added to the rear.

The brick dwelling, perhaps originally a shop, next to it was built in 1834–35, and shares the east wall of the stone building. (It was, therefore, most likely built by the same owner.) The style is, however, somewhat more sophisticated even though there are no elaborate cornices or decorated lintels (flat brick arches are used). The three-bay facade, with the wide door in the center— the second floor door is an altered window—has the general proportions of a Federal style house of the 1820s. Again stepped gables, somewhat more elaborate in form, are used, a feature which is known in many localities in the Federal period. The Barker House of 1821, now much remodeled, originally had stepped gables as well. The brick walls, though painted, showed signs of some re-working; 19th century iron tie rods helped hold the building together.

The interior here deserves special note. The ground floor was opened up as one large approximately square room, with a chimney at the east wall. The ceiling to this unobstructed space is formed by the original 8" x 10" beams, making a clear span of 28 feet. The beam edges (a plaster ceiling was never inserted) are all decorated by beading. A stair to the second floor was against the rear wall. Because of this clearly original open space, it is supposed this was built as a tavern or shop. Later, as a dwelling, the first floor had light partitions, but these were removed by 1972. The second floor was divided into rooms by more recent partitions. Except in 1867, when the building seems to have been owned by a Mr. Parker, Lester is shown as the owner (1854, 1881). Both of these venerable structures were demolished in 1977 (along with numerous other nearby buildings) to make way for the new Fire Hall now located on this site.

54. *Lester House and Hamilton House (both demolished; photo 1975).*

55. *Rear view of Hamilton House (1829), late 19th century photo.*

56. *Row of Federal style commercial buildings, c. 1815, in Newburyport, Mass.*

57. *Detail of stonework, rear facade of Hamilton House.*

Zattu Cushing House 171 *Eagle St.*
Richard Woleben House 46 *West Main St.*

By the time Fredonia's early settlers had amassed enough wealth to build more high-style (rather than just vernacular) houses, and there were craftsmen and materials available for elegant work, the Federal style (popular between about 1790 and 1825 in urban centers) was near its end. But there are still a number of dwellings that can be pointed to that represent this style, or influences from it.

The Federal style superseded the 18th century Georgian mode after the Revolution and simplified it by the use of thinner moldings, less elaborate surface treatments, and interiors which got away from overall paneling, or heavy orders, and tended toward larger areas of painted or plastered walls. Mantels were of more classical design. There was considerable flexibility and variety in its house types, as these two examples suggest.

The Zattu Cushing House was erected in two campaigns. The rear wing, visible at the far right in the photograph, was built first, around 1812 (the porch is later). The exterior was probably a simple vernacular design, and the plan turns out to be a very old one too: the front door leads into a small lobby with a closet, behind which are stairs, and a chimney. To the left and right are the main chambers, with small rooms along the whole back—thus a typical 17th and early 18th century vernacular plan. This portion has a cellar, and the floor joists visible there are made of logs.

In late 1817 Cushing, a widower, remarried and (according to a *Censor* article of Dec. 1, 1909), "built the front part of his house after he married his second wife," or about 1818. This portion shows the Federal-style detailing. The ends of the simple two story three-bay block have the gables treated like classical pediments, but with cornice moldings very thin and delicate—a Federal approach. The semi-circular fan louver visible here is also a popular Federal motif. The simple doorway in the first facade bay, with side- and over-lights, and even the delicate porch supports, are appropriate to the style. This front wing provides a new and grander entrance hallway with stairs, and a large parlor with fireplace to its right. The Zattu Cushing House is a rare survivor of this "colonial" style brought to the rustic frontier.

The second example is, technically, no longer extant: the body of the house still stands, but a commercial front was added in 1913, and no trace of the original facade survives—except in this old photograph. It was built about 1850 by Richard Woleben and his son Edward—very late for Federal style, but since the first major Greek Revival dwelling did not appear until 1839–40, if by an older, or conservative builder, understandable.

This facade is a more elaborate, and canonical, Federal mode. (This motif, slender pilasters across the facade and a fan light in the pediment, probably can be traced back to the work of Charles Bulfinch in Boston, in buildings of the decade 1799–1809.) At least two other houses similar to this survive in Chautauqua County—the Cyrus D. Angell House in Forestville, and 826 N. Main St., Jamestown (neither are firmly dated). Both have delicate pediment cornice moldings, and attenuated pilasters across the facade—though these two have segmental arches linking the capitals at the top, unlike the Fredonia example. But 46 W. Main had a full range of other elegant Federal motifs: a semi-circular lunette (which seems to have had slender metal glazing bars) filled the pediment,[11] and the doorway in the first bay was of traditional Federal style and finesse. Although the craftsman who built it would have known all this from apprenticeship and experience, one can also find such details in Federal-style architectural pattern books. The pedimental fan light is like plate 38, fig. F in Asher Benjamin's *American Builder's Companion* (first edition 1806, sixth edition as late as 1827), and the doorway with side and fan lights is the same type as shown in plate 32, fig. 1.

Fredonia has a few other houses with Federal-style detailing in some degree (such as 53 and 59 Forest Place), and there were probably more, for it was easy to give a simple vernacular dwelling some sophisticated Federal elegance with the proper doorway or gable light (either oval or semicircular); but later remodeling and "updating" usually removed such features.

58. *Zattu Cushing House, c. 1812 and c. 1818.*

59. *Woleben House, in detail of c. 1913 photo.*

Smith-White House   *35 Center St.*

This dwelling shows how persistent certain traditional forms could be, for the house combines elements of the older Federal style, with the Greek Revival. The building seems to have been erected in 1851—well after the Federal style had largely died out—by William Smith, and is depicted thus on the 1851 village map.[12] No information about the owner is given on the 1854 county map, though in 1867 the owner was D. A. White. In 1881 it was owned by G. Nelson Frazine.

The well proportioned three bay facade, with the door at one side, is typical of the Federal style, as are the still surviving 6/6 sash windows, quite possibly original. The gable walls are treated as sloping parapets (not stepped as in the Hamilton and Lester Houses) and the space between the two chimneys is bridged, not uncommon in Federal architecture.

But it will be noticed that the cornice is large and rather elaborate—not just classical dentils under the eaves, which would be typical of the Federal style, but now also has a classical frieze band below, a Greek Revival feature. This same classical feature is found on the brick Woleben Block, an impressive commercial building 15 bays long, which was erected in 1850–51 on W. Main Street north of Forest Place. In both cases, the dentils and frieze band make a sophisticated capping feature to an otherwise straightforward brick facade.

It is inside, however, that the Greek Revival details are most prominent; the doors and windows have crossetted (eared) casings in a simple Greek style, with six-panel doors.

The plan is also a later type than what one might find in a Federal house (a side hallway with straight stairs, and two rooms to the right). Here, rather, the stair hall to the left (the stairway curving upward), is only half the depth of the house, with a bedroom behind it. On the right side of the house are two chambers connected by a wide doorway. The brick addition to the rear of the house is probably original.

Some remodeling was done, to judge from the Academic Revival fireplaces of oak still in place, around 1900. The interesting stained glass window on the stairway was clearly also added at this time. Verandas (of c. 1900?) from the front and side were removed in the 1950s. About 1987 the house was carefully renovated. Copper flashing now protects the inner faces of the parapet, and a two-color paint scheme brings out the simple stone lintels over the windows. The 24 x 40' two-story carriage house behind (1850s?) and an adjacent one-story 19th century shed (15 x 24') were demolished around this same time. About 1991 the stone hitching post formerly in front of the house was removed after being damaged.

The new Greek style, inspired by ancient Greek temples and monuments, began in this country with Benjamin Latrobe in 1798, and was expanded by his pupils Mills and Strickland, and others. The appeal was partly artistic (the impressively formal style which could dignify even the smallest dwelling), and partly political and social (a break from the English-based Georgian and Federal; and its associations with the ancient democracies of Greece, and with that country's struggle for independence in the 1820s). Several outstanding Greek Revival buildings are explored in the next five sections.

60. *Smith-White House, facade view, 1972.*

61. *Federal houses with parapeted (left) and bridged (right) gable walls, in Chambersburg, Pa. (detail of c. 1843 print).*

62. *Late 19th century stained glass window on stairway.*

39

William Risley House   *63 Risley St.*

In the early 1840s, John Jones constructed three imposing Greek Revival mansions in a row, along what is now Risley Street, for the three Risley brothers. The Elijah, Jr., and William Risley Houses were probably built in 1843; Levi Risley's in 1845. Two of the three still stand, the Levi Risley House having burned in December, 1878 (see Fig. 39). The William Risley House is located directly across from the juncture of Center with Risley Street so that a formal, nearly axial, approach is possible.

The Risley brothers, sons of Elijah Risley who arrived in Fredonia in 1807, established a number of early businesses (grocery in 1808, an ashery in 1811), but are best known for founding, in 1834, an important early seed company. Their prosperity is reflected in the sumptuous, formal and very much up-to-date houses they had constructed.

The Greek Revival style, as is immediately apparent, is based mainly on the Greek temple form, though it did not, except in a few rare cases, attempt to reproduce the exact temple shape —rectangular, with columns around all four sides. Here the facade with triangular pediment supported by free-standing Doric columns, the symmetry and compactness, and white-painted wood to suggest marble—all are adapted from the true Greek temple. Some variety in plan was indeed possible, especially if one had flanking wings, in spite of the apparently rigid form. But, after all, the preceding Georgian and Federal periods had formal plans, and the Greek Revival, in a way, "purified" these styles, returning to even more simple architectural forms in the classical vocabulary. Although Federal style buildings had indeed drawn much from a renewed interest in ancient Roman domestic architecture, the Greek Revival went back even farther.

Major public structures, such as the Treasury Building in Washington, begun by Mills in 1836, used many Greek features—pedimented porticos, long peristyles of columns, antae and pilasters, and in this case, the Ionic order from the Erechtheion on the Acropolis—creating a sense of the imposing monumentality and compactness of ancient Greek temples without actually copying their shape. The interiors, vaulted for fireproofing throughout, also carried out the idea of simple geometric forms.

For more modest dwellings, in wood rather than stone, a carpenter-architect such as John Jones would have had recourse to carpenters pattern books, such as published by Lafever, which gave detailed engravings of the orders and their proportions, of doors, door and window enframements, moldings, fireplaces, and a few elevations and plans for entire buildings. But the Risley House overall design, while similar to Lafever's famous Plate 75 (1833) was based on local tradition: this form of mansion had been built (with Ionic columns) in Westfield as early as *1830–31*, and a Doric example was erected in Panama about 1837. Both were models for Jones to admire —and emulate.

The Risley House has an entrance hall with curving stair at the right of the central block, with the living room, to the left, occupying the rest of the facade. The south wing contains the dining room, the north the library. Behind each chamber, along the rear elevation, are other rooms, including the kitchen and pantries. Interior details are restrained; corner blocks of door frames in the north wing are plain, but those in the central section and the south wing have a carved wood medallion of oak leaves.

The William Risley House was carefully restored in the early 1970s; in the early '80s new owners removed the 6-panel doors and their crossetted frames from the two facade wings, and added a large brick chimney to the end of the north wing.

63. *William Risley House (photo 1972).*

64. *View of central living room, with dining room (south wing beyond).*

65. *Stairway in entrance hall.*

66. *Dr. Cornelius Ormes House, Panama, N. Y., c. 1837.*

67. *Treasury Building, Washington, D. C., by Robert Mills and others, 1836-1869.*

John Jones House *430 East Main St.*

Built in 1839–40 by John Jones for himself and his family, this house was originally located at 135 West Main Street, and was subsequently dismantled and moved to its present site in 1938. The house is composed of two sections, a hipped roof front block with five majestic Doric columns across the facade, and a rear wing or ell projecting behind it, which may be the older house he remodeled. The retention of older structures (and their remodeling in the latest style) when subsequent improvements were made was a common practice.

It will be noticed that unlike the William Risley House—but *like* the Elijah Risley House—the facade does not have a pediment. This was a perfectly acceptable variant in the Greek Revival style, the facade thus being more like a side peristyle, rather than a front portico, of a temple. The small panels in the frieze, with attractive scroll-work, are here either purely decorative, or cover ventilators for the attic. In many houses, actual tiny frieze windows, to provide some light for attic rooms, would be found in this location, the openings masked behind a cast iron grille of appropriately classical design.

The front door, which prior to its move in the early 20th century was in the second bay of the four-bay facade, is of special interest. Not only is it attractively detailed, but it also affords an example of how engravings from pattern books could be adapted. Here an interior door illustrated in Lafever provided the model for the enframement. A carpenter would naturally vary the original some as his sense of design—or the cost—might dictate.

The exterior finish of the Jones House, clapboards painted white, was usual for Greek Revival houses. Just as in the case of the doorway, Jones based his beautifully executed and proportionally correct Doric columns on models in some pattern book—probably Minard Lafever's *Modern Builders Guide* (1833) since Jones adapted the front door from it. Lafever's plates 44 and 45 provided two large engravings of the Doric order, one from the "Temple of Theseus," in the Athenian agora, and another from "The Temple of Minerva, at Athens," complete with highly detailed proportional notations, and line drawings of features not visible in the three-dimensionally rendered elevation views. As a further aid, Lafever's plates 52 and 53 provide line elevations, with dimensions, of the order, and a cross section of a column showing how the fluting was to be made. Such books were a gold mine for carpenter-architects aiming for the most accurate and up-to-date motifs.

Lived in for many years by his daughter (who was two years old when it was built) it is often called the Anna Jones House.

It might be worth mentioning here that not all houses with Greek columns on the facade are Greek Revival. The Noah Snow House, at 194 Central Avenue, had its columns added in 1907 (see Fig. 257). A brief discussion of the style of this house, and its transformation, will be included later.

68. *John Jones House, 1839-40.*

69. *Front door of the Jones House.*

70. *Detail of plate 69, "Elevation of a Parlour..."*
from Lafever, The Modern Builder's Guide
(1833).

Abner Clark House *128 W. Main St.*

The previous two examples have shown the Greek Revival house in its more elaborate form; but the style was equally popular for even the smallest dwelling. By utilizing the Greek Revival sense of compactness, perhaps its proportions, and classical details, almost any house could be given greater dignity. The Abner Clark House, built in 1842 or '43 (the land was purchased in August, 1842) is one such example.

It will be noticed that in spite of its diminutive size, the Clark House does indeed emulate the shape and proportions of a Greek temple. Although no freestanding columns are used, the pediment form is adapted for the gable; the cornice edges turn inward for a couple feet to suggest the lower cornice of a full pediment. The door is framed by a casing which takes the form of a section of entablature held up by tall pilasters at either side of the door. As in the pediment (and also frieze band running the length of each side of the house below the cornice), closely spaced dentils give it greater archeological correctness and enriched visual appeal.

The interior of the house reveals its heavy frame construction by boxed posts in each corner. The windows have simple Greek Revival moldings around them. The interior is essentially one large room, with the stair boxed in at the rear; an ell projects beyond that. Some of the floor joists, 6" logs with the bark remaining, and only the top portion hewed off, can be seen in the cellar. In 1960 the ell was considerably remodeled. In 1995 a Victorian-style front porch was added, at which time the classical door casing was removed.

While this house has only clapboard strips at the exterior corners, in other small dwellings the effect of classical corner piers is created by having wide pilasters at the edges, as at 22 Spring Street. This considerably enhances the temple-like effect, as the corner piers visually appear to support the entablature and pediment. This house also shows a side porch with square columns (thus, technically, piers). This was a common builders solution, far easier to make than the more correct round columns.

While many of the Greek Revival houses in Fredonia are of the preceding types, there were also other variants. One that is found more commonly in Massachusetts is the house with gable parallel, rather than perpendicular, to the street, and a one-story porch on the street side, as found at 120 Eagle Street.

An engraving of 1854 shows this house, then owned by Alford Stoddard, when located at 101 Eagle Street. It had been built in 1841 (attributed to John Jones) and had a *six* column porch, with the door in the center, at that time. It later became the Eagle Street school. In 1909 it was partially dismantled and three of its five bays were moved across to become 120 Eagle. In the move, it lost its frieze band (with attic windows) under the cornice, but retained its attractive pedimented ends with extensive dentil moldings throughout. The doorway is enframed by pilasters with palmettes at top and bottom, a high-style design found in Asher Benjamin's *Practice of Architecture* (1833), pl. 29 — and taken up by other pattern book authors thereafter. This door frame remains. The Ionic porch was rebuilt in the 1980s and now has modern columns; but the originals were especially fascinating: below the very correct Ionic capitals are columns with *convex* fluting — made from half-round moldings applied to the drum! This was an inexpensive, yet visually effective way to suggest the more canonical (and difficult to execute) *concave* fluting.

71. Abner Clark House, facade view in 1972.

72. The Hephaisteion, Athens, 449–444 B. C.

73. House at 22 Spring St.

74. House at 120 Eagle St. in 1972.

75. Detail of porch, 120 Eagle St.

Forbes-Cushing House   *23 Forest Place*

The Forbes-Cushing House was built in 1842 by Thomas G. Abell, who owned the stagecoach route from Buffalo to Erie, Pa., for his daughter, Katherine, and her husband, D.S. Forbes. In the late 19th century (after 1881) and until about 1960, the Forbes house was occupied by the two daughters of Commander William Barker Cushing (who had married a Forbes daughter), noted for his Civil War exploits, especially the torpedoing of the Confederate ram the *Albemarle* in 1864.

Although not of the temple-inspired form, as the previously examined houses, it is still Greek Revival. The type is rather traditional, going back to Federal house types, with a hipped roof, a three bay facade, the entrance in the first bay. The general blockiness, and especially its details, are strongly Greek, however. The front door, now hidden under a porch added in an appropriate style in the 1930s, is flanked by decorated piers, supporting a carved entablature; the door itself is decorated with egg and dart moldings, and the frame decorated with rosettes, as shown in Lafever (1833), pl. 65. (The doorway at 100 Eagle St. is based on this same plate.[13]) The original stone steps, with coffered cheek pieces, were removed in the 1930s, and replaced by brick—which in turn were redone in wood about 1995. The tall first floor windows, with crossetted frames, stand behind a particularly beautiful cast iron balcony (see also Fig. 277) of Greek-inspired design. Pierced frieze openings, on the facade and sides, ventilate the attic. The side porch, with square columns, appears original.

But it is inside that the finest Greek Revival features are to be seen. The plan of the front block is very simple; a hallway, with straight stairs, on the left, and a double parlor, connected by wide sliding doors, on the right. To the rear is a wing which appears to be a much earlier structure (it has considerably lower ceilings and boxed corner posts) which was incorporated into the new house. It contains sitting room, dining room, kitchen, pantries, etc.

The interior trim of the front portion is especially good. The front parlor has a very wide ceiling cornice, visually supported by the pilasters which flank the doors and windows; the space between the capitals (over the doors and windows) is decorated with symmetrical plant scrolls. The six-panel doors are common in Greek Revival houses.

The older rear portion has attractive 19th century wood graining in a variety of hues (dark for doors and panels under the windows, light for the door frames and base boards). The skillful graining includes trompe l'oeil paneling for the dining-room china cabinets! This house also has its original Greek Revival outhouse (now a tool shed), to the rear.[14]

When D. S. Forbes' sister Julia Ann married L. B. Grant they were given (probably by the elder Forbes) a nearly identical house at 74 East Main St. in 1848. It was designed and built by John Jones, so perhaps he was responsible for 23 Forest Place too.

74 E. Main was extensively added onto and somewhat remodeled inside in the 1890s. The front door, with side and fan lights in Federal style, was added in the 1920s. But the plan of the front portion of the house, though a mirror image, is the same as the Forbes-Cushing House. The general arrangement, and many details—the capitals, the six-panel doors—are identical, but the decorations above the doors and windows are heavier: the plaster enrichments are attached to the surface, rather than appearing to be molded reliefs. The stairway, though still a straight run, has been altered several times. Grace S. Richmond, a late 19th century writer, lived here for many years.[15]

76. *Forbes-Cushing House, facade view (photo 1987).*

77. *Interior, front parlor (1972).*

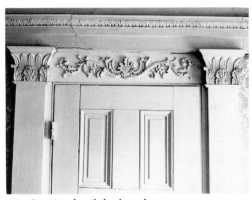

78. *Interior detail, back parlor.*

79. *Front door of Cushing House prior to addition of front porch in the 1930s.*

80. *Interior view in Grant-Richmond House, 74 E. Main St.*

Baptist Church   *19 Church St.*
Presbyterian Church   *formerly Church St.*

The Greek Revival style lent itself very well to public buildings, for the sense of monumentality and bigness of scale that the Greek temple form conveys is especially appropriate for an official, public structure. Two Fredonia churches in this style were erected in the 19th century.

The Baptist Church, built between 1852–53 to replace an earlier, rather blocky wooden edifice of 1823, was designed by John Jones. The tower of the original structure was quite different from the present one, added in 1886, having had a low parapet above the cornice (which hid the slope of the roof), above which was a square base, supporting an octagonal, louvered tower, with an extremely tall pointed spire (see title page). The spire was taken down apparently in the 1860s.

The problem of towers on Greek Revival buildings was a bothersome one, since few ancient Greek structures were vertically oriented. The two ancient monuments that did find adaptive use in this line were the circular 4th century B.C. Choragic Monument of Lysicrates in Athens (used twice by William Strickland as towers on public buildings), and the octagonal 1st century B.C. "Tower of the Winds," also in Athens. It seems likely that the church spire base, with antifixae at the upper angles, was indeed inspired by this octagonal Hellenistic monument.

The lower part of the church, essentially unchanged from cornice down except for the windows (1881), follows the proportions of a Greek temple. The facade and the sides are articulated by Doric pilasters of brick, which suggest the columns that would have surrounded a temple, and give unity to the structure. The facade is divided into five bays by pilasters just as the sides, but the spacing is narrower. The central three bays, both to visually create a base for the tower and to emphasize the central entrance, project somewhat. The interior of the church has been remodeled, some in the 19th century, but primarily in 1914 (when the attractive pressed metal ceiling was installed), and in the early 1920s when the sanctuary was rebuilt.[16]

A bit earlier was the Presbyterian Church, built on the corner of Church and Day Streets in 1835–36, also by John Jones. As old photographs show, it had an impressive Doric portico of four fluted columns, the wide steps in front being of stone (as the foundation of the church), and the body of the building brick. The sides were left plain, without pilasters. The tower had an octagonal central section, but which was divided into four large louvered panels, and four smaller plain ones, separated by slender columns, thus quite different from the "Tower of the Winds." This building was demolished in 1874 so that a second church, in Victorian Gothic style, could be erected on the site. It in turn was demolished in 1956; the present church edifice on Central Avenue is freely based on the original building, though smaller. As the photographs show, the tower added to the Baptist Church in 1886 owed something to the Presbyterian one in style.

There were, however, other public Greek Revival buildings which should at least be mentioned. The Johnson House (later called Taylor House, Park House, and finally—after rebuilding in 1892—Columbia Hotel), design by John Jones in 1837, was a good commercial example. The first floor was supported by tall stone Doric piers, allowing wide shop windows at the ends, and a five-bay entrance at the center. Above this entrance was a similar recessed space, a balcony with cast iron railings between Doric columns. The details and proportions, as well as the general compactness, reveal its Greek Revival form.

As we saw in Fig. 46, small, temple-shaped Greek Revival commercial buildings were formerly located on E. Main Street. By great good luck, two similar ones have survived on W. Main. The spaces between pilaster or piers, apparently removed in the right hand example, made logical and appropriate openings for doorways and shop windows.[17]

81. *Baptist Church, 19 Church St.*

83. *Park House, West Main St. at Park Place, now replaced by the Russo Building.*

82. *Presbyterian Church, formerly Church St. at Day St.*

84. *Greek Revival shops, 69, and 71–73 W. Main St. in 1972.*

Trinity Episcopal Church   *19 Day St.*

The only surviving Gothic Revival public building in Fredonia is the Episcopal Church, built in 1834–35. No indication of who designed the building has been located in the church records, which are missing for the year 1834, though it is thought to have been John Jones.[18] The structure was the result of almost 10 years of agitation by the congregation for a church building, and numerous fund-raising attempts. Finally in 1832 the site was selected, a building committee formed the following year, and the construction begun early in 1834 after materials had been collected. When completed in 1835, the cost had been $4,000.

The first major changes were made in 1848 when it was decided to lengthen the church by half its original dimension, add two new windows, and a brick vestry. The design for this addition was supplied by Dr. William E. Coates, a physician interested in church architecture whom Rev. Thomas P. Tyler had met in Boston. Painting, repairs, and minor remodeling took place in 1873, 1878, and 1888; in 1904 a new ceiling and floor were installed, following plans by Enoch Curtis. In 1925, however, after new windows had been installed, a fire destroyed most of the church; the tower which had been of wood, had to be removed. The church was rebuilt, however, in the following year using the old walls with a new tower in brick copying the old one; the architect was Paul Mann.

The Gothic Revival style, introduced into the United States by Latrobe in a house outside Philadelphia in 1799, was at first a decorative style only, "gothicizing" essentially symmetrical, classically planned buildings. But the style was soon taken up with larger churches. It was most appropriate for churches because of the associations the style had with some of the grandest religious edifices ever erected, during the late Middle Ages throughout England, and on the continent. In the 1830s, with the flourishing of certain English ecclesiastical movements, the style became more archeologically and correctly used.

The Episcopal Church emulates the sort of small country church which is known throughout England in countless numbers; most have a central facade tower, with the body of the church directly behind. Typical pointed arches are used throughout the Fredonia church for windows and other openings; buttresses, here structurally useful, are found at the sides of the building, and finials cap edges of the tower. The symmetry and regularity of all the forms indicate its early, less fully Picturesque, style.

Records reveal the names of the painters, masons, and glazier for the 1848 changes, and that the carpentry was by John Jones (who also supplied the estimates for the work in 1847). A newspaper account of February 6, 1849 records that the church, "beautiful in its style of architecture, has been rendered more symmetrical in its external proportions by a considerable addition to its length; and [that the] internal aspect is almost entirely changed by carrying the altar and desk into a recess, which together with the whole interior is lighted and ornamented beautifully by stained glass windows. The walls are painted in close imitation of stone, and the ceiling covered with elegant fresco and panel work, real and imitation." (This was all changed in 1904 when the ceiling was paneled, and heavy brackets added along the sides.) As rebuilt after the 1925 fire, the interior now has an open timber truss ceiling, and a central aisle. The louvered facade lancets were reinstated in 1993.

A second Gothic Revival public building, also facing the Common, was the Fredonia Academy building (1822), which had two pinnacled towers gracing the facade added in 1850 by John Jones (see title page, and Fig. 42). The site is now occupied by the Village Hall.

85. Trinity Episcopal Church, facade (photo 1994).

86. Village Church of Abbotsbury (Dorset), England, 15th century.

87. Trinity Church interior (photo c. 1905)

Ensign Baker House   *63 Central Ave.*

The Baker House, built in 1854–55, shows the Gothic Revival style in one of its most popular forms, that of the small house or "cottage," a type built in the United States between about 1840 and 1860. The 1867 and 1881 atlases record that J. B. Forbes ("dealer in dry goods and millinery goods") owned the house. The architect is not known.

As is apparent by the pointed window and the rather steep roof, the building is based on Gothic forms. The style for such small houses was begun in this country by New York City architect Alexander Jackson Davis in 1834, but was popularized by his friend Downing in his books of the 1840s and '50s, which included designs by Davis as well as his own. The source is English (not surprising, since Downing drew many of his ideas from British books) though in that country such a small building would have been designed as a gate lodge for a larger estate; this is an American adaptation. Many of its features, however, such as bargeboards under the eaves, steep roofs, oriel windows, tall chimney pots, verandas, and bay windows, were occasionally used in England in consciously rustic and picturesque country retreats, such as the one designed by Wyatville in 1810.

The Gothic cottage, thanks to Downing's books, became very popular throughout America. Sometimes a local carpenter might duplicate line for line a cottage shown in Downing (one such, built in 1850, is outside Newark, Ohio), but more usually some freedom was taken with the design. In a country with a rapidly expanding middle and working class, such well-designed houses, the plans carefully thought out, yet given a distinctive style that called up the bucolic country life of rural England and of age old estates, were very popular indeed.

The Baker House is based on these Downing models. The steep gables, at both the front and ends, are filled with Gothic bargeboards (a *sine qua non* of the style), and originally also had projecting finials at the peak of each gable. As shown in the early photograph of the house, the original porch was more Gothic in style (and less Picturesque) than the more open one added by J. B. Forbes in 1887. The grouped Gothic-style chimneys are also now replaced; but the bay windows that are found at the end of each first floor parlor, remain. The original siding seems to have been horizontal clapboards. For decades covered with wide aluminum siding, the narrower clapboard effect was reinstated in 1993 when tan 4" vinyl siding was installed.

The house has been added onto in several stages to the rear, and extensively remodeled, so that the original plan is not clear. It appears, however, that the front section consisted of two parlors separated by a wall at the midpoint, in which were connecting doors and the central chimney. Interior door casings are in simplified *Greek* Revival style—a curious stylistic admixture, but perhaps then (during the Greek Revival era), considered appropriate for formal parlors—no matter what the outside of the house looked like.[19] An ell extended to the rear. A further rear addition, in a style that successfully echoes the Gothic period, was made in 1993.

Another Gothic cottage, The Forbes-Judson House, with particularly fine bargeboards, and square label moldings over the windows (a feature Downing felt more appropriate than pointed arches in domestic structures), is at 39 Forest Place. In the vintage photograph, though the shutters obscure the label moldings, we see the original front porch supported by clustered Gothic colonettes, and that the rear porch originally consisted of three slightly pointed arches. At some later time it was (carefully) rebuilt as a single-bay stoop, retaining the three arches on each side. The house is now attractively painted in multiple colors—as in the olden days. The darker body color sets off the moldings and trim effectively, as originally intended. Though the detailing here is excellent throughout, the overall shape reveals this as an adaptation of the "pattern-book mode" to a local vernacular tradition. Interior trim, somewhat surprisingly, is in Greek Revival style, just as in the Ensign Baker Cottage.

88. *Ensign Baker House, facade view (photo 1994).*

89. *"A Cottage in the English, or Rural Gothic Style," from A. J. Downing, **Cottage Residences** (1842).*

90. *Endsleigh Cottage (Devon), by Sir Jeffrey Wyatville, 1810.*

91. *Old photo of Baker House showing original porch and chimneys.*

92. *Forbes-Judson House, 39 Forest Pl. (photo c. 1900).*

Robert Wolfers House *178 Central Ave.*

Another Gothic cottage, this time in brick, is found further north on Central Avenue. It was built in 1868 by Robert Wolfers, local brick-layer and contractor who had just finished erecting the Fredonia Normal School (1867-68). Alas, in 1871, Wolfers' house burned, though it was soon rebuilt. Later it was the residence of M. M. Fenner, the noted Fredonia doctor whose patent medicine became so popular.

As the house stands today, it is missing its porches, gable finials, ridge cresting, as well as its bargeboards (of a style somewhat later than those advocated by Downing). But even so, it is evident the house was based on the Gothic Cottage mode. The paired chimneys are similar to those used by Downing, based on Tudor forms, and the projecting oriel at the second floor is also found in many published designs. The taller proportions allowed for greater interior space in the second floor chambers; the house also has a large ell to the rear.

Unlike the previous example, this house is made of brick. One of Downing's esthetic tenets (a Picturesque ideal also advocated by others) was that country houses should be of natural materials—stone or brick preferred—with the natural surfaces and colors exposed. Wood houses, whose siding he felt should be vertical board and batten since the verticality expressed more "honestly" the vertical supportive timbers inside, were to be painted in earth colors—grays, browns, ochres, and so on. In this way they would blend in more with the rural, picturesque setting that such dwellings ideally would have—curving walks and drives, and carefully planted trees to create vistas from the house, as well as define and shape the grounds.

It will also be noticed that the Wolfers House, as the Baker House, has bay windows at the end of each front parlor. These bays were popular features, not only for the Picturesque animation of form they provided, but also because, contrary to popular belief, mid and late 19th century architects liked to let sunlight into houses. Vaux, in his 1857 treatise, objected to verandas on all sides because "most healthily-constituted persons like to have the opportunity to admit a stream of glorious, warm, genial sunlight into their rooms whenever they feel inclined to enjoy it, and this cannot be obtained if the veranda entirely encircles the living apartments." Twenty years later, Orson Squire Fowler (about whom more later) speaks of sunshine as "this great necessity and luxury," and somewhat cryptically writes, "one often needs to lotch [sic] in sunshine and [the] sitting-room is its place. This a bay window…promotes."

Wolfers House has been somewhat altered; but, according to a former resident, the plan originally consisted of a front entrance vestibule, with the stairs curving up at the left hand side, from which one could enter, by separate doorways, either the south or the north parlor, which were also joined by doors. A fireplace, still extant, was against the separating wall in the south parlor. Behind this parlor was the dining room, and, next to it (behind the north parlor), the library. Behind these were the rear stairs, and lavatory, the kitchen and pantries, and a back porch across the rear.

The carriage house, which originally had a picturesque louvered ventilator at the apex of the roof, was demolished in 1984. All major homes in Fredonia in the 19th century would have had such buildings, some of considerable architectural pretension; several will be discussed in a later section.

The rear wing, and parts of the front, were badly damaged in a fire April 8–9, 1979, but the house was skillfully restored and renovated as the Fredonia State University College Admissions Office in the early 1980s.

93. *Robert Wolfers House, facade view (photo 1972).*

94. *"A Symmetrical Country House" by Downing and Vaux, from Vaux,* **Villas and Cottages** *(1857), design 12.*

95. *Late 19th century view of the Wolfers House. The rear side porch is original; the front porches appear to be c. 1885.*

96. *Chimneys, in imitation of Tudor chimney pots, on the Wolfers House.*

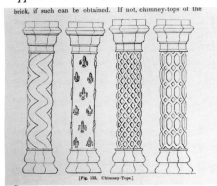

97. *"Chimney tops" from Downing,* **Country Houses** *fig. 155. These designs, in terra cotta, were available from James Lee and Co. of New York and Boston.*

Lorenzo Morris House 67 E. Main St.

Two major styles of the Italian Villa became popular in the 1840s and '50s; some were irregular and asymmetrical, and others were rectangular or square, and compact.

The asymmetrical Italian Villa style became popular in England just after 1800, where some important country villas were built in the style. Based on Italian vernacular, and certain Renaissance forms, the asymmetrical villa is noted for a prominent tower (largely based on Italian Romanesque bell towers), around which low and blocky units of the house would be arranged. It is also characterized by wide eaves with prominent brackets, windows often shaded by hoods or canopies, low pitched roofs, and verandas or loggias. The sources of this style were travelers' and architects' drawings and descriptions of the vernacular buildings of 18th century Italy, but also, equally important, the small, blocky buildings pictured in the landscapes of Nicolas Poussin and Claude Lorrain, 17th century French masters whose Italian paintings were avidly collected by British travelers.

The asymmetrical Italian Villa was the more canonical form. The irregularity of silhouette presented by the tall tower, the asymmetrical arrangement of rooms around it, and the projecting bays and bay windows, all provided the ins and outs, and contrasts of shadow and form, that the Picturesque esthetic advocated. The tower contains paired arched windows, a standard feature going back to Italian bell towers of the Middle Ages. Like all early Italian villas, this has a low pitched roof.

The Lorenzo Morris House was built in 1866.[20] Morris was one of the most important inhabitants of late 19th century Fredonia. Born in 1822, he graduated from the Mayville Academy in 1836 and remained in the county seat to study and later practice law. Between 1855 and 1872, however, he was in partnership with Judge Warren in Fredonia; he was a State Senator from 1868–1869. He lived in Fredonia until his death in 1903.

The exterior of the house is little changed except for the porch, which was added probably in the 1880s. A view of this house published in the Sept. 24, 1879 New York *Daily Graphic* (together with a number of other Fredonia buildings) shows that the original porch was very small, located in front of the entrance door at the base of the tower. Outline traces of the original porch, and the section of its balusters, can be seen in the brickwork. Otherwise, compared with the 1879 view, the building is unchanged—a particularly good example of the irregular Italian Villa as published by Downing and many other architects from the 1840s on.

The interior plan is very compact. The entrance hall has a stairway curving upward; directly to the right, off this hall, is a front parlor and behind the hall (and parlor) is a larger living room with an especially sunny bay, glazed from floor to ceiling, at the eastern end. At the western end (separated by a wall with a fireplace) is a first floor bedroom. Behind these rooms came the dining room (to the left) and the kitchen, and lavatory, to the right. A pantry was located behind the dining room (off the kitchen); a frame woodshed (removed 1992) was attached to the rear of the house. The interiors (mainly upstairs) were altered in 1935, and the living room fireplace was rebuilt. The house was carefully restored, and the kitchen remodeled in 1992–93.

This seems to have been the only asymmetrical villa, with low roof, built in Fredonia, though Second Empire houses, which have mansard roofs, sometimes continue this Picturesque villa plan.

98. Lorenzo Morris House, facade and east side (photo 1995).

99. "A Villa in the Italian Style, Bracketed," from Downing, Cottage Residences (1842), design VI.

101. Etched glass window in front door, Morris House.

100. View of stair hall, Morris House (photo 1972).

E. F. Warren House   *123 Central Ave.*

In 1854 this property is listed under J. H. Havens; the house was built, however, for E. F. Warren in August, 1855. In 1867 and 1881 it was owned by H. C. Lake.

As can be seen, when the Italian villa style is adapted for regularly shaped edifices of more modest size, as in this example, the prominent eaves, heavy brackets, and low sloping roof—and often the loggia—were utilized, and give much of the Italian flavor to the houses. Thus while the forms are compact, the details are Picturesque.

Italian villas of this type usually have a cupola on the top. These were mainly decorative, but also served as little chambers from which to view the countryside, or on occasion, served as light wells for the central portion of the house (as at 429 Central Avenue, Dunkirk). Though this feature has been removed in the Warren House, old photographs show that it did indeed exist.

The wide eaves are decorated with extremely elaborate paired brackets which provide much of the Picturesque animation for the house. The porch, with square piers rather Greek Revival in style, suggests the slightly transitional nature of the building.

It is particularly interesting to note that this house is built of poured concrete, the famous "gravel wall" construction advocated and popularized by Orson Squire Fowler (see below) about this time. The surface is scored to resemble large blocks of ashlar. The windows, curiously for an Italianate house, appear to lack lintels. In fact, there is a slightly arched molding in concrete 6–8" above the window; when this, with the space below it, is painted a contrasting color—a window lintel is visually created![21] In brick villas of this type such lintels were often in cast iron (as at 54 Risley St. or 284 E. Main St.). Another square villa, the Willard McKinstry House at 87 Central Avenue, is also of concrete; it was built in 1857 and enlarged (also in concrete) in 1868.[22] A third concrete villa of the 1850s, with fine detailing in wood, is at 187 Water St.

The plan of the house has been slightly altered, but appears to have been a central hallway plan, slightly off center, with straight run stairs. A major formal room is located to the left, and a smaller sitting room with dining room behind on the right of the hallway. Across the back of the house (behind these rooms) was a kitchen (left), and rear stairs and pantry (right). The interior trim is slightly Greek Revival, again suggesting that the builder, quite at home in that earlier style, felt it appropriate for formal interior details.

The partition separating the dining room from the hall has been removed, and the ceilings have been lowered (1920s); a large rear porch has been replaced by a smaller one.

As can be seen, the Warren House is quite similar even in plan (see Fig. 2) to a "suburban cottage" published a few years before by Downing, both in general size and shape. The published building was to be of masonry. That the house could really be directly inspired by A. J. Downing is not as remote as it might at first appear: an ad by Fredonia bookseller Henry C. Frisbee in the October 23, 1843 *Censor* notes that "Downing's Landscape Gardening [1841]…also his Cottage Residences [1842], two very desirable works, for every person of taste, and especially to those intending to build and improve their grounds" were now for sale at his bookstore. The influence, via books, of the most famous designers of the day, was remarkably widespread.

102. *E. F. Warren House (photo 1871).*

103. *Warren House, current view.*

104. *"A Suburban Cottage in the Italian Style," from Downing,* **Country Houses** *(1850), fig. 33.*

Daniel Fairbanks House · *4587 W. Main Rd., Fredonia*

A more elaborate example of this square Italian Villa form is the Daniel Fairbanks House, just outside the village limits to the southwest. It was built sometime between July 1861 and July 1868. In 1881 it was owned by Sayles Aldrich.

Compared with the previous example, the house is somewhat more elaborate. Brackets of two different types are used, in the cupola and under the eaves; the present porch was apparently added in the 1880s, the earlier one being somewhat simpler. It will also be noticed that round-headed windows (first floor) and segmentally arched windows (second floor) are employed, features which were a popular Italianate form. The original board and batten barn still stands to the rear, but without the original cupola. The engraving of 1881 also gives a good idea of the arrangement of a late 19th century farm of the area; vineyards, orchards, and grazing seem to be the main uses of the land.

The plan of the house is considerably more irregular than in the Warren House—as perhaps befits a later, more Picturesque, version of the type. The front block is occupied, across the facade, by an entrance hall with curving stair (to the left), and a small front parlor (to the right). Behind these is a large living room, with a smaller chamber at the right end. Behind this main block, as the engraving and photograph show, is a large ell, which includes a dining room with bay window to the left, and, to the right, a small chamber, with the kitchen behind. A pantry, plus wood additions and sheds, are at the rear of the house.

The interior trim of the stair hall and front parlor is Greek Revival, but the other rooms have heavier painted and grained moldings around the doors and windows. Again, perhaps the Greek Revival mode even at this late date, was considered appropriate for a formal front parlor by the local builder. Curiously enough, in view of the very elaborate and prominent nature of the cupola, the interior of it is not finished, and access is made only through the attic.

A similar villa is located at 54 Risley St., the William H. Chaddock House, built a few years earlier in 1858–59. The elaborate cupola is almost identical to that on the Fairbanks House, suggesting that the same designer, or perhaps carpenter (or mill work company!) was involved.[23] An impressive castellated tower was added to the end of the Chaddock House (to "update" the design, and make it even more Picturesque) sometime between 1881 and 1889. The current Queen Anne porch, with concrete block piers and base, is more like 1905—again, keeping the design up to date, and functional (large porches being in vogue at the time).

The square villa was very popular in Fredonia, and fine brick examples can be found on Central Avenue as well as East Main. A small wood version is at 187 Water Street.

105. *Daniel Fairbanks House, Route 20 (West Main) just beyond village limits.*

106. *View of Sayles Aldrich residence from* **Illustrated Historical Atlas of the County of Chautauqua, New York** *(1881), facing p. 58.*

107. *Interior, showing also front stair hall and rear parlor.*

108. *Detail of exterior brackets.*

109. *Painted glass fan light over the front door.*

Kellogg House   *64 Central Ave.*

Because the Italianate style contained a number of features easily adaptable to even the simplest house—wide eaves with brackets, round-headed and segmental-headed windows—small dwellings that otherwise would be very plain could be given a sense of architectural sophistication by their use. One good example is the Kellogg House illustrated here. It appears to have been built about 1865; it is not on the 1854 map, and in both 1867 and 1881 is listed as occupied by a Mrs. Kellogg. The original porch extended the entire length of the facade, but was removed, except for a section left as an entrance porch, many years ago.

If we compare the brackets on this house to similar brackets from a late 19th century builders pattern book, we will see how close some of the suggested shapes come to brackets on Fredonia houses. This is not to suggest that this book by Bicknell was actually used—in fact it is a little later than this house—but is the sort of manual which local carpenters, or local mill-work firms, would have employed to design appropriate brackets, bargeboards, window frames, dormers, balconies and railings, and cornices, as well as a host of interior details (mantels, doorways, etc.)

This sort of simple, but richly detailed, Italianate house was popular in Fredonia. The 1881 Atlas shows T. S. Hubbard's residence at 29 Central Ave. (now somewhat remodeled) in this style. The George W. Lewis House, 211 Chestnut St., built in 1868, is similar (the wing at the far left is a bit later). Although the design by Hussey is a few years later, it shows that the Italianate features—wide eaves, brackets, circular attic window, bay window at the side,[24] and enframed windows—were widely known in national publications.

113. 211 Chestnut St.

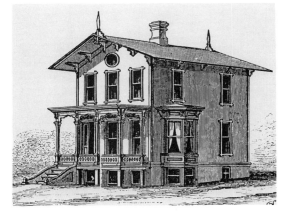

*114. E. C. Hussey, **Home Building** (1875), pl. 3.*

110. *Kellogg House, 64 Central Ave.*

111. *Detail of brackets, Kellogg House.*

112. *"Designs for Scrolls and Brackets," from Amos J. Bicknell, **Detail, Cottage and Constructive Architecture** (New York, 1873), plate 35 (detail).*

Levi L. Pratt House   *99 Chestnut St.*

One of the most interesting houses in Fredonia is the octagonal one shown here. It has the brackets, wide eaves, and central cupola which are Italianate, but the most distinctive aspect of the house is its shape.

The property was bought from the Holland Land Co. in 1840 by Levi L. Pratt, who for seven years was Editor of the *Fredonia Censor*, and later of the *Fredonia Advertiser*. Pratt seems to have built his house in 1866–67; he left the area in 1871 to work on the *Watertown Daily Times*.[25] The house had been sold by 1881 to I. A. Saxton, whose son continued to live here until 1917. Details of its style—the window caps with a hint of the classical pediment, and the corners of the house finished in pilaster-like strips—confirm the continued influence of the popular and long-lived Greek Revival.

Octagonal—and many sided and round—structures have occasionally been built since ancient times; even in America, circular and octagonal barns and school houses are known from the early 19th century. But the development of the octagonal house of this form is due to the efforts of Orson Squire Fowler (1809–1887). This remarkable man, who had early studied for the ministry, was introduced to the pseudo-science of phrenology in the early 1830s, and became so successful in reading character from the shape of one's head, that he began to lecture and write on the subject extensively. He was immensely popular and prolific, and had a long career, not only in phrenology, but in other fields—temperance and abolition, home life, self-improvement, and so on. He published over thirty titles, in many editions, and had an international fame—at least two of his volumes were translated into German. One of his most successful books was *Creative and Sexual Science, or, Manhood, Womanhood and their Mutual Interrelations; Love, its Laws, Powers, etc.* ... first published in 1875. This remarkable book of over 1,000 pages, dealt with every conceivable aspect of marriage, sex, and physiology.

Always aiming at improving humanity, Fowler also invented the octagon house, first made public in *A Home for All; or, a New, Cheap, Convenient, and Superior Mode of Building* (1848). In his 1853 edition of this little treatise he introduced the use of "gravel wall" construction. This was essentially poured concrete, using any aggregate available—stones, gravel, sand, brickbats, cinders or clinkers, even bits of glass, sticks, and so on. (He had earlier advocated plank walls, composed of boards laid horizontally, and pinned together, thus forming a solid wood wall.)

The octagonal shape arose from philosophical and practical reasons. The circular (and spherical) form was nature's most beautiful and perfect shape; thus the architectural form approaching it was the most beautiful. Furthermore, for the amount of space an octagon encloses, it has less exterior wall surface (for heat loss, and original material cost) than a rectangular house. The compact interior plan further saved steps, as well as awkward corners. Concrete was considered a perfect material since it was cheap, extremely durable, a good insulator, and fireproof. Quite a number of octagon houses were built throughout the United States and Canada, mainly in the 1850s and '60s; over 400 survive today. Their construction, however, varies considerably, from traditional frame, to brick, and concrete.

The Pratt House is a particularly good example of the Fowler Octagon mode, and is in good condition, even retaining its octagonal carriage house. The exterior finish was scored to look like ashlar; the walls, 24" thick, are composed of lime grout with stones, brick fragments, and even small sticks as aggregate. The walls are extremely solid.

The plan of octagons varied considerably. Often there were two large rooms through the center (with a wall separating them at midpoint), with another square room to each side. The triangular spaces left would provide closets and stairways. But Fowler preferred a plan that provided vertical ventilation, carrying warm air upward, and out the cupola in hot weather. In the Pratt House there is both a central stairway, and a second flight just inside the front door. Interior finishes, as would be expected, are quite plain.

115. Levi L. Pratt House, facade view.

116. Pratt House, showing octagonal carriage house and rear of dwelling.

117. Composition of concrete, as visible in cellar.

118. Detail of window and cornice brackets.

119. Stairway in entrance hall.

Spencer L. Bailey House   *42 Central Ave.*

The Bailey House introduced a new and more formal style to Fredonia, the Second Empire mode, which became immensely popular during the decades after the Civil War. The house was built in 1868 to designs of Enoch Curtis. In 1882 Bailey sold it to Albert C. Putnam, Sr.

The Second Empire mode—the dominant feature being the use of tall, often curved, mansard roofs—is named after the reign of Napoleon III (1852–70), and indeed, one of the most impressive structures in this style, the New Louvre, was done under his aegis, beginning in 1852. But the style had been revived (mansard roofs had been used centuries earlier) by the 1840s, and by 1850 it was becoming popular in England for major houses and public buildings. From there it spread quickly to the United States. Probably the most famous early example in a public building was the Corcoran Art Gallery by James Renwick Jr., begun in 1859 (and finished after the War); [26] but the mansard roof—concave, convex and straight sided— was already well known from published accounts, and some houses, by that time. Several such roof styles are illustrated as early as 1857 in the first edition of Calvert Vaux's *Villas and Cottages*.

The mansard roof (named after François Mansart, 1598–1666) was especially popular because it allowed almost a full story of useable space to be included in what was normally the attic, and at the same time provided a visually successful capping to a building. Second Empire houses of the more formal sort, such as the Bailey House, are symmetrical and blocky, often with a central pavilion; but the roof could also be adapted to more irregular villa forms.

The Bailey House, of brick with dressed stone hood molds over the windows, originally had a slate roof, as the view of c. 1885 shows; the present porch replaced the earlier one in 1929. Features such as the bull's-eye dormers in the bays flanking the central pavilion, and the balustrade in front of the paired central windows on the second floor, added to the sense of formality and symmetry. Curtis could well have based his design on that published by Vaux in 1864; if so, it shows how quick he was to adopt new national trends to local dwellings, and how up to date, thanks to architectural books, local building could be.

The imposing quality of the house is to be seen inside as well. The front section is actually only one room deep. On either side of a central hallway with stairs (curving at the upper end) are two large parlors with especially tall ceilings. The sense of formality is emphasized by semi-circular niches (for urns, statues, etc.) at either side at the front of the hallway, and on the stairway at the point of curvature. Behind this front block the ceiling heights are lower, and the house a few feet narrower. The hall leads to the dining room on the left side of the dwelling (with a solarium at the side), and to the right is the music room, with lavatory behind. Running across the rear are the kitchen and pantries. Originally there was a frame ell on the rear, but this was removed when some remodeling was done to the house in 1956–57. The interior fireplaces are of two forms, a standard white marble type with arched opening and carved keystone, common in the 1850s and 1860s, and later oak mantelpieces in 1890s Classical Revival style. Two of a most interesting group of photographs, taken of the interior of the house in the 1880s, are reproduced here; they were obtained with the house by the present owners.

The other Second Empire house in Fredonia of this formal, central-pavilioned type, was built in 1868–69 by Curtis as his own home, but it was soon sold to H. L. Taylor (see Fig. 40). Two flanking porches on the facade, shown in an 1879 view, have been removed, and the cornice (and upper windows) altered some. It has a more complex plan (the stairway is to one side and perpendicular to the central hallway), and more elaborate detailing; the newel post is astonishingly complex.[27] The house has a fine tile-faced fireplace of c. 1905.

120. Spencer L. Bailey House, facade view (photo 1995).

121. Bailey House, with original porch (photo c. 1885).

122. Design for mansarded house from Vaux, "Villas and Cottages," 2nd ed., 1864.

123. Interior of house, c. 1885, looking from left parlor, through the stair hall, to right parlor.

124. Interior view, c. 1885, from the dining room into the music room.

Masonic Lodge *formerly 14 W. Main St.*

The Second Empire mode was especially well adapted to public buildings, since the high roof gave an appearance of dignity and formality to buildings which otherwise might be rather plain. It is also provided a further rentable floor while still providing a roof at that level. Often decorated, especially in the later 19th century, with bands or patterns of colored slate, and capped with cast iron cresting, they provided an especially Picturesque roofline.

The Masonic Lodge was originally matched on E. Main Street by the similarly mansarded Odd Fellows Hall (Enoch Curtis, 1869–70; after a fire, on Sept. 16, 1923, the mansard roof was removed and a plain brick parapet built in 1924). Prior to its destruction by fire on Feb. 28, 1973, the Masonic Lodge gave a prominent focal point to this stretch of commercial buildings on W. Main directly opposite the Common. As early photographs show, the original 16-bay brick structure which was built here in 1852–53, had a completely uniform roofline. In 1854 it is listed as the "Centre Block" and apparently had a large hall at about the middle; in a photograph of c. 1870 the legend "Concert Hall" is read at that point. Thus the original division was into a middle seven-bay block containing the concert hall, flanked on the west by a three-bay structure, and to the east by two three-bay buildings (chimneys mark the interior dividing walls), all with a uniform facade. The style is late Greek Revival, with a prominent brick cornice approximating Greek triglyphs below a row of dentils. The windows have cast iron caps with embossed decoration.

The concert hall section of the block was bought by Forest Lodge and Fredonia Chapter, Royal Arch Masons, on Feb. 4, 1873. Plans for a new roof and windows, by Enoch Curtis, were announced in the *Censor* December 17, 1873. Remodeling as a lodge was carried out as funds were available until 1878, when the first meeting was held. Thereafter, at considerable cost, further work was done; thus the roof may not have been added until the late 1870s. In the 1880s and early 1890s Enoch Curtis did some more interior work.

As the photographs show, when the mansard roof was added the brick triglyphs were removed below it, so that its own bracketed cornice could be constructed. Because of this difference in cornice form, and different color of this section of the block, it conveys the appearance of a separate structure rather than just a portion of the longer block re-roofed.

The Lodge building consisted of the following divisions: first floor, shops; second, present Lodge kitchen, stairs to main Lodge room, and other chambers; third floor, the Lodge anterooms across the front and, occupying virtually all of the remaining space, the spacious Lodge hall itself, which extended up to the fourth floor (into the roof). This last floor also had the old (very small) dining room, and kitchen, in front of and to the side of the upper part of the Lodge room.

The Lodge hall was most impressive. The coved ceiling was decorated with painted masonic motifs, and the center of the ceiling had an octagonal ribbed dome extending even higher. To the left side was a niche which, by the style and motif (a muse-like female embellishing the central keystone), is possibly a remnant of the original concert hall. The classical tabernacles on three walls of the chamber are of uncertain date.

It is said that some time around 1950 *Life* magazine did a story on the Lodge and building.

125. *Masonic Lodge, West Main St., in 1970.*

126. *View of "Centre Block," Aug. 8, 1867.*

127. *Masonic Lodge about 1880, showing original cast iron roof cresting.*

128. *Interior of Masonic Lodge, looking south (photo 1972).*

129. *Interior of Masonic Lodge, detail of niche in east wall.*

William H. Greene House   57 Central Ave.

How well the mansarded Second Empire mode could be adapted to all sorts of houses is shown by the ease with which it became popular as a means of updating the Italian villa form. In fact, this asymmetrical mansarded villa type is often popularly considered *the* "Victorian" dwelling.

The house has a complicated history of ownership and remodeling. According to the *Fredonia Censor* for June 1, 1867, this lot was purchased by William Greene; on July 17 the *Censor* noted that his house was in the process of construction. But a year later (*Censor*, Oct. 28, 1868) Greene sold the nearly-completed house to a Mrs. Lydia Vinton for the princely sum of $12,000. The architect (according to a *Censor* article a month later) was Enoch A. Curtis.

The vintage photograph shows what the mansion looked like about 1870. The similarity of this house shape to the asymmetrical villa type previously discussed (Fig. 98) is at once apparent. The massive central tower, appropriate to the Italianate origins, has two round-headed windows on the second level, and three on the third. Other windows are also round-headed, and the wide cornice is elaborated with brackets. With the more Picturesque mansard roof, the older mode has been updated to conform to evolving esthetic standards. The Second Empire style's details (balustrades, bay windows, arched porches and entrance doorway) are also close to the Italianate style, revealing the essential formality of this richly Picturesque composition. The small porch at the right makes a "semi-enclosed" transition between the mass of the central tower and the side wing.

By March 1872 the house was owned by W. S. Lines, who had it thoroughly redone inside (*Censor*, March 24, 1872). Most of this was "redecorating"— painting, papering, and wood graining; but there was also plasterwork and making ceiling medallions, and "woodwork and ... double parlor doors" by Robert Wolfers. Lines also purchased "elegant" new furniture for his beautified residence.

In 1890 the house was bought by Frank Tarbox, who in 1899 sold it in turn to Dr. John A. Waterhouse. But by May 1902 it had been sold again, to George L. Knight. It was Knight who built the wrap-around veranda in classical style (and had "the whole building" repainted). The purpose of this capacious porch was two-fold: first, to provide a shady retreat, a sort of "outdoor living room" for the warmer days of summer; and second, to de-emphasize by its scale and uniformity, the Picturesqueness of the ground level. By 1902 tastes had changed, and Academic ideals and classical restraint had returned to favor after the animation of the late 19th century styles.

For over 30 years, since the glazed storm enclosures for the porch remained in place year-round, the porch has seemed to "cut off" the house, visually, at the first floor—far more than it really does. But now (in 1997) the glazing has been removed, and one can clearly see the original articulation of the base of the house, and the disparity between the first floor and those above is mitigated.

The major stylistic remodeling inside seems to have taken place in 1909 after a Mr. McManus bought the house from George Knight. He made "great improvements in some of the rooms, especially with new windows," according to the *Censor* of May 12. This apparently was when the large second-story facade bay window was added, and the first-story window swept away for a new main entrance. Inside, the former small entrance hall was remodeled into a majestic oak-detailed stairway, the space now being opened up to the new entrance chamber by a pair of tall fluted Tuscan columns on pedestals. Oak fireplaces with tile facings and classical columns replaced the earlier white marble surrounds. This sort of up-dating, both artistically and spatially, shows how conscious new owners were of "the latest style" in interior planning and design, as an expression of both their taste, and their wealth.

The house still holds down the corner lot with great authority, and like a dozen or so houses along this side of Central Avenue, is located about 75' back from the sidewalk.

130. William H. Greene House, facade view (photo 1997).

131. Greene House, photo c. 1870.

132. Interior view of remodeled stair hall.

Nathan A. Putnam House   *30 Central Ave.*

The Stick Style, a fascinating mode which flourished from the 1850s to the 1870s, was never as widely built as, say, the Greek Revival, Italianate, or Second Empire styles, but has sometimes been considered more distinctly "American" than these other modes. Fredonia has a few houses which reflect this style.

We know a good deal about the construction of the N. A. Putnam House since the architect's specifications, discussed below, have survived. The house was built in 1880; a small cornerstone is inscribed "N-A-P-1880." The architect was Enoch Curtis.

The sources of the Stick Style (not a contemporary term, but one coined by Vincent Scully, who "discovered" the style) seem to go back to Downing, and his interest in expressing the wood framing of the house to an extent in vertical board and batten siding, as well as by vertical dividing strips, seen in some of his designs. Other architects of the 1850s, also influenced by so-called Swiss architecture, developed the "stick esthetic," in which the vertical and horizontal interior beams are echoed in comparable bracing, real as well as decorative, on the outside. Board and batten, vertical siding, horizontal clapboards, attenuated brackets, and bargeboards now composed of stick-like members, are other features that the style uses to create its distinctive sense of wood-ness and timber construction. Major architects constructed houses in this mode as early as the 1850s and '60s; the Griswold House is a good example. The growing use during this period of balloon frame construction (still used today), a type of framing using light but numerous pieces of wood, rather than fewer and heavier beams and corner posts, may have encouraged the style.

The Putnam House reflects this mode. Especially in the gables it can be seen that horizontal bands, with vertical boarding between them, are a prominent feature, standing out from the clapboards. The house should really have more such bands, but the mystery is resolved by a note penciled in the margin of the specifications: "All the belting courses to be left off the building, except the courses across the gable ends." The gables are decorated with beams and struts, the forms often lathe-turned—a wood esthetic. As can be seen, Bicknell and Comstock published this sort of treatment as late as 1881. Bicknell's book of 1873 is full of designs that are largely, if somewhat maladroitly, Stick Style. The porch on the Putnam House, especially the balustrade made of short pieces set at right angles, recalls the style. The roofs of most Stick Style houses, as here, were quite steep.

As mentioned above, 12 pages of handwritten specifications for this house are preserved by the present owner, and indicate the sort of detail to supplement drawings (now lost) that were provided by the architect.

> *Specification* of Carpenters and Joiners work to be employed and used in the erection and completion of a wood dwelling for the use and occupancy of N. A. Putnam Esq. on his lot on Central Avenue…& in accordance with the plans Elevations sections & detail drawings & these written specifications made & drawn by E. A. Curtis archt.

All facets are specified: the exterior dimensions; height of stories; nature of timbering, sheeting, outside covering and dressing; the roofing; interior flooring, stairs, doors, and finishes. Specific features such as the china closet, pantry, water closet, bath room, closets, etc. are outlined, even to such details as that the "cover and casing of bath tub to be walnut," and that "Gilbert's Patent" locks should be used. Interior finishes were "to be made in accordance with detail drawings from clear face thoroughly seasoned pine lumber smoothed up after the machines." The contractor was to "complete the building according to a fair and liberal interpretation of the drawings and these written specifications."

The house has been sympathetically converted into several apartments, with old molding used where shifting of doors was necessary. The former plan had a stair rising from the hall at the right side of the house, a front parlor (reached from the hall through a wide doorway) to the left, with a second living room, the end treated as a bay, behind it. The kitchen was opposite this, behind the stairs, with other rooms beyond.

133.   Putnam House, facade and north side (after siding in 1986).

134.   Griswold House, Newport, R. I., by Richard Morris Hunt, 1862.

135. Detail, eaves of Putnam House, before siding (photo 1972).

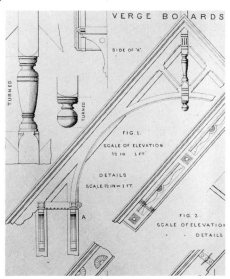

*136.   "Verge Boards" (detail of plate 70), from Bicknell and Comstock, **Modern Architectural Designs and Details**, 1881.*

Aaron O. Putnam House   134 Temple St.

This house is rather similar in design, but more elaborate than, the previous example; it was also designed by Enoch Curtis. Built in 1878, it was illustrated in the 1879 New York *Daily Graphic*. Together with his cousin Nathan Putnam, A. O. Putnam ran a successful drygoods store (J. B. Putnam & Co.).[28]

The early photograph shows clearly the Stick Style band of vertical boarding which wraps around the house at the second floor level. The side gable as well as the front originally had Stick Style details now missing; the open work railing above the front porch was also in this mode. A porte-cochere was formerly at the north side.

Curtis provided Putnam a complex yet sophisticated design. The overall form, and hipped roof, are based on a dwelling in Cambridge, Mass. by Peabody and Stearns (well known Boston architects) which was illustrated in *The American Architect and Building News* Jan. 13, 1877. But the shape of the porch, two-story bay, and other features are from two house designs in *Palliser's Model Homes* (1878), a book by a Bridgeport, Conn. firm. Since the Putnam House cellar hole was dug in June of 1878, Curtis was keeping right up-to-the-minute in drawing on national designs to inform his stylish Fredonia work.

The original plan of the house (it has been changed slightly on the first floor) consisted of an ample entrance hall with north and south parlors reached through wide doorways. Behind the north parlor is the stairway, and the side entrance hallway, perpendicular to the main hall, and behind the south parlor a small room. The large dining room was entered through a door at the end of the hallway (visible in Fig. 140). Behind the dining room are large and spacious kitchens.

The interior views of c. 1885 record the house's opulence, and show Putnam's pride in his material success. Today most of the interior details and finishings remain and give a good idea of the richness of many of the more elaborate homes. The original hall chandelier is still in place, as well as the branched light on the stair newel. Elaborate ceiling medallions are found in each parlor, and the jambs of these doors have inset polychrome encaustic tiles as decorative motifs. The hardware of the front door is particularly elaborate, the knob having a raised relief of a flying hummingbird and the plate curvilinear and palmette designs. Door and window casings (just as the furniture, designed in Renaissance Revival style) are finished in natural wood, and handsomely carved. The fireplace illustrated, as many found in Fredonia, is actually slate or some other hard but inexpensive stone, which has been skillfully *painted* to resemble marble. It is similar to ones suggested about this same time in Bicknell's pattern book.

In 1893 the Women's Christian Association, founded that same year (with Mrs. Enoch A. Curtis as vice-president), purchased the Aaron O. Putnam House, Mrs. Lorenzo Morris, the president, contributing $4,000 toward the purchase price (which was about $8,000); their aim was to establish a home for elderly ladies. The building, with a later, and sympathetic, addition to the south, serves the same purpose today. An article in the Nov. 17, 1894 *Grape Belt* which tells about the Association, and the current "inmates" of the home, also mentions that the house ("large, roomy and conveniently arranged...[presenting] an imposing appearance") was purchased with much of its original furniture. Thus many of the pieces visible in the series of interior views taken about 1885 are still to be found in the first floor parlors of the WCA Home. It was repainted in Victorian-style colors in 1989.

Because of many original furnishings still in the house, and the excellent condition in which the building is maintained, the Aaron Putnam House is especially interesting as a document of late 19th century architecture and design.

137. *A. O. Putnam House, now Women's Christian Association Home; facade view (photo 1993).*

138. *A. O. Putnam House, c. 1885 view of side prior to the addition of a south wing.*

139. **Pallisers Model Homes** *(1878), pl. 7, detail.*

140. *Front hall, c. 1885.*

141. *North parlor, looking south into hall.*

142. *South parlor, looking south.*

143. *Fireplace in north parlor.*

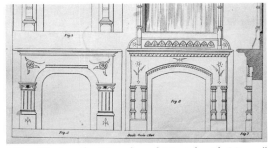

144. *"Designs for Mantels and Mantel with Mirror," from Bicknell, (1873), pl. 45.*

White Planing Mill   *formerly 63–69 Water St.*
Colburn Bros. Grist Mill   *formerly 19 Norton Place*

Mills were important in the early life of Fredonia, and continued to remain so into the 20th century. As we have seen, as early as 1807 a grist mill was set up on Canadaway Creek, and a saw mill soon thereafter.

The appeal today of such vernacular industrial buildings arises from several sources: first, as part of the historic structures of any era, they have interest as do high-style expressions of the building art; second, the fascination with old technology, of which these were the "envelopes," appeals to many (and in the past decades has become a whole field of scholarly endeavor); third, there has long been a delight in vernacular building, for its simple bold construction, use of natural materials, and its aura of "frontier life." But surprisingly enough, it has been the success of modernist architecture, in which concerns of form, texture, and three-dimensional composition are dominant issues, that have awakened many to the appeal of vernacular industrial building.

The mills of 19th century Fredonia produced more than just the milled grains and finished lumber (and later windows, doors, and other woodwork) for use by its citizens; they helped provide the wealth for building more elaborate dwellings! But here it is their architectural appeal that we can focus on. We already examined briefly (in the Preface) the McCleur Mill; here we can turn to a couple others.

As the 1881 map shows, Canadaway Creek was dammed in several spots to provide water power for these mills. Adjacent to the creek on W. Main St., G. W. Teft (by 1881) owned a grist mill and across the street a planing mill (the former McCleur Mill). A branch of the creek crossing under Spring St. powered G. W. Wiley's foundry. Further up Canadaway Creek, where Water St. crosses it, was G. H. White's planing mill. The photo shows it in 1977, when its lofty chimney was still standing (later cut down; entire mill demolished 1996). Though with some later additions, this functional structure (nucleus 1840s?) in its simple volumetric forms, has strong visual appeal. On the other side of the creek was the Colburn Brothers Grist Mill, which from the print of 1879 is seen to have been a tall gambrel-roofed building with *its* tall smoke stack; the adjacent structure undoubtedly housed specialized machinery.[29] The low wing next to the feeder stream is of stone; the mill seems to be vertical board and batten; often odd-shaped structures (as that next to the chimney), were shingled; and the chimney was of course brick. Such a variety of textures, colors, and shapes have a strong visual appeal to the modern eye, if they were not really appreciated in their own time.

Further up the creek the map shows two other industrial structures. The Wilson & Colburn Ice House was on the upper end of their feeder stream; and between Canadaway Creek and Liberty St. was the E. Roberts & Son Grist Mill. Alas, every one of the buildings cited here is now gone, though the visual record of a few reminds us of a less well-known, and certainly less well-understood or appreciated, part of Fredonia's cultural and architectural heritage.

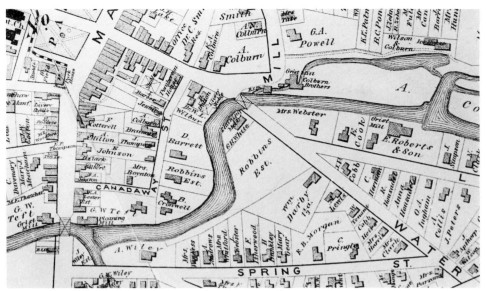

145. Detail of 1881 Atlas showing Canadaway Creek mill sites.

146. White Planing Mill ("Tadt's Old Mill") in 1977 (demolished 1996).

*147. Colburn Bros. Grist Mill, from New York **Daily Graphic**, Sept. 24, 1879 (demolished).*

Clark-Johnson House   *44 Temple St.*
The Day Building   *4 West Main St.*

One of the most interesting and colorful of late 19th century styles is High Victorian Gothic (often called just Victorian Gothic); several local buildings reflect this movement.

The sources of this mode should be at least touched on. The style is noted for its use of polychromy (red brick, black brick, light-colored stone, colored slate roofs, even colored decorated tiles) in construction; irregular and bold silhouettes, sometimes using elaborate cast iron roof cresting; and, in more elaborate buildings, carving of capitals and other motifs based on natural plants forms rather than pre-existing models. High Victorian Gothic was based largely on medieval Gothic examples, especially on those of Northern Italy. Growing out of the earlier Gothic Revival, the use of these forms was inspired largely by John Ruskin's book the *Seven Lamps of Architecture* (1849) in which he discussed at length many ideals of architecture (truthful materials, "simple, grand massing," bold and irregular silhouettes, hand-crafted materials rather than machine-made, etc.) and found much to emulate and admire in the early architecture of Northern Italy, especially Venetian Gothic. His *The Stones of Venice* (1851–53) gave further impetus to this creative use of new Gothic forms and polychromatic building. The noted architect George Edmund Street was inspired by these volumes to travel to Italy himself, and his book *Brick and Marble in the Middle Ages* appeared in 1855; in it his enthusiasm for use of undisguised brick, often with alternating bands of light stone around windows (the book had many illustrations) furthered the style.

At the same time, William Butterfield constructed, beginning in 1849, the first of these High Victorian Gothic buildings, his All Saints, Margaret Street, London. The red brick walls banded with black brick and tan stone were a startling innovation; the shape was irregular and Picturesque. His extensive academic complex, Keble College, Oxford, begun in 1867, is also notable. The style was launched in this country in the early 1860s, and lasted in some areas into the 1880s. Two Fredonia buildings that reflect this style are the Clark-Johnson House and the Day Building.

The Clark-Johnson House was built in 1877–78 for H. C. Clark; it was occupied later for many years by Fredonia lawyer Oscar W. Johnson. The architect was Enoch Curtis, who seems to have got some of his ideas for this unique house from Hussey's book, of two years before. Many Victorian Gothic features can be seen on the exterior, notably the red brick accented with light stone for lintels, sills, and other details. Some of these blocks (as flanking the transom) have incised floral motifs, common to the style. The alternating stone and brick voussoirs above the second floor window are a basic motif. The house originally had a small front porch, a side porch, and ridge cresting; the slate roof had alternating bands of color.[30]

Inside, the plan is quite formal, with a central hallway, rooms ranged along each side, with the stair in a side entrance hallway on the south. Repartitioning makes the original disposition a little unclear. The attractive newel post, when compared to plates from Bicknell, suggests the type and source for many of the interior details.

A commercial building in this style on West Main is the Day Building, built in 1879–80 (according to a party wall agreement) by Mrs. Mary P. Day, widow of Stephen O. Day, who had bought the property in 1867. Here again is the use of contrasting colored materials—tan stone trim and red brick. Bricks set at angles in order to create pockets of shadow, which give further richness and animation to the surface, is seen around the second floor windows. The cast iron cresting (see also Fig. 278) creates an irregular and highly decorative topping to the facade. The interior of the second floor office has robust moldings around all three windows.

148. *Clark-Johnson House, east and north side in 1970 (a modern front porch was added in 1982).*

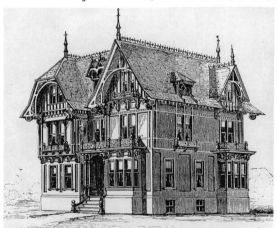

149. *E. C. Hussey,* **Home Building** *(1875), pl. 35.*

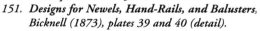

150. *Newel post in Clark-Johnson House.*
151. *Designs for Newels, Hand-Rails, and Balusters,*
Bicknell (1873), plates 39 and 40 (detail).

152. *The Day Building, elevation view.*

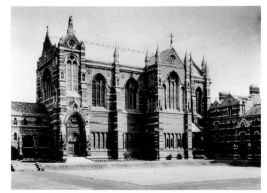

153. *Keble College, Oxford by William Butterfield;*
constructed 1867–75.

St. Joseph's Church   *143 East Main St.*

High Victorian Gothic was especially popular for churches in the United States, and Fredonia had three in this style. Only one stands today. Although a good number of important public buildings in the style, often quite lavish in execution, were erected in America, only a fraction survive—the three most famous ones being Memorial Hall, Harvard University (1870), Jefferson Market Courthouse, New York (1875), and the Pennsylvania Academy of Fine Arts, Philadelphia (1876).

St. Joseph's Church is remarkably late for this style, having been built in 1900. The salient features of the style are, however, apparent—red brick with contrasting bands, moldings, buttress caps and other features of light stone. The silhouette, appropriately varied, has the asymmetrical composition (the tower at one side) which so well suits this mode. The buttresses, raised arch moldings, etc. provide further surface interest.

This design, while ultimately going back to English models, has an American source: Minard Lafever's Strong Place Baptist Church in Brooklyn, New York (1851–52) which was well known through engravings. Its fame is confirmed by noting that in E. C. Hussey's popular volume, *Home Building* (1875) an engraving of it is provided as a model for emulation. The asymmetrical massing and commanding facade tower assured it of many imitators.

Two other churches in this mode were the Presbyterian Church (second edifice, built in 1875 by Enoch Curtis, demolished in 1956) which also had one corner tower, and the second Methodist Church (1868–69). This latter church, even though employing two facade towers, kept them unequal in size so as to prevent a monotonous facade.

The interior of St. Joseph's does not reveal any High Victorian Gothic features; rather, it is more an essay in Neo-Gothic. It should be remembered that the High Victorian Gothic of Butterfield, as in All Saints, Margaret St., provided an interior even more colorful than the exterior. In that church the interior glowed with colored encaustic tiles (based freely on medieval examples) which covered the walls; tile murals; lavishly used colored granite, marble, and other stones for paving, interior furnishing, etc.; richly painted beams; and a retable of burnished gold. Flooded with colored light from the stained glass windows, such an interior had an almost Byzantine—almost otherworldly—richness and opulence.

When the spire was reshingled about 1979 the decorative gablets near the top, which provided a bit more vertical emphasis and Picturesqueness, were removed. The brickwork of the whole church was cleaned about 1983, restoring the original vivid contrast between light stone detailing and rich red brick.

157. Interior view, St. Joseph's Church.

154. St. Joseph's Church (photo 1972).

155. Strong Place Baptist Church, Brooklyn, 1851–52, from Hussey (1875), pl. 42.

156. Methodist Church, built 1868–69; destroyed by fire, Dec. 1922.

John A. Waterhouse House   *71 Central Ave.*

Although there are only a few elaborate or "high style" Queen Anne houses in Fredonia, the influence of this mode of design was considerable, and a great many smaller dwellings have a tincture of Queen Anne in their massing, variety of surface textures (such as shingled gables), elaborately turned porch posts, or chamfered bays for rooms.

The Queen Anne style traces its origins back to country estates built by Richard Norman Shaw in England in the 1860s and '70s in a style recalling rural country houses of the late medieval period and early 17th century. These quite original houses (which used some half timbering; overhangs; tall, paneled chimneys; hung tiles; etc.) were widely published and their informality of composition fitted them well to the Picturesque esthetic. The style received impetus in America from the British government buildings at the Philadelphia Centennial Exposition (1876), though half-timbering was not a feature that Queen Anne, as it developed in this country in the 1870s and 1880s, used very often.

In America, the style took on its own distinctive qualities. Round or polygonal corner towers were favored; inset panels (in brick walls or chimneys) of cast terra cotta with rosette or floral patterns were incorporated; posts were elaborately turned, often with downward tapering forms; informal—almost casual—composition and massing were common too. Often bands of shingles, or gables filled with them, were employed (an echo of the British hung tiles). Details were often very freely adapted from the classical tradition (American Georgian or Federal), so that pediments, balustrades, or Colonial-style windows, are found.

The Waterhouse House shows many of these features: the tower with shingled top, the steep pediments with prominent modillions or dentils, small terra cotta insets in the front porch, and window frames (like the side porch) fancifully classical. Originally the front arched entrance bay had a balustrade at the top. What is fascinating to learn, however, is that this stylish Queen Anne mansion was created out of a far simpler Square Italian Villa by a thorough remodeling!

The original dwelling was built in 1853. Although only three bays wide, it was given sophistication by its paired brackets, roof balustrade (in place of a more canonical cupola), and cast iron lintels. In 1888 Dr. John A. Waterhouse, a physician from Michigan who had moved to Fredonia in 1883, transformed the house. A tower was added to the northwest corner of the original building, a brick entrance porch (and stairway extension) added near the center, and the south side completely rebuilt, extending it outward somewhat.[31] Cast iron lintels on the south and west sides, but not the north, were replaced by stone, and the roof was completely rebuilt. Except for the remaining 1850s style lintels, and some noticeable changes in brickwork, one would never have thought the house was once an Italian villa. The architects for this transformation were Curtis and Archer.

Why would Dr. Waterhouse so radically remodel his dwelling? One reason was surely that the house was too small for his needs (or *appeared* too small for a man of wealth). Furthermore, in 1888 such an Italianate house was in an "old fashioned" style. In 35 years "picturesqueness" had increased considerably, and the older dwelling lacked the visual variety and interest then fashionable. Nowadays we are able to appreciate a dwelling's original style, with the refinements and character appropriate to the period, thanks to broader historical perspective—and perhaps, esthetic maturity. But in the 19th century, with the crescendo of Picturesqueness growing throughout the decades, the earlier house would have seemed "lacking" to tastes of the 1880s. Probably for similar reasons, the old Thomas Higgins House (1829–30) was remodeled into a Queen Anne mansion about this same time (see Figs. 259 and 260).

158. *John A. Waterhouse House, facade and south side.*

159. *Porch at south side, detail.*

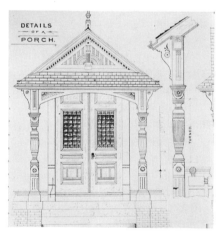

'. *"Details of a Porch," Bicknell and Comstock,* **Modern Architectural Designs and Details** *(1881) plate 7 (detail).*

161. *Facade of house, photo c. 1895.*

162. *F. S. Edwards House from the 1854 Chautauqua County map.*

A frame version of the Queen Anne, built 15 years after the Waterhouse remodeling, but complete with comparable corner tower is found at 96 E. Main St. (A duplicate of it, in mirror image, but with a later porch, is at 35 Hamlet St.) The animated combination of vernacular tradition and formal detailing continues. The asymmetrical form, with two gabled wings bending around the pivotal corner tower, suggest vernacular design, as do the patterned shingles in the two gable ends. But the Queen Anne love of classical features is seen here too—in the attic windows (both based on Colonial models, one semi-circular with apex keystone, and the other oval with *four* "keystones"); and in the Tuscan style fluted columns for the porch.

Houses of this style were included in pattern books of the day. Some of the most famous were published by George F. Barber, a Knoxville, Tenn. architect. In fact, a house (now much remodeled) at 4728 W. Main Rd., Fredonia, is based on design 39 in his *The Cottage Souvenir No. 2* of 1891, a model without corner tower.

The interiors of a few Fredonia houses have their details and decorations recorded in vintage photographs. The Waterhouse House is one such lucky example. The photos reveal how many of the ideas and motifs of the exterior are reflected in the interior too.

The plan as remodeled was open and intricate. The entrance stair hall led directly to the living room (south side) through a wide doorway; from here one could enter the library behind it or, also through wide doors, the parlor on the north side. This room was one of the most spatially intricate. The front portion had, of course, the corner bay jutting out providing a cozy viewing point. About midway in the rather long room, probably where an old partition had been, the chamber was divided by a section of wall that projected slightly, and had tall turned columns against the ends, again, suggesting a division in the space, but not really closing it off. Behind this room (corresponding to the library on the south) was the dining room. Kitchen, pantries, etc. were at the rear of the house.

The photograph of the parlor is especially revealing. The elaborate spindle-work screen framing the bay window provides just the sort of spatial complexity and transitional planes as seen on the outside, in the various porches. The slender columns at the edges of the photo echo the turned posts on the exterior porches as well. What is interesting to note is that such elaborate screens could be ordered from specialty mill-work companies. For example, the E. L. Roberts & Co. *Number 500 General Catalog* (Chicago, 1903), in their "Grilles and Arches" section (pp. 257–292) depict 68 different grilles, large and small. Item R 2230 shows columns on pedestals, and a grille embellished with fabric swags, as found in the Waterhouse House. Such catalogs made the work of local architects a great deal easier, for customers could select from the myriad examples the ones that appealed most strongly to their individual tastes.

Dr. Waterhouse, who did not practice in Fredonia but was apparently in the oil business, sold his house in 1898 to a Mr. Kirkover from Buffalo, but bought it back in 1903. He finally sold it five years later.

The Waterhouse House, and its large carriage house, were both converted into apartments over 35 years ago. The exterior of the house was essentially unchanged; inside original detailing, and at least one fireplace, still survive.

Three good examples of frame Queen Anne houses which dispense with a corner tower can be found at 79 Central Ave. (1887), 131 Central Ave. (1910); and 25 Day St. (1910).

163. *96 East Main St., 1903.*

164. *Southwest living room, Waterhouse House, and front stairs, photo c. 1895.*

165. *Northeast parlor, Waterhouse House, photo c. 1895.*

166. *Design for room grille, from 1903 trade catalog.*

Warren Scott House   *160 Temple St.*

This style of house is sometimes called "Builder's Eastlake," though some might categorize it as a type of Queen Anne. As can be seen, the house has some similarities with the previous essentially Stick Style examples, but the decoration has less of the general structural sense of banding, X-brace panels, etc. of mature Stick Style, and consists more of isolated details (porches, bargeboards, braces, etc.) with chiseled and turned elaboration.

The Warren Scott House was built in 1885. According to a former owner (granddaughter of Mr. Scott), a house originally on the site was divided into two parts and moved down Risley Street to the adjoining lots, where two smaller dwellings were constructed from them. The contractors for the Scott House are said to have been Sly & Coddington ("carpenters and builders," who had a planing mill on Water Street). Mr. Scott, a retired farmer (and also math teacher) built it for his retirement. Photographs of the house taken in 1906, plus the recollection of a former owner, indicate that originally it was painted a tawny yellow, with the trim dark brown. After many years of being a monochrome hue, it was returned to a contrasting paint scheme—which brings out the details far better—in 1985.

The color schemes of late 19th century houses were quite varied. While some, such as this house, originally had traditional earth colors of contrasting hues, others had the most astonishing color combinations. An 1894 Queen Anne house in nearby Brocton, for example, was originally painted light lavender, with the shingle band around the middle a reddish-yellow; the shingled roof was painted slate gray, the cornice and window casings dark and light brown and the window sashes black.

The "Eastlake" style in which we might class this house, is named after the English architect Charles Lock Eastlake, well known in this country after his book *Hints on Household Taste, in Furniture, Upholstery and Other Details* (1868) came out in an American edition (1872). His designs became immensely popular. A reformer of over-decorated, inappropriately-designed, and poorly-built furniture, his book advocated a return to simpler, somewhat medieval forms, sturdily built, with the decorative forms achieved by wood turning, gouging, grooving and chamfering of the panels, legs and other parts with other features (hinges, locks, etc.) also done in a simple, straightforward, style. The somewhat blocky pieces of furniture, in natural wood finishes, were imitated widely, and there even developed a style of architecture (Bicknell illustrates a house "showing East Lake Features" in 1881) named after him, but which Eastlake himself disavowed. Features include the use of porches, bargeboards, etc. with elaborately turned, chamfered, and perforated forms, based presumably on the wood esthetic from his furniture. It is thus more involved than the more straightforward detailing of the Stick Style. In a way the style is a carpenter's version of the Stick Style, since the sort of decoration natural to wood (turning and gouging) comes to the fore. Some of these features can be seen also in the A. O. Putnam House.

The Scott House has the openness of plan that we often find in the late 19th century. The small entrance hall has a straight run stairway; to the left, through wide doors, is the front parlor, connected by a wide opening to the living room (which is expanded outward by an ample bay), which in turn connects with the dining room. Along the other (north) side of the house is a den off the living room, and a lavatory and kitchen off the dining room. Across the rear of the house is a storage room, and back stairs.

As can be seen from the illustration on the Sears House Catalog, this was a popular style into the early 20th century. A somewhat similar, though smaller example, but also with very open connection of rooms, is found at 142 Temple Street.

167. *Warren Scott House, south side and facade (photo 1997).*

169. *Detail of gable, bargeboards and corner bracing, south side.*

168. *Interior view, looking from front parlor to living room, and into dining room (photo 1972).*

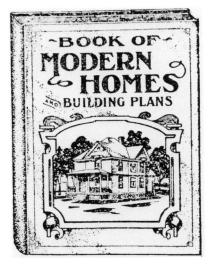

170. *Front cover of Sears, Roebuck & Co.'s* **Book of Modern Homes and Building Plans** *as illustrated in their 1908 general catalog.*

171. *Similar dwelling at 142 Temple St.*

In the architectural fabric of Fredonia we have concentrated on some of its finest houses and public buildings—with a glimpse at mill buildings—but we should not forget that no dwelling was complete without its "outbuildings." These might include a carriage house, gardening or work shed, outhouse, and other structures. Some were treated with architectural sophistication, while others were simple vernacular structures; but all served a particular function in domestic life and in the architectural hierarchy. It is interesting to highlight some of Fredonia's carriage houses, since many of these survive pretty much intact, having been converted in the early 20th century to garages for automobiles.

Examine Figure 48. Those dozens of horses and carriages had homes, as did the people milling about next to them. Not everyone could afford to own a horse, or a carriage; many walked where they needed to go, and others took horse drawn trolleys (see Fig. 83)—or if necessary, hired a horse (from a livery stable). But most prosperous residents, with substantial homes, had a carriage house to take care of their horse or horses, keep its feed, store and maintain all the harnesses and equipment, shelter the carriage, and often lodge the "hired man" who would take care of all this.

Frequently carriage houses were built to reflect the style of the dwelling they served. One of the grandest carriage houses in the area, and most perfectly preserved, is that for 3761 Route 60, just outside of Fredonia. The house is a major Second Empire dwelling; the carriage house by its arched windows, Picturesque board and batten cladding, and sheer size, comports well with it. Located in the country, this extra-large structure probably had some agricultural uses as well.

We have actually glimpsed carriage houses behind Fredonia dwellings all along the way: see for example Figs. 93, 98, 105, 116, and 120—all built, coincidentally, in the 1860s. Here we can examine a few other interesting examples.

That formerly at 36 Center St. appears to have been a Greek Revival *house* first (1840s?), with the later carriage entrance replacing the original front door and window to the right (partly filled in). Another early one, *built* as a carriage house, was formerly behind 35 Center St. The slightly gabled window lintels seem to be an 1850s holdover of the Greek Revival, but the eaves trim reflects coming "Picturesque" movements (the entrance canopy may be later, from the 1870s). The many front windows suggest a residence for stable hands, or perhaps office space; at the rear we see two small windows which provided light and air—and a view—for two horse stalls; above, mid-way down, is the door for loading in hay to the loft. (Note the ancillary work building to the left, by contrast in a plain vernacular style.) A decade or so later, the wide eaves and curved brackets of the carriage house at 150 Central Ave. reflect the main house, in Italianate style; the left two doors could be original, since in the era before electricity, natural illumination was important. The right-hand door indicates refitting for the automobile age.[32]

A final example, at 346 Central Ave., by its steep gable and thus more animated design, echoes the Picturesqueness of the Queen Anne dwelling it serves. And our next entry provided a splendid carriage house in Shingle Style treatment. All of these reflect varied architectural solutions to functional needs, but also depict how, in most cases, careful design was applied to "lesser" domestic buildings.

In the early 20th century some attractive automobile garages, often emulating the style of the "main house," were erected here too. That at 150 Central Ave. (1903), is very good, as is the one at 29 Risley St., for a Stickley Bungalow of 1929–30. Some appear to be professionally designed mail-order garages; the one-car unit at 38 Barker St. is almost identical to (though a bit narrower than) a garage sold by Bennett Homes of North Tonawanda in their 1927 catalog (p. 76), even to the hinges and hardware. The two-car garage at 165 Temple St. is likewise nearly the same as a model in *Architectural Economy*, published by a Chicago lumber dealers organization in 1930 (p. 101), helping to assure high quality design.

172. Carriage house/barn for 3761 Route 60, Fredonia.

173. Carriage house formerly at 36 Center St.

174. Carriage house formerly at 35 Center St.

175. Carriage house for 150 Central Ave.

176. Carriage house for 346 Central Ave.

Shingle Style Carriage House   *formerly 300 Central Ave.*

Although Fredonia does not have any true Shingle Style houses (some good ones can be found in Jamestown, however) this wonderful carriage house is extremely close and can be used to illustrate this fascinating style. Since the Shingle Style *influenced* a lot of Fredonia houses—Foursquares, Bungalows, and Colonial Revival houses reflect this treatment—it should be considered here.

The Shingle Style (a term coined by Vincent Scully, not a contemporary appellation) can, in a way, be traced back to the late 1840s. A cottage built by an Albany architect which Downing illustrated in 1850 (there called "Swiss," mainly because of the balconies and overhangs) shows that the beauty of houses completely shingled was appreciated, as one might expect in a period when "natural materials" were advocated. Although it is the only shingled house he illustrates in the volume, Downing clearly liked the treatment: "This mode of covering wooden houses with shingles is a very durable mode, and when the shingles are cut in ornamental patterns, it has a more tasteful and picturesque effect than common weather-boarding." He also realized that shingles were a common American cladding treatment, mentioning "shingle-covered Dutch farmhouses in our vicinity, more than a hundred years old, and still in good preservation."

The true Shingle Style, however, was developed in the New England states about 1880, and was popular for over a decade. While some influence may well be due to the renewed interest in older American buildings of the time, spurred by the 1876 centennial as well as studies by architects, another undeniable influence is from the previously mentioned British houses by Shaw, in which the hung tile was translated into an American idiom—shingles—when adapted in this country. The style was extremely popular for seaside houses, undoubtedly influenced by the many shingled houses to be found in New England seaports, especially Nantucket. These informal, capacious Shingle Style dwellings frequently used boulders or rough stonework in conjunction with the natural shingle surface, as in Emerson's Loring House of 1881. Sometimes details (the form of a window, or its glazing pattern, for example) were based on Georgian- or Federal-style models. The interior plans of Shingle Style buildings were often quite free.

Thus the Shingle Style draws on a number of threads: 17th and 18th century American Colonial houses (especially near the ocean, where shingles stood up best); use of shingle work in Queen Anne dwellings (parallel to hung tile in the work of R. N. Shaw in England); and a revived vernacular treatment at mid-century (as Downing's Swiss cottage) as part of a love of Picturesque texture. During its heyday the Shingle Style was probably seen primarily by most people as a form of Colonial Revival—understanding architecture in anything but historic terms was difficult before the 1880s. But with modern hindsight we recognize that it is actually an early "abstract" or "modernist" mode, in which texture, volumes, surface treatment, and overall composition of forms can be appreciated in more-or-less pure esthetic terms. Its appearance in the 1880s was one of the harbingers of emerging non-historical modernism in America architecture.

The carriage house for 300 Central Ave., which was probably built in 1899–1900 along with the main house, expresses well this Shingle Style esthetic. Large, bold, simple shapes, which are at the same time expressions of function, articulate the capacious four-bay carriage house. The long slope of the rear does indeed suggest 17th century Colonial houses, but the projecting facade gable and large roof ventilator give it a more robust, late-19th century feel. The beautifully weathered brown shingles added visual richness to the building.[33] Trim in many Shingle Style buildings was often dark green. These earth colors continue the naturalistic trend begun by Downing in the 1840s, and augmented by Shingle Style designers such as H. H. Richardson, Peabody and Stearns, or W. R. Emerson in the 1880s.

177. Shingle Style Carriage House from the southeast (demolished; photo 1973).

*178. "A Swiss Cottage," in Downing, **Country Houses** (1850), fig. 46; designed by G. J. Penchard, Albany, N. Y.*

179. Charles G. Loring House, Pride's Crossing, Mass., by W. R. Emerson, 1881.

Forest Hill Cemetery Gate Houses   *55–57 Lambert Ave.*

One of the most popular, and highly successful, styles of architecture in the late 19th century —from the late 1870s to the mid 1890s—was Richardsonian Romanesque (not to be confused with the earlier 19th century Romanesque Revival, which does not happen to be represented in Fredonia), named after its originator and major practitioner, Henry Hobson Richardson (1838-1886). The Forest Hill Cemetery Gate Houses are very good examples of this style.

The Cemetery chapel (left hand building), the superintendent's residence and office (to the right), and the handsome gates and pillars, were designed by Enoch Curtis; the cornerstone on the chapel is dated 1896.[34] The designs were published in an attractive perspective rending in the Oct. 13, 1894 *Grape Belt* ("Proposed Entrance to Forest Hill Cemetery"); plans of both buildings were also included. This article also mentions that the estimated cost would be $10,000; one of the six trustees wanted the buildings to be constructed of brick, since it would be cheaper, but fortunately the stone design was executed.

The Forest Hill Cemetery Association was formed in 1854 after a group of 39 local residents, including Levi and William Risley, Lorenzo Morris, and George Barker, met to form a Village Cemetery Association; the current name was chosen at a July meeting, and the first land, nine acres of the present site, was purchased. Dedication services were held in 1855. According to the 1915 *Annual Report* of the Association, the land was then surveyed by Lucius Hurlbut ("engineer and surveyor") and "after visiting some of the more modern cemeteries, [Hurlbut] made an excellent plan for laying out the ground.... Most of the lots mapped were with curved lines adapted to the topography of the ground." It was, thus, based on the Rural, or Garden Cemetery plan then being developed, which followed the model of Mt. Auburn Cemetery in Cambridge, Mass. (1831). Though the land here is not as hilly as the name might imply, it does indeed have gentle undulations to which the curving roads conform. Further land (15 acres) was added in 1870 when the old fairgrounds were purchased and finally, in 1911 and 1914, about 10½ more acres were bought.

After rather difficult beginnings, the Cemetery Assn. prospered, so it is not surprising that by 1896 the present imposing gate houses were built (to replace earlier, apparently frame, buildings). The style was based on that solid and massive mode developed by Richardson, beginning about 1870, in which the apparent style, based on European Romanesque forms, was actually subservient to the bold massing and composition, and the rugged yet varied stonework which, in his best buildings, would be differentiated in treatment, finish and detail depending on the location. Contrasting types of stone, such as light granite and dark sandstone, were generally used to help mark major divisions. These gate houses, however, are of reddish Potsdam sandstone with dark mortar (a common feature) on a foundation of lighter, contrasting, stone. Richardson's buildings, as mentioned previously, often tended to be conceived more as form and material, rather than in a conscious "style"; so that while many architects could — and did — imitate his stylistic features, many actually missed the more basic element, that of bold composition and massing. Because of the handsome materials used in this style, the rough, tactilely appealing surfaces, and its extremely solid appearance, Richardsonian Romanesque buildings often have a sense of authority, and a visual interest, far greater than their actual size might suggest.

The chapel, which was essentially an open rectangular room with large fireplace (in a style not unlike that used by Richardson and his contemporaries) at one end, and stained glass windows at the other end, had lavatories (with doors directly to the grounds as well) added in 1915. The chapel is now partitioned, and used for offices. The superintendent's house, which originally had a simple balustrade over the front porch roof, has a central hallway containing stairs with the parlor to the left. To the right is the dining room with square bay; behind it is the kitchen, and at the very back a room for the Superintendent's office.

180. *Forest Hill Cemetery Gate House and Chapel (photo 1972).*

181. *Ames Memorial Library, North Easton, Mass.,*
by H. H. Richardson, 1877–79.

183. *Fireplace in Chapel, east wall.*

182. *Detail of stonework on Chapel, north side*
(photo 1972).

93

Enoch A. Curtis House   50 Central Ave.

Two styles previously illustrated, the Shingle Style and the Queen Anne, drew some of their (often quite different) features and ideas from earlier colonial architecture. The former's use of shingles, natural finishes, beamed interiors, and large fireplaces, have some links with 17th and early 18th century buildings; the latter's rather freely adapted pediments, modillions and dentils, and some decorative features, are from the later 18th century. But during the 1870s architects began to study 18th century colonial buildings more closely, and especially after the Centennial Exposition of 1876 a renewed interest in the more orderly, and nostalgically appealing, colonial forms was apparent. By the mid-1880s a number of houses in a clearly Colonial Revival style were being erected.

Enoch Curtis bought this property in 1875 for $6,000, a price which indicates that a house was already on the lot. In fact, the 1879 *Daily Graphic* has a view of the Curtis residence which shows it to have been a cross-shaped, gabled vernacular house with first floor front porch and slightly arched windows. According to *Censor* articles, a major remodeling campaign began in the summer of 1900, and was completed in the spring of 1901.[35] The Curtis House can be considered a good example of the early Colonial Revival style; its links with the Picturesque Queen Anne can still be felt.

As can be seen, in spite of the large corner tower (actually projecting only slightly from the body of the house, but given its tower effect by the roof), the house is conceived of as a rectangular block, gable parallel to the street, with the gable ends finished off as pediments, a common early 18th century feature (see Fig. 212). The front porch, with paired Roman Doric columns and corner piers, is clearly more academic and correct than the more freely treated Queen Anne. The general regularity and compactness of the shape of the house (the first floor wing to the left was added in the 1920s) reveals this trend toward more ordered form. It will also be noticed that corners are marked with tall Ionic pilasters; other details, such as the scroll pediment with urn over the second floor tower window, and the pedimented projecting bay on the south side, are also based generally on 18th century Georgian buildings. The prominent modillions decorating the cornices come from the same source.

The interior continues this classical motif. The plan was originally quite open. After passing through a small vestibule, one entered a large hall with the stairs (the landing occupying the projecting facade bay) against the south wall. The hall is divided at the center by a beam supported by Roman Doric columns at each end, which provide a visual division of the space. To the north, through a wide doorway (now closed up), one could pass from the hall to the library, which originally had built-in shelves to a height of about 5 feet—as we have seen, Curtis appears to have had quite a library of architectural books and journals! Behind the hall, also on the south side, one entered the living room; this has now been extended and much remodeled. To the north of this room, behind the library, is the dining room, with a high paneled wainscoting, and china closets at the north end decorated with Doric pilasters—with whimsically squat Ionic pilasters above them. The beamed ceiling recalls 17th century interiors, though the academic details and symmetry of the room are based on later 18th century classical forms. Behind this compact front block of the house was a kitchen and pantry wing, and rear stairs, all now somewhat remodeled, apparently between 1920 and 1937. Shifting of doorways and other changes in the dining room and library probably date from this period.

The building was converted into several apartments between 1947 and 1953. The colonial details, however, are essentially all on the first floor.

184. Enoch A. Curtis House, facade and south side.

185. Entrance Hall, Curtis House, looking southeast.

186. Dining room, looking northwest.

Scott-Card House   *150 Central Ave.*

By the late 1890s more historically correct, and more formally and symmetrically arranged, Colonial Revival houses were common. F. W. Scott built this house in 1903; it is a good example of this later, more mature phase. Henry Card, who achieved success in the wine business, was a later owner.

The greater formality of the exterior is at once noticeable. The brick dwelling is compact and contained, with the truncated hipped roof clearly defining the cubic mass. The corners, and the central entrance bay, are articulated by tall Roman Doric pilasters. The original roof balustrade was removed about 1962, but a replacement was reinstated (with similar ones on the porch roofs), about 1982. These features—the shape of the house, pilasters, roof balustrade—are, as a comparison with the Vassall-Longfellow House shows, prominent colonial features which are here revived. Although the Scott-Card House does not have a central pediment, as the colonial example does, the central bay is emphasized by a large pedimented dormer at this point. The Palladian window below it, giving further formality to the facade, was also an 18th century feature found in more elaborate houses. The front porch, with paired Doric columns, is original (as is the side porch).

The interior also has an ordered arrangement. The plan returns to the old central hallway form, although its 12' width and the inclusion of a fireplace make it a useable living space. The stairs are located at the far end, running up against the west wall. The main living room, on the south side of the hall, was entered through a very wide doorway with square piers at the edges; as in the hall, the fireplace here is based on Federal (not Georgian) models, and is considerably larger in size than the original type would have been. As can be seen, the stair railing, interior paneling, and beamed ceiling, were intended to call up Georgian models. Behind the living room on the south side is a second chamber, entered from the hall. On the north side are two rooms, connected by a doorway, with pantries against the rear wall. The second floor also has considerable Colonial trim. The attic is a large open space, unfinished.

Another Colonial Revival house of this type is found at 193 Central Ave. The hipped roof cubic form is articulated at each corner by slender pilasters in more-or-less Tuscan form; the front porch (and a side one not visible in this view) are embellished with finely detailed Ionic capitals on fluted columns.[36] The contrasting body color permits the detailing of cornices, pilasters, columns, and window frames to stand out clearly. Here are only a few Queen Anne reminiscences —the stucco-work reliefs in the attic dormers, and their diamond pane upper lights.

This house was built in 1907–08 by local contractor William S. Sly as his own home, and reveals another source for well-designed dwellings in Fredonia other than a local architect, or a creative carpenter. The firm of Sly & Coddington were "contractors & builders," who also provided building materials and manufactured "sash, doors & blinds," according to the 1912 Fredonia directory. Such companies would often use mail-order plans in constructing houses; clients could leaf through catalogs with hundreds of designs to find the style, size, and plan that suited them best. In this case Mr. Sly selected Design No. 569 from *The Radford American Homes: 100 House Plans*, published by Radford Architectural Co. of Chicago in 1903. The firm employed a number of licensed architects specializing in house designs who turned out these models in great numbers (the architect for this one was G. W. Ashby).

Such mail-order plans when built were often customized. Mr. Sly enlarged the living room by cleverly extending it onto the porch, and raised the side bay to two full stories—and widened the house a bit too. But the origin of the design as created in Chicago by a successful national house plan company is still evident.

187. *Scott-Card House, facade and south side (photo 1984).*

188. *Vassall-Longfellow House, Cambridge, Mass., 1759.*

189. *Scott-Card House, interior hallway.*

190. *193 Central Avenue, 1907–08.*

191. *Design No. 569, **Radford American Homes** (1903), p. 227.*

Manufacturers and Traders Trust Co. *1 East Main St.*

The Academic Revival style (also called Beaux-Arts Classicism) was extremely popular after 1893, and well into the 20th century, for buildings such as banks, railway stations, and post offices which wanted to appear traditional and impressive. Fredonia's M & T Bank, though a bit late in date, is a fine example. The bank was originally built as the Citizens Trust Co. (founded in 1906) in 1929; the cornerstone indicates that it was "Designed and Erected by Hoggson Brothers," of New York and Chicago. The engineer in charge was W. J. Banks.

The Academic Revival style received its main impetus from the Columbian Exposition of 1893, held in Chicago. Although new and innovative design was going forward at this time for commercial building under Louis Sullivan and other Chicago architects, most of the architects for the Fair were from the east coast where the revival of more traditional forms had been growing. The particularly monumental and classical style chosen for most of the Fair's buildings had its immediate source in the academic classical tradition of the Ecole des Beaux-Arts in Paris, whose prize-winning students were sent to Rome for additional study. It is thus not surprising that the buildings found at the Fair recall to mind something of the scale, grandeur, and style of Imperial Rome. Richard Morris Hunt, one of the chief architects of the Fair, had lived and worked in France from 1843 to 1855, and had studied at the Ecole des Beaux-Arts.

The highly decorated classical style of the Fair was immensely popular. Undoubtedly part of the appeal was the superb organization and arrangement of the buildings, creating urban spaces of impressive grandeur. And to many, the strongly classical style, obvious and somewhat pompous, was a welcome change from the apparent confusion of the latter decades of the century. The facade of the Citizens Trust Co. was based on the form of a huge Roman triumphal arch with its central archway flanked by columns, and capped by a cornice and parapet with inscriptions. The motif is probably adapted from Beaux-Arts designs, or possibly the Columbian Exposition directly. The central feature of the immense peristyle closing the end of the main court of the Fair has such a triumphal arch (an inflated version of the Arch of Titus in the Roman Forum), and the rows of Corinthian columns flanking it are even picked up in the side columns of the Fredonia bank. The overall effect—blocky, massive, big in scale—is very Roman indeed. (That this sort of Academic Revival bank was an established type in the early 20th century is suggested by a similar, but simpler, version from 1916 located in Charlottesville, Va.)

The beautifully carved details of the Fredonia bank are more eclectic than its overall design, however. While the lettering, the crouching griffin and floral rinceau found at each upper corner of the facade are Roman, the decorative panel between the pilasters below it is Renaissance in origin. The handsome composite capitals containing acanthus leaves, seated winged lions, and helmeted heads, seem to be original creations of the Hoggson Brothers.

In keeping with the grandly impressive exterior, the interior was on an equally imperial scale. The banking chamber was one vast room, with tall arched windows (with pilasters on each side) to light the hall. Above, suspended from the paneled ceiling, were two huge brass chandeliers. The tellers' counters, tables, and other fittings were also in classical design, of marble and brass. At the back of the hall was the vault, prominently situated in the center, and above it, appearing as if a balcony, the directors room.[37]

The interior was completely remodeled in 1969. The chandeliers and remaining original fittings were sold, the ceiling dropped by about 12 feet, the east windows blocked up, and the west windows (because of the lower ceiling) made shorter.

192. *Manufacturers and Traders Trust Co., facade and west side (photo 1985).*

193. *Detail of Peristyle, Court of Honor, Columbian Exposition, Chicago, 1893.*

194. *Bank in Charlottesville, Va., 1916.*

195. *Detail, Manufacturers and Traders Trust Co.*

Otto F. Hakes House *219 Central Ave.*

We have seen before that there were a number of developments in the late 19th century that we can consider sources for the distinctively modernist architecture of the 20th century—a mode of design which is non-historically based, and deals rather with materials, interior and exterior form and space in a wide variety of ways. Development in the buildings of Richardson, Louis Sullivan, and others in the late 19th century, together with influence from industrial and engineering work, are other sources. In the early 20th century Frank Lloyd Wright, who had worked for Sullivan, was the major architect to continue this non-historical thread in America.

But as we have seen, there were parallel trends, culminating in the Academic Revival of the 1893 Fair, which gave a new impetus to various historical approaches which were, for most people, the style of choice.

One of the revival styles which became popular in the 1890s, perhaps almost in reaction to the overly formal Academic Revival style, was the Elizabethan Revival. Though the term "Jacobethan" is preferred by some historians—to suggest its varied sources—in 19th century architectural works the style is usually (if not quite correctly) called Elizabethan. Although some houses generally in this mode were published at mid-century by Downing and others, the Elizabethan Revival here considered began only toward the end of century. Some of its sources are the already mentioned work of Richard Norman Shaw, and some of the very early Shingle Style houses of Richardson and others which used half-timbering, and other consciously late medieval features. British publications aided in the more accurate adaptation of the picturesque forms.

Elizabethan style houses, from their associations with rural England of the olden times, were especially popular for homes on large lots suggesting "country living." Designs in this mode with steep roofs, brick or stone bases, and plenty of half-timbering, were perennial favorites in the American professional press. For example, as early as 1877 (inspired by contemporary work in England by Shaw) noted architect Charles F. McKim published a design in this mode in *The American Architect and Building News*. A similar house, by Cram and Wentworth, was illustrated by them in 1893, and even in 1900 a large, rambling country seat by a W. A. Bates was given a two-page photographic spread.

The Hakes House took its current form in 1916. It was actually a drastic remodeling of a house of 1866 built by H. L. Taylor. The half-timbering in the gables, the grouped windows with heavy mullions, the projecting bays, and the carved doorway with Tudor arch, all recall the informal late medieval country house that the style wished to emulate.

The interior, as the many gables and bays on the exterior might suggest, is quite open. The wide entrance hall containing the stairs, running up against the north wall, gives access to the dining room (and kitchen and pantry wings) through an ample doorway to the east, and the large living room, ending in a bay, to the west. Off the living room to the south is a solarium, and to the north two smaller rooms.

Another house in this style (built in 1899–1900) is at 300 Central Avenue. The narrowly spaced half-timbering on the second floor emulates a mode of construction popular in southern England, especially Kent, during the 16th and early 17th centuries. How close the Fredonia house comes to work by a master like Shaw is suggested by the comparison with his Merrist Wood, Surrey, built 1876–77. Note that in the American esthetic, the brick of the lower story, and hung tile of the wing at the left, are rendered in wood shingles. With its large chimney (a second at the far end has been removed), it really does suggest an Elizabethan manor house. Now converted into apartments, the interior still retains much of its original paneling and beaming.

196. *Otto F. Hakes House; Cottage Street (north) facade, and west end.*

197. *Design for the Thomas Dunn House, Newport, R.I., by Charles F. McKim, published in* **The American Architect and Building News,** *1877.*

198. *300 Central Ave.*

199. *R. N. Shaw, Merrist Wood, Surrey, 1876–77.*

Aladdin-type Foursquare   *63 Cushing St.*
Alton M. Loomis House   *49 Maple Ave.*

The Foursquare—a modern term for this straightforward and solid-looking dwelling—was "reform" domestic design of the 1890s through the 1920s which were popular in Fredonia, as well as nation-wide. The type obviously owes much to the square Italian Villa of the 1840s and '50s; by 1886 a Foursquare-like house complete with hipped roof and shed dormer, plus spacious porch was published in *The American Architect and Building News*. Denver architect Frank E. Kidder published an early Foursquare in 1891, and a popular builders magazine illustrated a brick version by 1895. Then everyone began designing these capacious, dignified, and "foursquare" houses—which were far simpler to build, and less "Picturesque" than the contemporary late Queen Anne dwellings. William Radford had mail-order plans for one by 1898, and Robert Shoppell's "Co-operative Building Plan Assn." of New York City by 1900.

The house at 63 Cushing is actually a radical remodeling of 1928–29 of an earlier frame dwelling of 1909–10, making it into a perfect example of the popular Foursquare. The contrasting clapboards below and shingles above, the beam-ends projecting on the porch, and the triple-window grouping for the front room, gave the simple geometry of the house visual and textural interest. A similar house shown in the 1918 *Aladdin Homes* catalog was called "The Standard," and indeed it was.

Homeowners could order Aladdin houses complete: all the lumber precisely cut and fitted, to be erected with no waste of material or time. The Cushing Street house is thus a local carpenter's skillful version of a "catalog" house, following in his remodeling the sort of stylish dwelling offered by Aladdin, and a host of other companies.

When Sears, Roebuck & Co. began issuing their big general catalogs in 1893, building materials and components were simply one of their departments. To boost flagging sales they began to offer in 1908 free house plans and specifications: when the prospective home-builder studied their materials carefully (such things as doors, windows, staircases, mantels, flooring, finished lumber like clapboards or shingles, plumbing, furnaces, sinks, and so on) they would see how economical it would be to order them from Sears. "Rough lumber" and of course masonry was specifically excluded.

The 1908 general catalog explains this service, and urges the reader to order their *Book of Modern Homes and Building Plans* (sent free) which would illustrate "a large variety of completed houses, together with the floor plans of each" similar to the three examples shown in their general catalog. The "vast number of beautiful completed houses" in their special catalog were, they noted, designed by "the most skillful licensed architects in the country." The book, they asserted with ingenuous hyperbole, "would convey more ideas to you in five minutes than an architect would in a year," enabling the prospective builder to select an appropriate house, "plainly marked with a price."

By 1911 Sears began selling *all* the materials ("rough lumber" included, but still excluding masonry), needed to erect a house, though it was not "cut and fitted" at the factory (as was Aladdin's) until after 1915. Because Sears manufactured all the building material and components themselves, they could provide highest quality material at the lowest possible price.

Several concrete block houses similar to the one illustrated in the Sears catalog are to be found in Fredonia. This mode of building, claimed to be cheaper, and "more artistic in design" than other materials, permitted the blocks to be made in a wide variety of surface designs and patterns. One of the most common, "Standard Rock Face," is used at 49 Maple Avenue, built about 1910. The similarity with the illustration published by Sears is striking. Since the furnace, apparently original, is marked "Sears," this may well be a genuine Sears house. A similar house, at 37 Newton Street, built in 1910, even has the bay for the living room on the facade as shown on the Sears plan. A third example found at 33 Curtis Place (built about 1908) was constructed by a local builder for himself. The blocks used here are smooth faced, but with rusticated corner blocks.

200. *Foursquare at 63 Cushing St.*

201. *"Aladdin Homes," Catalog No. 31, 4th ed. (1918–19), p. 22.*

202. *49 Maple Ave., facade and east side.*

203. *Concrete block house illustrated in 1908 Sears, Roebuck & Co. catalog, p. 597.*

Harry P. Beebe House   *266 Central Ave.*

A style which became extremely popular during the first three decades of the 20th century, and which was especially well adapted to smaller, conveniently planned houses, was the Bungalow Style. Its great popularity in Fredonia is attested by the dozens of houses in, or based on, this mode. A particularly good example of this style is the Harry P. Beebe House, which was built in 1914. The architect is know to have lived here, and a steel beam in the basement has "H. P. Beebe, Fredonia" painted on it.

The term "bungalow" comes from India, where it was a low house with a veranda on all sides, built as a rest house for travelers in the 19th century. In the late 19th century in America the term was used occasionally to suggest the informal quality of a vacation home. The bungalow—characterized by low, usually one-story form; wide eaves and porches; convenient and informal plan; often built with natural materials like shingles or stone—found its most fertile ground in California. The sources of its style there are varied, including Spanish and indigenous architecture of the southwest, and even Japanese buildings. It also fitted well into the tradition of informal small houses that Downing had championed a half-century before. The climate, and willingness to experiment, seem some of the reasons that California was an early home.

The style soon became widely popular. Many books and articles were written about its style and its virtues, and the mode was exported to all parts of the country. By 1908 California architects were offering plans, which one could order by mail, for a great variety of bungalows.

The Harry Beebe House is of a type best called a "Stickley Bungalow," characterized by the one-and-a-half story height and two distinctive features: a wide porch across the whole front, and a prominent dormer in the roof slope. This type seems to have been developed first by New York State furniture maker and design reformer Gustav Stickley. He published bungalow designs of this style in his *Craftsman* magazine as early as 1905.[38]

The Stickley Bungalow type favored shingles as their cladding, but the Beebe bungalow consciously refers to California associations: the surface (originally white) is stucco, suggesting whitewashed adobe; the red-shingled roof echoed terra cotta tiles of the southwest; and the prominent beam ends under the eaves reflect adobe (and even Japanese) construction. Large planters on the porch also can be found on California bungalows. The interior plan of Beebe's house is quite open. The large living room extends, as common in bungalows, nearly across the entire front, with the dining room, through wide doors, at its north end. The entry vestibule is to the south of the living room. Behind the vestibule and living room is the ample central hallway, with straight run of stairs, and to the west of that, a library or den. To the west of the dining room is the kitchen and pantry, and rear entry. The interior has numerous closets and storage spaces under the eaves; a skylight over the central stairway contributes to the general air of openness. There has been some remodeling, notably the second floor at the rear, which has been expanded.

There are several other bungalows in Fredonia (and eastward on Route 20) of this same distinctive type with rounded ends; they may all be by Harry Beebe. A fine example is at 138 E. Main, built in 1918.[39] The exterior finish of tan brick suggests more the Eastern, rather than Californian, naturalistic esthetic.

The bungalow could take many forms. A simple gabled type from 1915–16, with side roof dormers, ample front porch, and side bay window—and beautiful natural-stained shingle cladding—is at 39 Barker St. The row of bungalows (two of Stickley Bungalow type) on Water Street is especially attractive.[40] The first, more informal one, is actually a design from Sears ("The Kilbourne," sold between 1921 and 1929).

204. *Harry P. Beebe House, facade view (photo 1972).*

205. **Living room, looking south from dining room.**

206. *Bungalow at 39 Barker St.*

207. *Bungalows at 199, 197, 195 Water St. (photo 1983).*

United Methodist Church   *25 Church St.*

The Neo-Gothic style, quite distinct from the Gothic Revival of a century earlier, became popular in the first three decades of this century for churches, naturally, as well as for a good number of college campuses. The Methodist Church of Fredonia, which replaced the High Victorian Gothic structure formerly on the site, was constructed in 1923–24.

The Neo-Gothic style is easily distinguished from the older Gothic Revival by its less consciously Picturesque treatment, as well as the style being more archeologically "correct"—English Perpendicular Gothic was a favorite. The use of brick and masonry, or masonry alone (but not wood), is characteristic. Among the most famous examples are the collegiate buildings erected at Yale University during the 1920s. There the educational usage was sanctioned by the many late Gothic structures to be found at the universities Oxford and Cambridge in England.

The use of Neo-Gothic for churches was appropriate especially in a period when stylistic revivals were still practiced by many architects with considerable originality. The Methodist Church is said to have been modeled on King's College Chapel, Cambridge, perhaps the most famous of all Perpendicular Gothic structures in England. Actually, because of the entrance projections to the sides of the main facade, the design is closer in form to a church such as Bath Abbey (16th to early 17th century) which has side aisles, lower than the central nave. Originally the Fredonia church was designed without the wood entrance porches, but difficulty with snow and ice, shed from the roof directly above the entrance, necessitated their installation about 1971.

The large Perpendicular Gothic window at the facade, the two flanking towers, the lancet windows at the sides between stepped buttresses, are all appropriate to the style. The wing at the rear, containing classrooms and offices, has a more domestic flavor, however, with square label moldings over doors and square-headed windows, and a cornice decorated with battlements, commonly found in non-ecclesiastical buildings in the Neo-Gothic style. An attractive, freely-composed, version of the Neo-Gothic can be found in Dunkirk on Central Ave. in the First Christian Church, built in 1925.

208. *United Methodist Church, facade and east side.*

209. *Detail of corner tower.*

210. *Abbey Church, Bath (Somerset), 16th century.*

Lathrop-van der Voort House	*272 Central Ave.*
U.S. Government Post Office	*21 Day St.*
Mason Hall	*State University College*
Middlesex Garden Apartments	*1–6 Middlesex Dr.*

The Neo-Colonial style thrived in the United States at about the same time as the Neo-Gothic —in fact, was a popular alternate style for college campuses in the 1920s and '30s. Obviously it had its roots in the Colonial Revival, but the Neo-Colonial is more archeologically exact, often copying parts (or all) of well-known colonial buildings in their design. Like the Neo-Gothic, the forms tend to be more smooth, and less robust, than previous essays in this style. When built by the best architects, with ample funds—such as the dormitories at Harvard College of the 1920s—the results could be very good, with excellent craftsmanship lavished on the interior Georgian- and Federal-style woodwork as well as the exterior details. It was also a style popular for country estates, and even smaller houses, because of its associations with a nostalgically attractive and stylistically appealing period in our own history. Especially after the major reconstructions at Colonial Williamsburg of the Governor's Palace (as of 1706–20) and the Capitol (as of 1701–04) were completed in 1934, the style met with wide approbation. The heyday of the Neo-Colonial style ended with the Second World War, although some good Neo-Colonial work is found in the late 40s.

A number of Fredonia buildings show the various manifestations—and the persistence—of this style. The Lathrop-van der Voort House, built in 1918, is a good early domestic example. Originally erected for Daniel W. Lathrop, an executive with the Atlas Steel Corp. of Dunkirk, it was bought by J. Nelson van der Voort, Jr. in 1923, who added the rear section, in similar style, in 1933. The general shape, the white trim in contrast with the red brick, the cornice enriched with classical dentils, the prominent chimneys—they are all Georgian features common to dozens of 18th-century buildings. Distinctly 20th century, however, is the pergola at the right side, which runs across the facade and joins a comparable structure (glazed as a sun porch) on the south side. This sort of treatment would never have been found in a real Georgian house, but was a pleasant addition to the 20th century incarnation.

The interior retains many of the features we associate with Georgian mansions, such as a wide central hallway divided at the middle by a keystoned arch. The stairs are at the rear of the hall. To the left is a large living room, the entire depth of the front portion of the house, and to the right, two rooms, separated by service stairs. Interior woodwork and fireplaces are all in Neo-Georgian and Neo-Federal style.

A good number of Post Offices were erected in the Neo-Colonial mode (it has both Georgian and Federal style features) during the thirties, such as the Fredonia example (Louis A. Simon, supervising architect). (A rear wing in compatible style was added in 1997.) Because of its traditional and historical associations, this mode was popular for government buildings. But the Colonial design here has a thinner treatment than either true Georgian example, or more elaborate versions of Neo-Georgian. This can be gauged by comparing its most prominent feature, the doorway framed with pilasters and capped by a broken scroll pediment (with urn), to a real Georgian example of 200 years before.

Mason Hall, built in 1940, is also quite good Neo-Colonial, and compares well to a genuine late 18th century structure of this general type. The carved stone doorway is particularly good. A late attempt at Neo-Colonial is nearby Fenton Hall (1953).[41]

Among the latest Neo-Colonial buildings in Fredonia are the Middlesex Garden Apartments, six buildings arranged to form attractive groupings with interior "courtyard" effects. Built in 1948, the different roof forms (gabled or gambrel), use of red brick, and a variety of classical door casings, provide much appeal.

211. Lathrop-van der Voort House, facade view.

212. Berkeley Plantation, Virginia, 1726.

213. Mason Hall, State University College, 1940.

214. Old North (begun 1792) Georgetown University, Georgetown, D. C.

215. U. S. Government Post Office, Fredonia, 1935.

216-17. Doorway of Fredonia Post Office (left), and front doorway of Westover Plantation, Va., c. 1730 (right).

218. Middlesex Apartments, 1948.

Edward H. Freeman House   *26 Cottage St.*
William T. Kerr House   *135 Temple St.*
John F. Luke House   *134 E. Main St.*

In the 1920s and '30s some of the most pleasing forms of domestic architecture in the historically based mode adapted to smaller homes were the so-called "period houses" which consciously attempted to evoke historic types of dwellings. The Neo-Colonial style was readily adapted to smaller houses; like larger dwellings and public buildings the associations with historic Americana gave it an added lustre of appeal. In Fredonia, Neo-Colonial houses take many forms, but three types are typical and representative.

The gabled two-story house three bays wide was erected in some numbers: that at 26 Cottage St. (built in 1923) is a good example. As the comparison suggests, one way local builders arrived at these designs was through mail-order plans. In earlier days architectural treatises, carpenters manuals, and pattern books (such as Palladio, Lafever, or Downing) provided drawings of complete buildings that could be adapted by carpenters or architects. But beginning, it seems, with a pattern book published by Cleaveland & Backus Brothers of New York City in 1856, readers could order printed "working drawings and specifications" for designs in the book. Thereafter plans by mail became a common American phenomenon. *The Books of a Thousand Homes* (volume I containing "500 small house plans") edited by Henry Atterbury Smith, AIA, was published by the Home Owners Institute of New York in 1923. Design No. 864 is the sort of model from which 26 Cottage St. could have been built. Another fine example of this two-story three bay type (which here even has a side porch) is at 288 E. Main St., built in 1932–33. Though designed by an Erie architect, it was actually based on mail-order plans from Standard Homes Co. of Washington, D. C. Real colonial types like this are ubiquitous; the center part of the St. George Tucker House in Williamsburg, Va. (a remodeling of 1788–1795), is a close match.

For smaller homes one-and-a-half story dwellings were erected. The brick example at 135 Temple St. dates from 1947. At first, purists might argue that the asymmetrical placement of windows—two at the right of the central doorway, and only one at the left—was "un-Colonial" and smacked of 20th century functionalism. But in fact that composition was not unknown in the 18th century: the frame Captain Orr's Dwelling (c. 1726) in Williamsburg is one, and shown here is a brick example, an outbuilding at Elsing Green Plantation, Va., from 1719. A similar brick Neo-Colonial house—but with symmetrical bay treatment—is at 40 Risley St.; it was erected in 1949.

Specifically coastal New England associations are conveyed by the shingled house at 134 E. Main St., of 1920. The gambrel roof type was found throughout the colonies, but the shingle cladding suggests a seaport town where unpainted shingles stood up to the salt air best. The Gott House in Rockport, Mass. (1702) is the sort of cozy, nearly vernacular model that evoked such charm to home-builders of the 1920s—as it still does to us today. The original builder of the Fredonia dwelling, John Luke, was a local contractor; he obtained plans for the house from some outside source, according to his daughter-in-law. The sloped dormers are an 18th century feature appropriate to this sort of design. The house even has its original gambrel-roofed garage.

219. 26 Cottage St.

*220. **Book of 1,000 Homes**, vol. I (1923), pl. 127.*

221. 135 Temple St.

222. Kitchen wing, c. 1719, Elsing Green Plantation, Va.

223. 134 East Main St.

224. Gott House, Rockport, Mass., 1702.

Anthony F. Drago House   *135 Central Ave.*
Charles R. Farnham House   *38 Leverett St.*

Almost as popular as Neo-Colonial period houses were those based on English models—homes with half-timbering, perhaps a large facade chimney (often found on the fronts of vernacular Tudor houses to which a main fireplace had been added), steep roofs, even bits of wall that suggest buttressing. An alternate source was the English thatched cottage, with lower roof pitch. The aim was to create an attractive, well-designed house with a consciously "period" flavor, the emphasis more on coziness and quaintness than on historical accuracy. The plans were generally good—in more elaborate versions might be quite adventuresome—and the details often very competent.

The Anthony F. Drago House is an excellent example of the little "Tudor" cottage which was quite popular. The remarkably tall entrance gable, the contrasting brick (or stone) and half timbering (on the front and on both ends), the tall, quaintly designed chimney, all bodied forth old world charm. Plans for such houses could be ordered by mail. A page from a 1920s catalog, compiled by a Mr. Floyd A. Dernier (who proudly stated that it was his 22nd annual edition) is shown in Fig. 4. Such catalogs, with illustrations of attractive young couples embarking on establishing their Home, make delightful if sometimes vacuous reading: "Appreciative of its distinctiveness and cheery atmosphere—grateful for the comfort and protection it bestows—thankful for the blessings and privileges which make it a 'world of its own'—your home," etc. It appears that the Drago House was built from such purchased plans. The elevations of the house are distinguished by "left," "right," etc. rather than cardinal directions; no company or architect's name is given, however.

Mr. Drago (who was an officer and manager of the local Bison Canning Co.) took a lively interest in the construction of the house, and made a good number of changes in the plans and elevations, suggesting that he was dealing with a local contractor, not an architect. Fortunately, all the original papers and correspondence are preserved by the present owners. He raised the main roof by two feet, lowered the dormer window on the front (and altered other windows), redesigned the slope of the right side of the chimney, had the iron balcony installed, and made a number of other emendations. The contractors for the house were Fredonia Builders' Supply Co., although Mr. Drago corresponded with a large number of firms himself for many of the details, in order to assure exactly what he wanted— the hardware, bathroom and kitchen tilework, exterior face-brick, steel casement windows, bathroom fixtures, the garage roof, and other features (including the front drive and walk) were all under his immediate care. The house was begun in 1930, and completed the following year.

Some of his interior changes were for greater openness; an arched partition originally separated the stairs and small hallway from the living room. This opening he made wider, thus giving the room more space. The overall plan, however, is very compact. The living room occupies most of the front, with the stairway at the south end. Behind the living room, through an arched opening, is the dining room, and next to it, behind the stairs and small hallway, the kitchen. A solarium and dining alcove were originally across the back of the house. Rear additions were sympathetically added in 1963.

A house rather similar to this in style, though with rustic stonework around the doorway, is found at 29 Curtis Place (designed in 1924). Another good Tudor Cottage is at 97 Forest Pl. (built 1940–41).

An English Cottage house which draws on the vernacular thatched roof tradition is the 1931 Charles R. Farnham House at 38 Leverett St. (Mr. Farnham was a clerk in the Main Street store of Ray Beck at the time.) While the most famous thatched-roof English dwelling everyone—in those days, anyway —would have known is Ann Hathaway's cottage (from the late 16th century) near Stratford-on-Avon, the direct source for the Farnham House was a set of plans ordered from the *Home Builders Catalog*, published in Chicago. As built, it follows the plans very closely; like the design, it once had facade window boxes (removed in 1977). A rear addition, continuing the general lines of the house, was built in 1985.

225. *Anthony F. Drago House, facade view.*

226. *Interior view, looking from dining room.*

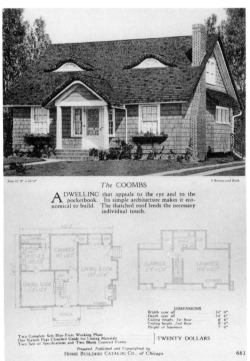

228. **Home Builders Catalog (1927), p. 661.**

227. *38 Leverett St.*

Willard Guntner House   *340 Central Ave.*

International Modern was the first 20th century architectural design, not based on past vocabularies of style, to have been employed by leading architects in both Europe and America. The mode of design was based on the desire to construct efficient, well-planned and composed buildings, using the latest materials and techniques, and avoiding all factors except those that bear directly with form, space, shape, texture, and planning. Thus, while some architects might design in the "style" of International Modern, the movement itself (at least as handled by its most notable practitioners, such as Gropius, Mies van der Rohe, and Le Corbusier in the early 20th century) was not aiming at a conscious *style*, but rather developing functional buildings of the simplest uncluttered form, which spoke of the 20th century and its new machine technology and mass production, not of historical associationalism. It was the affirmation of radically new beginnings, not simply the reinterpretation or "modernization" of older styles.

International Modern can be said to have begun with the construction of the Fagus Factory, Germany, by Walter Gropius and Adolf Meyer, in 1911. Like other buildings in this mode, notably the Bauhaus at Dessau (1925–26) by Gropius, it was characterized by clean crisp lines, contained cubic masses, new industrial materials (such as steel sash windows, pipe railings, etc.) used unabashedly, and walls that might be plain curtains of glass, the supporting piers set back from wall surface. International Modern was, then, clearly a forward looking style, and, like the work of Frank Lloyd Wright, dealt only in abstract form, not historically associated styles.

One outstanding example of an International Modern dwelling was constructed in Fredonia, the Willard Gunther House at 340 Central Avenue. It has been altered somewhat (including the adding of a hipped roof and a later one-story addition across the rear), but is otherwise an excellent representative of the style. It is made of concrete block, with nearly flush joints, accenting the overall cubic mass of the structure, into which the windows are cut in a pattern that reflects interior function. Industrial materials are seen in the use of steel sash; the corner windows, emphasizing the continuity of the exterior surface, are a popular International Modern feature. The simple flat canopy over the front door eschews all historic stylistic antecedents. The Guntner House was built in 1937, the decade in which this style became common in the United States.

The Ralph B. Jones House, in Harrysbourg, Dunkirk, is the other good local example of the style. Built in 1946, it was designed by the owners, according to Mrs. Jones, from ideas they gathered from seeing similar houses in Florida. Edgar Schulenburg (Dunkirk) drew up their ideas and plans.[42]

The only other Fredonia house from this era reflecting the International Modern mode was built in 1947–48 at 199 Lambert Ave. One story high, again of concrete block with nearly flush joints, the simple rectangular dwelling has a projecting entrance porch.[43]

Obviously, with only two examples in the village, despite the mode being bruited in the 1930s as the "style of the future" by the architectural profession, for most people the evocative associations that historically based styles body forth were almost universally preferred. That only two houses in Fredonia, out of over 2,300 extant dwellings, are in this style speaks volumes as to what most people want for their homes. Only in the 1950s and '60s, when less austere modernism was adapted to houses, do we find non-historically based designs in abundance.

Although the International Modern mode of design was too radical for most, it had a strong effect in the simplification and "modernization" of more traditional styles. The Dunkirk and Fredonia Telephone Co. of 1940 is based on Neo-Colonial forms, but it is modernized by now interpreting the pilasters flanking the door as vertical, fluted panels. The cornice is only hinted at by horizontal masonry strips, and the windows, though still framed by moldings, are now filled with steel sash. The result is quite successful.[44]

Later attempts modernized traditionally inspired brick clad buildings by stripping down the details, as in the 1950s. McGinnies Hall on the Fredonia State campus is an example.

229. Willard Guntner House, facade view.

230. The Bauhaus at Dessau, Germany, by Walter Gropius, 1925–26.

231. Dunkirk and Fredonia Telephone Co., 1940.

232. McGinnies Hall, State University College, 1959–60.

Lynn A. Hawkins House   *309 Central Ave.*
L. Walter Schultze House   *38 Birchwood Dr.*

The developments of Frank Lloyd Wright, Walter Gropius, and other modernists, which revolutionized the nature of architecture in the early 20th century, were reflected in some degree by houses erected after the Second World War by builders and contractors, often on speculation (as the Hawkins House was). One might call the style "Contractor Modern."

Many of the homes built in our growing suburbs during the 1950s and '60s could be so classed. One which can represent this mode is found at 309 Central Avenue. Many features found in Wright's early dwellings can be sensed here—the long, low profile; the low gable roof which covers both house and garage; the combination of several materials in one structure. But the Wrightian motifs, are, really, very faint—they are taken as stylistic features, not as a mode of building. While Wright used strip windows, or window walls, to help integrate the interior with the outside, many development houses use the older concept of a window—a hole cut in a wall—and just enlarge it. Wright did often use contrasts of material—natural wood siding, rough-cut stone, etc.—in constructing a house, for they aided integration with the land around. Here, however, the band of stone up to the window level is actually Permastone, and the clapboards above are made of imitation wood (pressed fiber). Thus the whole idea of "natural materials" is sidestepped, and only visually approximated.

However, the interior plan of the Hawkins House (built in 1965 by Fredonia Home Improvement Co.) picks up many modernist ideas quite successfully. The large living room, occupying much of the facade, is linked to the dining space by a wide opening, and this space in turn to the kitchen by an ample doorway. The dining space flows into a hallway connecting the rooms along the rear of the dwelling, so that a pleasantly open and convenient plan is achieved. This certainly employs modernist developments we have mentioned before. In fact, this sort of house—with many stylistic features drawn from work by Wright and others, but with a compactness and simplicity dictated by the experience of builders or contractors, and by judicious economy—has become a 20th century vernacular modernist mode. This house type is often called a "ranch style" home—a term which comes from the "ranch bungalow" of California of the decade before the First World War.

Another option for homebuilders of the 1960s was to choose a traditional dwelling type and adapt it to contemporary needs. This was the case with the L. Walter Schultze House a block away. The house was built in 1966; the owners brought the builder/developer, Sam Castiglia, an illustration from a magazine of a Cape Cod-style home they liked; but Mr. Castiglia did not have any plans for such a dwelling. So combining their ideas with the ground plan of a nearby house they liked, preliminary drawings were prepared. Dr. and Mrs. Schultze then modified these, and gave it the second floor overhang. Seven pages of blue prints were drawn up by D. E. Schulenberg. The exterior turned out to reflect a long-popular Colonial type—which still, even today, evokes traditional "home life" and straightforward American design. The plan is more "high style" than the exterior—a central hallway containing stairs, with rooms on each side: a living room with dining room behind it on the right; a den on the left; and behind this and the stairs, a spacious kitchen.

These were two popular approaches—modified modern and adaptations of traditional—in the 1960s. A third option was to design a house in thoroughly contemporary style—usually with the aid of a professional architect or designer. If, for example, one desired the monumentality, symmetry, formality, and sense of tradition of the Greek Revival, a contemporary house utilizing simple clear volumes, symmetrical composition, masonry or stucco finish, and a roofline and fenestration that is regular and orderly, can be designed. Or, if one prefers the natural wood finishes, irregular silhouette, bay windows, porches and so on of a Downingesque cottage, a modern house using these same ideas in a contemporary vocabulary is the logical solution. Our next entry is an example of this sort of approach.

233. Lynn A. Hawkins House, Carol Ave. at Central Ave.

234. 38 Birchwood Drive.

235. Stanley-Whitman House, Farmington, Conn., c. 1720.

Therold Lindquist House   *227 Chestnut St.*

The term "contemporary" does not, as do many of the other stylistic rubrics, give any idea as to what such a building will look like, since the stylistic possibilities in the continually evolving field of 20th-century architecture are extremely varied. But in houses at least, a mode that is very popular—and which, obviously, continues a tradition going back through Wright and Richardson to Downing and even before—is one that employs a rich variety of natural materials, such as wood (often redwood, cypress, or cedar), brick (available in a wide variety of textures and colors), and stone (usually left so as to give an appealingly rough surface, as in many of Wright's houses). A good example of this sort of approach is the Therold Lindquist House, designed by Nelson J. Palmer of Dunkirk, and built in 1968–69.

Such a house does not consciously attempt to imitate any historical style—unless it is "Wrightian"—but solves the requirements for interior space, arrangement of rooms, lighting, desire for exterior views, preferred materials, surface treatment, and so on, in a vocabulary of abstract form which grows out of structure, materials, and design. A certain Japanese flavor is traceable more to a similar sensitive treatment of natural wood surfaces—and the siting perhaps —than to any real stylistic influences.

The two most prominent materials here are a sandy-colored brick, reminding one more of sandstone than of traditional red brick, and redwood, which is used for trim, eaves, and other features. The two divisions of the house (a garage, studio, and guest room section on the upper part of the hill, and the living room, kitchen, and bedrooms at the lower slope) are unified both by the shape of one part echoed in the other, and by the consistent materials. The combination of natural materials in the exterior—just as Wright in his Pope-Leighey House used brick and stained cypress—continues the effect of natural materials one finds elsewhere on the property—stone paving, timber retaining walls, and of course, natural rock outcroppings and trees.

The interior of the house, as mentioned, falls into two logical sections, separated so that work in the studio does not interfere with activity in the rest of the house. These logical divisions, apparent in studying the exterior form of the house, are linked by a hallway with the entrance at its center, so that one can go into either unit of the dwelling with equal convenience. Just as the exterior has a sensitive use of natural materials, so the interior uses slate for floors and counter tops, natural-finished cherry for cabinets, floors, and other features, and a plain plaster finish which sets off these rich materials to advantage. As the view of the living room shows, exterior nature is brought into the house by large windows, carrying on the tradition of integrating the dwelling with the natural site promulgated by A. J. Downing over a century before, and seen also in many of the houses of Frank Lloyd Wright.

This house also indicates how the creative interaction between owner and architect can develop distinctive features. Certain basic requirements, set out by the owners, had to be welded into a coherent design by the architect. For example, they wanted as much window space as possible in the living room to take advantage of the view of trees and Canadaway Creek; yet at the same time, needed a considerable amount of wall space, readily visible, to display paintings and photographs. Furthermore, the studio area had to be somehow out of the way so as not to disturb the household. The solution was to conceive of the house as two units. By making the hallway connecting the two sections into a sort of gallery, with no windows and thus plenty of wall space, it was possible to give the adjacent living room an entire wall of windows looking toward the creek. As we have seen before, in the Drago House, the active interest and imagination of an owner can often contribute to the design of the house.

236. *Therold Lindquist House, east side (photo 1986).*

237. *Pope-Leighey House, Va., by Frank Lloyd Wright,*
1940.

238. *Lindquist House, west side (photo 1986).*

239. *Living room of Lindquist House, looking southwest.*

State University College campus *Fredonia*

Undoubtedly the most striking group of buildings in the village is the campus of the State University of New York College at Fredonia. Both as individual structures, and group planning, they are an especially good example of the best in contemporary architectural design.

Higher education has been important in Fredonia since its early days. The Fredonia Academy (1826) facing the Common has been mentioned before. Later in the 19th century the academy was absorbed into the State Normal School (established 1867) and moved to a new vernacular Second Empire building (1867–68) on Temple Street at Central Avenue. This edifice burned in 1900, and in 1901–03 the present Old Main was constructed. It ceased to be used by the college in 1975, but as senior citizen housing still provides a prominent landmark at this intersection.

With the construction of Mason Hall (1940, by architects Beck & Tinkham of Jamestown), the college began expanding on its current site off Central Avenue, further from the center of town. During the next dozen years other buildings were gradually added, notably two more Neo-Colonial structures: Gregory Hall (1949–51), a large dormitory forming two wings of a proposed quadrangle off of Temple Street; and Fenton Hall (1953), a large classroom building. Both have attractive brickwork and detailing in cut stone. U-shaped Fenton Hall was placed east of Mason Hall, creating a sort of quadrangle—a *sine qua non* of college planning at this time. Had Fenton been constructed with its gabled roof, as originally planned, it would have been a more effective "match" for Mason Hall facing it. By 1964 ten buildings, in Neo-Colonial style or a semi-modern red brick mode, had been constructed. Only one of these, the old heating plant, has since been demolished.

During 1967–71, however, this number was doubled by major new construction in a contemporary style. The overall plan and most of the buildings were by I. M. Pei & Partners, of New York, Henry N. Cobb the partner in charge. Kirkland Complex and Andrews Complex (dormitories and dining halls), the Heating Plant, Reed Library, McEwen Hall (classrooms), Maytum Hall (administration), Houghton Hall (sciences), the Michael C. Rockefeller Arts Center, and the Williams Center were designed by the Pei firm, and built between 1967 and 1971.[45] Other buildings in similar style but by other firms were also erected at this time: the infirmary—one of the finest of these non-Pei buildings—was by Pederson, Heuber, Hares and Zlavin (1967); the Mason Hall addition (music) by Ira Kessler and Associates (1971); and Thompson Hall (education and social sciences) by Heuber, Hares and Zlavin (1971–73). The new buildings (integrated with the pre-existing structures on the site) form one of the finest architectural complexes in New York State. By briefly examining I. M. Pei and his firm, the plan and the siting, and then the style and treatment of the buildings, we can better appreciate the architectural excellence of the campus.

Fredonia was one of the State Normal School campuses which, in the early 1960s under the aegis of Governor Nelson A. Rockefeller, were expanded to full undergraduate liberal arts college status. Different noted architects were chosen for each campus. The firm of I. M. Pei & Partners was selected for Fredonia—a happy choice since they were experts in both planning as well as building design. The founder of the firm, Ieoh Ming Pei, with degrees from MIT and Harvard, had worked during a dozen years (1948–60) for Webb & Knapp, the architectural division of developer William Zeckendorf—so was an expert in building on tight budgets (always a concern for the New York State Construction Fund). Pei established his own firm in 1960, and when they presented their preliminary building and site plans for the Fredonia campus in 1964, he was already a well-known architect. Pei had just completed the Green Science Center at MIT, and the School of Journalism for Syracuse University (both 1964); his designs and plans for L'Enfant Plaza, Washington, D. C. appeared in 1965, and the area redevelopment plan for Brooklyn, N. Y. was prepared in 1966–67.

240. *State University College, view of Maytum Hall, Reed Library, McEwen Hall, from Rockefeller Arts Center (photo 1987).*

241. *Reed Library—original entrance front (photo 1984).*

242. *Secretariat Building, Chandigarh, India, by Le Corbusier, 1951–56.*

243. *East side of Reed Library (photo 1972).*

244. *South side of McEwen Hall (photo 1987).*

The Pei firm brought expertise as planners and designers with a distinctive contemporary architectural vision, inspired by the great modernist masters Walter Gropius, Mies van der Rohe, and Le Corbusier, but nonetheless very much their own manner—the "Pei style." I. M. Pei's experience in reinforced concrete construction, and his sensitivity to surface treatment and detailing, are evident in the Fredonia campus.

The difficulties of creating this enlarged college complex were increased by the existence of many older buildings, some of little architectural distinction, but which were still efficient and serviceable. New buildings had to fit in and around them, and, at least in part, attempt to make some sort of stylistic bridge. A further problem was the flat and potentially monotonous site.

The solution to the first problem was to design two types of buildings. The more domestic in size and scale (such as dormitories) were built of dark brick, with portions in poured concrete, which would pay lip service to the pre-existing brick structures, but, at the same time, be clearly different in both style and mass. Then, for the larger, main buildings, poured concrete—utterly different from the red brick buildings—was employed, to assert the new direction the architecture was taking and give a needed dominant focal point to the campus.

These concrete buildings—the arts center, administration building, library, classroom building, and student center—were located on a right-angled "spine" with the arts center at one end, the library at the angle, and the student center at the other end, with McEwen and Maytum placed tangent to the arms. This not only helped weave the buildings between pre-existing structures (Jewett, Mason, and Fenton) but the spine also provided axes of walks to visually and actually link the new structures. This angled spine was further used as a leitmotif in the design of parts of the various buildings, providing almost mysterious affinities: the angle cut in the first floor of the Arts Center follows the angle of this arm of the spine, as does one face of Maytum Hall; and the right angle is actually traceable in the library along the upper level balcony. Other buildings (those of brick) were aligned with the pre-existing structures, or along street lines.

The arrangement of the buildings at the center of the college formed a new spacious rectangular courtyard, oriented north-south. The small ring road provides access to this, where it is "cut off" at the northeast corner, which becomes the "grand entrance" to the courtyard and college. Maytum is given an imposing portal onto this entrance plaza, as is the Arts Center. The flat site was mitigated somewhat by several flights of imposing steps, from the area east of Maytum to the library terrace and spine, and another from the west up to the front of the library. The elevated walkway to the Campus Center adds further spatial interest. The band of trees along Ring Road—first poplars, now maples—were also intended to screen off the very flat site.[46]

It is the core academic buildings which attract most attention. The main structures are of poured concrete, of a light tan color. Their shapes are most striking. Like works of abstract sculpture, basic geometrical units—cubes and cylinders—are employed as a vocabulary of form, and the angles and segments cut from these basic shapes, the interlocking of several such units, the opening out as courtyards or enclosing as spacious entryways, provide spatial compositions of originality and interest.

But completely aside from the simple, grand massing of the buildings, and their striking geometry, a major feature is the treatment of the surface. Poured concrete can take the impression of whatever texture the form into which it is poured has. At the Fredonia campus, surfaces of great refinement are achieved by the use of forms filled with 3¼ inch wide wood boards, so that a faint but perceptible vertical texture is found on all exterior surfaces. Then, in keeping with the geometry of each building, the vertical and horizontal divisions are carefully calculated to mark off the surfaces into logical visual units. These complement the two-dimensional pattern that the judiciously placed windows form. Often the resulting patterns seem to have more to do with painting (perhaps a Mondrian) than with architecture. We recall that equal care was lavished on the

245. *View of central part of campus from elevated walkway (photo 1972).*

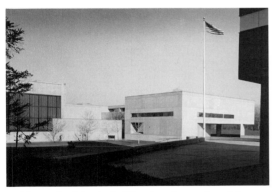

246. *Michael C. Rockefeller Arts Center from Maytum Hall (photo 1990).*

247. *Arts Center courtyard (photo 1981).*

248. *Stairs to walkway, and east side of Williams Center (photo 1997).*

249. *West side of Williams Center (photo 1997).*

composition of facades—every window, molding, cornice, column, etc. in careful relationship—in the Renaissance, so this approach is in a way no surprise.

Pei is not the only architect to use textured poured concrete, of course; Le Corbusier in France, in the late 1940s used it with force and originality. In fact, the simple, powerful shapes of Corbusier's concrete buildings for the Punjab capital of Chandigarh of the early 1950s may well have been an inspiration in the development of some of Pei's plastic geometric forms.

The material of the concrete buildings is relieved only by strips of windows, or in the Concert Hall, a section (forming a huge cube) entirely of dark glass—reminding us of the Shop Block at Gropius's Bauhaus of 40 years before. The dormitories combine concrete with dark brick. The choice of color—a rich, dark brown—and the use of a dark mortar, help give even these structures an extra compactness of design, to partake of some of the monumentality of the concrete structures. The use of bases and other details of concrete help articulate buildings, conceived as large simple volumes with angles and perforations cut into them. Yet the dormitories pay homage to nearby Gregory Hall in their massing and regular fenestration of vertical units. The courtyards of the dormitory complexes, attractively planted and paved, are especially successful.

The exteriors of the buildings, and their relationship on the campus, are the most effective elements of the Pei design. Less successful, perhaps, are some of the interiors. While some spaces, such as the Campus Center, the Concert Hall, or some of the dining halls are excellent, others tend to be a little monotonous—but then, it is perhaps too much to ask that all interior spaces be as visually exciting as the exterior forms. And part of the "bareness" of some interiors is due to economies made during construction, thanks to the procrustean Construction Fund. According to Harry Cobb, inside Jewett Hall, with its ample brickwork, displays best the firm's ideas of interior detailing—at least for the brick structures.

The campus is clearly a remarkable conception. The design of the individual buildings is especially good—the heating plant, a grassy sloping earth wall capped by slit windows and a thick concrete slab, is perhaps the most striking thing of its kind in the state.[47]

As can be readily seen, the campus bodies forth a mode of design more classically conceived and geometrically ordered than the more domestic approach we saw in the Lindquist House. Yet both of these examples show how some of the finest contemporary architecture is animated by principles of design grounded in the basics of building—geometry, materials, interrelationships of forms, nuanced surface treatment, and careful integration with the site.

Naturally, over the years, there have been some modifications to the Pei buildings, but these have generally been done with care and sensitivity, so that the original design concept is not significantly altered.[48] The buildings are, after all, works of art as well as functional architecture.

It should be pointed out, however, that one alteration significantly changes an original function and design. Reed Library's main entrance was at first on the elevated plaza facing Mason Hall. One entered the glass doors to a spacious lobby, from which one had a panoramic view of the entire library from an elevated position—and then descend to it via a "grand staircase." Due to security concerns in the 1970s, this entrance had to be closed, thus depriving visitors of the dramatic entry—and first striking view—planned for this core facility of the college.

Two major buildings have been added to the Fredonia campus after this flurry of activity of 1967–73. The first was the vast athletic building, Steele Hall, designed by Pasanella & Klein of New York in 1979–80, and constructed in 1981–82. A more difficult job was the same firm's addition to Reed Library, designed in 1987–88 and built between 1989 and 1991 (they also renovated Reed Library in 1992–93). The new unit is placed across the south end, and consists of five stories, primarily for stacks, archives, and additional offices. The dark brick blends well with nearby Houghton Hall, and the north side has concrete panels the same color as Reed Library.

250. *Maytum Hall from Reed Library Plaza (photo 1990).*

251. *Gregory Hall (left), and Kirkland and Andrews Complexes (photo 1997).*

252. *Interior courtyard and dining hall, Kirkland Complex (photo 1997).*

253. *Houghton Hall (photo 1971).*

254. *Addition to Reed Library (photo 1997).*

Just as in the early 20th century, and in the 1960s, so in the succeeding decades the duality of "traditionalism" and "modernism" runs parallel in domestic design. Two fine examples to represent this are these dwellings at 6 Bryant Place and 289 Central Avenue.

The Paul A. Bowers House on Bryant Place clearly represents the abstract modernism trend of the 20th century. Although one might find here allusions to 17th-century dwellings with their steep roofs, natural wood siding, and the overhanging second floor—even the "additive" quality of many early colonial vernacular houses—it is none-the-less a thoroughly modern design. The blocky gabled units, almost logos for "shelter" or "home," echo and repeat each other like theme and variation. The placement of windows, especially the asymmetrically shaped one in the facade, speak of interior function expressed on the outside. The vertical boarding of the exterior, by running in the opposite direction of clapboards, is another step away from tradition. But the love of rich natural textures and colors, and the integration with a wooded site, also has links with "advanced" theories from Downing to the Shingle Style and to Frank Lloyd Wright. The interior has plain plaster surfaces and refined woodwork that are a civilized contrast to the rustic exterior, with open planning reflecting the achievements of modernists of the past 100 years.

The house was designed by the owner, Paul Bowers, in 1979, and was constructed in 1980. The main influences, according to Mr. Bowers, were "Acorn Homes," designed by a Massachusetts company long involved in semi-prefabrication. The combination of rustic exterior treatment with clear, prismatic geometric forms is sometimes humorously called "barnyard Bauhaus." It represents a continuing trend of abstract design with a focus on natural materials we have seen for over a century in American domestic architecture.

Especially popular in Fredonia during the last decade have been "post-modern" designs, in which functional concerns are wedded with a careful study of historic buildings for forms, motifs, references, and allusions, that can give a traditional aura to a dwelling without trying to mimic or duplicate actual historic models. Post-modernism as an architectural movement developed in the 1970s and '80s, with key architects such as Charles Moore and Michael Graves turning back to traditional architecture for enlivening motifs, and to create a consciously—often self-consciously—allusive meaning in modernist architecture which some critics, by those dates, felt had lost much of its original élan.

The dwelling at 289 Central Ave., built in 1993, is three apartments conceived as one simple visual unit, the broad facade gable pulling together the whole form, and the echoing front porch fitted neatly into the design. Traditional motifs abound in this bold overall shape: gable returns on both features recall the Greek Revival; the gable louver may suggest Federal-style motifs; the 6-over-1 windows are a common Queen Anne treatment; and the great semi-circular opening in the porch—functionally to let more light in to the entrance door— is like a pedimental lunette in a Federal or Georgian building. The beautifully sharp, crisp clapboarding is cedar, stained in two tones of green. Low on the site, blending with the ample trees around, it "fits in" to the neighborhood full of traditional houses very well—a major concern of the owner and his wife, Wally and Joan Latimer, who worked out the floor plans themselves. The designs for the building were prepared by CCS Architects of Dunkirk (Carol Case Siracuse project architect) a small firm of two architects and a staff of seven, who worked closely with the Latimers throughout.

While these are not the only options of the '80s and '90s, they represent two of the most creative; though it should be pointed out that many feel that the "post-modern" movement is... historic preservation! in which actual historic buildings are returned to their formed glory by careful research and detective work (and at times scholarly intuition), and brought fully up-to-date mechanically by unobtrusive modern systems.

255. 6 Bryant Place.

256. 289 Central Ave.

Noah D. Snow House   *194 Central Ave.*
Thomas L. Higgins House   *20 Central Ave.*

The importance of architectural style as an expression of artistic taste, cultural values, and as an embodiment of one's wealth and social status, are reasons that, decade after decade, new and (in the 19th century) more Picturesque designs succeeded the architectural models of the preceding years. If one already owned a fine, if older, house, one could artistically "up date" it by a thorough remodeling.

We have actually already seen quite a number of these "updating" projects in Fredonia buildings. Early cases just added a stylish new front to an older vernacular home, as at 171 Eagle St. (transforming a c. 1812 house into a Federal dwelling in c. 1818), or John Jones adding a grand Greek Revival front in 1839–40 to a plain, earlier structure at 135 W. Main St. (now at 430 E. Main). And the vernacular Fredonia Academy (1822) was given a majestic Gothic Revival facade in 1850 by John Jones.

But Fredonia has also a fascinating range—and long history—of "thorough remodeling" too. The vernacular/Federal Barker House (1821) was nicely Italianized, apparently in the 1850s. Then comes the Centre Block (1852–53) on W. Main which was given its Second Empire configuration by Enoch Curtis in the late 1870s as the Masonic Hall; 1888 saw the rebuilding of 71 Central Ave., transforming an 1853 Italianate house into a Picturesque Queen Anne mansion. The remodeling of the Johnson House (1837) from a Greek Revival hotel into a Richardsonian/Queen Anne edifice—the Columbia Hotel—after 1892 was also Curtis' work. In many of these, the original building can still be seen, more or less; not so in Curtis' radical recasting of his own house from a c. 1870 modest Italianate home into a distinctive Colonial Revival dwelling in 1900–01.[49]

Good examples of successful remodeling are found in the 20th century too; we mentioned the Otto Hakes House, a 1916 Elizabethan Revival dwelling encasing an 1866 structure; and 63 Cushing St., a house of 1909–10 made into a stylish Foursquare in 1928–29. And we mustn't forget the Town of Pomfret offices, transformed in 1984.

That this approach was common in the 19th and early 20th century is suggested by national publications. Downing proposed—and illustrated—such remodeling to up date old fashioned houses in 1846, and Calvert Vaux also had before-and-after examples in *Villas and Cottages* (1857).[50] *Old Homes Made New*, published in 1878 by Albany architect William M. Woollett contained many examples of architectural updating, and *The American Architect and Building News* provided some plates in the late 1870s too. Amelia Leavitt Hill's *Redeeming Old Homes* (1923) contained many before-and-after comparisons, comparable in date to Fredonia examples.

Here we can examine two more excellent cases of this creative remodeling. Impressive 194 Central Ave. in Academic- or Colonial-Revival style, was originally a square Italian Villa with cupola, paired brackets, and symmetrical flanking wings, as the old photo reveals. A remodeling of 1907 took off many of the Italianate features (such as the brackets from the eaves and cupola), and gave it a more classical expression with a two-story pedimented Ionic portico.[51] It also had Colonial-style balustrades above the front door, and along the eaves of the south-wing's porch, but these were removed in 1930. The Italianate cast iron window lintels of the main block remain, however, as does the Italianate cupola, though with dentils of 1907.

Several remodeling campaigns—always keeping architecturally up-to-date—are revealed in 20 Central Ave. The original house of 1829–30 was vernacular Federal in style, but with a stylish Greek Revival cornice and frieze band, and with Doric columns and piers flanking the second floor central window (the original front door was probably also Greek Revival). A half century later this was a decidedly old-fashioned and un-Picturesque house, and was remodeled c. 1890 into an elegant Queen Anne mansion, complete with corner tower and numerous whimsically Colonial details (as in the central dormer). By 1923 such Picturesqueness was itself out of favor, and the sturdy dwelling once again was transformed, this time into an elegant Colonial mansion. It would appear that the local builder got his design from "The Magnolia," the most ambitious (and most expensive) of Sears' mail-order houses, offered only between 1918 and 1921. One might even mistake it for a Sears house, so close is the result, were one not privy to its earlier incarnations.

257. 194 Central Ave. (photo 1997).

258. 194 Central Ave. in the late 19th century.

259. 20 Central Ave. as depicted in the 1881 atlas.

260. The same house after remodeling of c. 1890.

261. The same house after remodeling of 1923.

262. "The Magnolia," Sears plan No. 2089 from their 1918 catalog Honor Bilt Modern Homes.

129

The attractiveness of a village is not restricted only to its buildings; there are other features which contribute to its "urban delight" which can be examined here, and in the following sections. In a way, they help provide the setting and framework into which the houses and other buildings fit so successfully.

A view down Central Avenue shows at a glance that even when a house is hardly to be seen, there is still much in Fredonia to enjoy.[52] The beautifully planted streets, the generous setbacks of houses, the richness of shrubbery and ornamental trees cultivated by the residents, all contribute to the overall appeal.

We often take our beautiful tree-lined streets for granted, but they were "created" just as were the buildings they frame. Early settlers found a wild forest, an oppressive dense canopy which needed to be eradicated so that crops could be planted and building sites created. The nearly total lack of substantial trees in the overview photo of the village from the 1860s (see Fig. 42) may seem surprising today.

A generation after the initial clearing of the land, the desire for shade trees—organized, carefully selected, the opposite of the chaotic jungle which met the first settlers—was felt. After clearing the Barker Common of its black walnut grove, trees were planted *back* on the Common as early as 1833. During the 1840s the civic-minded *Fredonia Censor* encouraged planting of trees along streets, and on April 30, 1850, William Risley proposed a village ordinance for a rebate on residents' property taxes for each maple, elm, basswood or walnut tree planted along the street. The fact that Fredonia today has such a wide variety of trees—including at least one surviving mature elm, several ginkos, beech trees, tulip poplars, white pines, and numerous mulberry trees —is a testament to that enlightened commitment, which continues to this day.

But details which often go unnoticed are the distinctive 19th century urban features which give much of the sense of history and tradition to a village. One of them is the streets themselves —the character of their paving. During the 1970s, and into the 1990s, among the most appealing historic urban amenities in Fredonia were its brick streets, which survived in numerous places in 1972, including—Day, Church, Summer, Gillis, Leverett, Newton, and White Streets, as well as Lambert and Porter Avenues and Curtis Place.[53] By 1994 only two survived—and remain largely brick today—Curtis Place and Leverett St. (though the entrance to Forest Hill Cemetery, a short privately-owned stretch, is the best preserved). As brick paving was a distinctive feature of Fredonia for 60 or 70 years, it is worth giving some background on it here.

Old photographs (such as Figs. 46 or 83) show that until the late 19th century much of Fredonia had unpaved, dirt streets. There was some attempt at paving major streets beginning in the 1850s. A plank road was built for Central Avenue in 1851, but it rotted away in the 1860s. Village Trustees Minutes mention "flagging and laying stones" (gravel) on Main St. in July, 1860, and in April, 1865 Central Ave. was to be "stoned and gravelled" from "the brow of the hill to the corporation limits." Twenty-some years later a new process was attempted: Central Ave. was "macadamized." This was a specialized form of stone-surfaced road developed by British engineer John L. Macadam (1756–1836). Its key ingredient was a surface layer 2" thick of *broken* stone (thus with sharp edges), of 1" size—not gravel. These stones, the roadbed slightly arched, would compact themselves as used over time, providing a dry firm surface.[54]

Various other road surfaces were possible too by the end of the 19th century: Trustees Minutes for July 24, 1899 advertised for bids for ordinary macadam, tarred macadam, Telford macadam, brick paving, block asphalt, and sheet asphalt! But there was no consistent paving program; in 1900 all Fredonia streets (except for parts of Main St. and Central Ave.) were dirt, with bluestone cross walks laid at intersections on some streets.

263. *General view, from 244 Central Ave. looking south (photo 1971).*

264. *Brick paving, formerly on Summer St. (photo 1993).*

265. *Chamfered paving bricks, formerly on Lambert Ave. (photo 1970).*

Although Dunkirk had major brick paving projects in the 1890s, Fredonia's streets of brick—the form ultimately selected as best—did not really start until the advent of the electric street railway in 1901 which caused West Main to be paved with brick up to Day St. Soon after Temple St., and others, began to be similarly paved.

Paving bricks are a bit larger than regular building bricks, and thicker—4" rather than 2". In paving a street, a foundation (later a mat of concrete 4" thick) was first put down, on which a ½" layer of sand was spread on which to bed the bricks. Bricks were closely laid on this surface, with the spaces filled in with hot tar.[55] On steep slopes (as on Lambert Ave. or Leverett St.) bricks with their lower edges cut off at an angle (chamfered) were used, so that a slight triangular depression was formed next to the adjoining brick, providing excellent traction. The gutters were five bricks laid parallel to the direction of the street, and the curbs were of 5" thick sections of siltstone (though sandstone was also used). In the 1920s the form had changed somewhat so that concrete gutters and curbs replace brick gutters and siltstone curbs.

Brick paving is extremely durable under light loads—even modern automobiles—and has the advantage that frost heaves and other damage can be replaced brick by brick, a smooth and perfect repair being effected. But, unfortunately, heavy trucks—for which it was never intended—break the tar seal on the bricks, create furrows in the road by their weight, and thus create a broken and uneven surface. This has ultimately led to most of our streets being paved over with asphalt.

Stone sidewalks are also a distinctive local feature. The Village Trustees encouraged residents to put in such walks by the passage in June 1882 of an amendment to the 1881 village laws, providing tax credit for putting in sidewalks. From that date onward there is increased mention in village records of cut-stone sidewalks being laid down, especially on Central Ave. These are about the widest ones in the village, and where they survive the slabs are about 5' wide, by 3½ to 6½ feet in length. The section illustrated here is on Center St.: the second slab in the photo measured 60 ½" wide by 46½" and is 2" thick. The material is siltstone from local quarries. Except where they have been broken by roots of trees (or heavy vehicles) they have survived in remarkably good condition.

One unique section of sidewalk pavement survives on Temple Street, possibly an "inexpensive" version of paving. The side pieces (each about 2' wide) provide smooth passage for a wheeled vehicle (such as a baby carriage), while the central strip, 20" wide, is composed of scrap pieces set on edge—perhaps better drainage was envisioned.

Stone also served for other distinctive features—carriage blocks and hitching posts. Two types of carriage block seem to have been common—a low, rather flat variety (as in Fig. 269) and a taller, more cubic form. Hitching posts of siltstone were also common, and a few good examples survived into the 1970s (see also Fig. 60).[57]

Cobblestones, a labor-intensive stone finish of great visual appeal, are not common in Fredonia, but can be found here and there. The foundations of 39 Forest Place which face Terrace St. (the foundations on the front were originally hidden by the full-width front porch) provide a rich surface texture, an example of the finesse of detailing that this Gothic Revival house bodies forth.[58]

These features of brick and stone, remnants of the horse drawn era for the most part, are tangible reminders of another age, but also of how natural materials could be skillfully adapted for many useful purposes.

266. *Stone sidewalk between 252 and 260 Temple St. (photo 1997).*

267. *Stone sidewalk behind Old Main on Center St. (photo 1997).*

268. *Stone hitching post, formerly at 35 Center St. (photo 1972).*

269. *Carriage block and stone sidewalks formerly at 80 Central Ave. (photo 1970).*

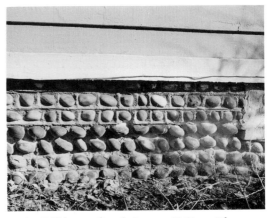

270. *Cobblestone foundations on 39 Forest Place.*

We have already seen changes in building technology in early Fredonia: log houses were replaced by traditional timber-frame construction, which was often modified, for economy's sake, by using vertical boarding instead of studs. In 1848 Orson Squire Fowler introduced his solid plank walls (horizontally stacked up), and in 1853 his "gravel wall" method—all intended to make domestic architecture easier and cheaper to build than traditional timber framing with its complex mortise and tenon joints, pegged carefully together.

The "new and improved" framing method that *did* catch on, and is still used today, was "balloon frame" construction. This was invented in Chicago in 1832 for a warehouse built by George Washington Snow. The secret was using 2x4s, nailed together (with cheap, machine-made nails), the whole stiffened by the exterior clapboards and interior lath nailed on horizontally.[59] The method spread to the rest of the country, though it did not completely replace timber framing till the end of the century.

The exposed frame of a Greek Revival house in Cassadaga (eight miles south of Fredonia) shows the traditional method well. This portion may date from the 1820s; when rebuilt as a two story, five-bay house c. 1840 it was incorporated as the left side. By contrast is the balloon frame construction of another Greek Revival house (c. 1850?) on Route 20, just outside Fredonia. Here the *original* form of balloon framing is clearly seen: the 2x4s run unbroken from sill plate to the eaves plate, and the joists for the second floor are rested on a 2x4 run horizontally at that level and just nailed to the vertical studs. No complex tools, expert cutting, or long apprenticeship training was needed—any capable workman with a saw and a lot of nails could carry this out. Economy and speed of construction were achieved and the slenderness of the 2x4 units made complex framing—as in a Picturesque Queen Anne house, for example—easier to effect.

With brick commercial buildings a concern in the 1820s was how to open up the facade for larger windows. One way was using a granite post and lintel system, popular through the 1850s (see Fig. 83). But that decade also saw the greater use of cast iron to support the brick wall above, and have truly large openings to light the shop within, and display goods effectively. Piers, lintels, and whole shop fronts could be purchased from specialty iron works in the 1850s and '60s; by the casting of the units in architecturally sophisticated forms, high-style touches could be produced at minimal cost. The ground floor of the Fredonia National Bank is an excellent example of this sort of treatment (other uses of cast iron are discussed in the next section).

Pressed metal—galvanized iron or steel sheeting—was also turned to decorative architectural use. Lighter than cast iron, it was used mainly as a veneer over wood or brick.[60] We have seen it enriching a cornice (see Fig. 24) but another popular use was as decorative ceilings. At a fraction of the cost of plasterwork, richly detailed metal ceilings (which were also thought to help in fire-proofing a building) could be produced in great variety. The ad below shows one example (plus borders and cornice); when the Village Hall Opera House ceiling was repaired in 1903, this was what they chose to use, and it still enriches the interior today (see Fig. 12).

271. *Mortise and tenon timber frame of Greek Revival house formerly in Cassadaga.*

272. *Balloon frame construction of Greek Revival house south west of Fredonia.*

273. *Cast iron front for Fredonia National Bank, formerly at 3 East Main St.*

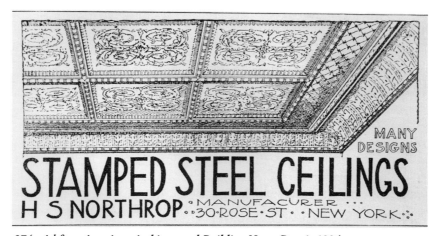

274. *Ad from American Architect and Building News, Dec. 1, 1894.*

The use of cast iron for all manner of things was firmly established in America by 1850, and until the end of the century the ways in which it could be used were continually explored. Often it could replace materials more costly to work, such as stone, or be used as a cheaper imitation of an expensive item, such as a bronze urn or fountain. Obviously it had wide usage in new machines and in industry, but here we are concerned with items that relate to the embellishment of the urban scene. Iron's ability to be cast into intricate shapes, both light in appearance and delicate in detail, made it especially useful for new forms of standard features, such as hitching posts or fences. But above all, the sheer variety of things that could be made of cast iron in the late 19th century is astonishing—fences and gates, cornice cresting and gable finials, balconies and railings, hitching posts, garden urns, benches, gazebos, lintels and sills for buildings, architectural columns and piers, cemetery monuments, statues and other lawn decorations, interior and exterior stairways, fountains, fireplaces, and so on (leaving out, of course, its uses for beams, piping, furnaces, radiators, stoves, shutters, machinery, and the like). Many of these features can still be found in Fredonia.

We have already glimpsed some of the uses of cast iron: as first floor piers and columns for buildings (Fig. 273), as roof finials (Fig. 148), and as cornice and ridge cresting (Figs. 127 and 158). We can now examine this more closely.

A number of houses and public buildings in Fredonia have cast iron lintels over their windows, usually cast so as to look like blocks of stone, carved or plain. Fredonia's Centre Block of 1852–53, part of which was later transformed into the Masonic Lodge, is a good early example of cast iron used for lintels and sills. These may have come from the Buffalo Eagle Iron Works (founded 1853), for their catalog has several similar designs.[61] A number of local houses have cast iron lintels too, such as 225 and 284 E. Main St., 29 Day St., or 54 Risley St.—all slightly later Italianate dwellings (see also Fig. 162). Showing its ability to create light, open forms, is the balcony of the Forbes-Cushing House, in an attractive Greek Revival design (see also Fig. 76). Frieze windows in Greek Revival houses often had grilles of cast iron.[62]

Cast iron was also popular for lawn decorations, and in many towns lots were regularly enclosed at the sidewalk by a handsome cast iron fence. These rarely survive, but local cemeteries are good places to find iron fencing, since the same patterns were used to enclose burial plots and often are still standing. Major garden cemeteries, such as Mount Auburn in Cambridge, Massachusetts, keep their iron work painted (flat or semi-gloss black), and when details or lettering are judiciously picked out in gold, the effect is very handsome.

Fences and fence posts were made in great quantities, and fences of the same or similar design can be seen in widely separated areas of the country. As the illustrations show, a fence post found in Forest Hill Cemetery is identical in design to one found in San Francisco, either sent out from a New York City foundry, or made there from the same molds. One of nearly this same design is in Petersburg, Virginia. As trade catalogs indicated, foundries would ship their wares anywhere.

Urns, in imitation of marble vases, as seen in European gardens, were popular embellishments for any well-kept lawn; again it is often only in cemeteries that they have survived. Forest Hill had a wide variety of types; the one illustrated here may be specifically a "cemetery urn," since grapes are a traditional eucharistic symbol. Benches of various types, both cast in imitation of rustic wood constructions, or (a more comfortable design) made of strap iron, were popular; again Forest Hill Cemetery has had both types. And hitching posts, replacing the more old-fashioned stone ones, were common. While the one depicted is quite plain,[63] others (apparently not used much in Fredonia) could be very elaborate.

275. *Detail of cast iron lintels on Centre Block (photo 1975).*

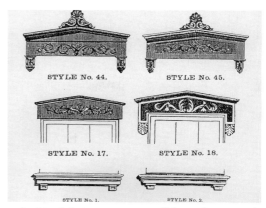

276. *Lintel designs in 1859 Buffalo Eagle Ironworks Catalog.*

277. *Cast iron balcony at 23 Forest Place.*

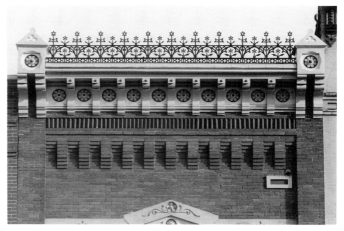

278. *Cornice of galvanized iron with cast iron cresting, 4 W. Main St. (photo 1988).*

279. *Cast iron urn, formerly in Forest Hill Cemetery.*

280. *Cast iron bench, formerly in Forest Hill Cemetery.*

Especially for public parks, cast iron was essential. Many parks had fences of this material (and cast iron sidewalks were even tried in some cities), and iron benches; but cast iron fountains are one of the most striking adaptations of the material.

Fredonia is especially lucky to have two elaborate cast iron fountains in Barker Common. The pair was given to the village by Charles Leroy Mark (the fountains have "Mark Fountains" in relief on their bases), the son of an early pioneer, who had become a prosperous businessman in Fredonia. As can be see in Fig. 291, there had existed earlier cast iron fountains, but not as grand in size; it is also know that some private residences had cast iron fountains gracing their lawns (one formerly stood at 23 Forest Place), but the two Mark fountains are the only survivors.

The fountains were installed in 1901, but their design goes back much further. A similar terra cotta version, based on marble (or bronze) fountains of preceding centuries, was exhibited in London in 1851, and was possibly a model for American foundries. The Mark fountain illustrated has, cast into the base of the uppermost figure, the inscription "J. W. Fiske/Manufr/New York." This was a well-known late 19th century firm manufacturing decorative cast iron. Both fountains were skillfully restored in 1991, at which time missing pieces were recreated, and damaged portions recast and replaced. They are now painted a bronze-gold color, their original hue.

These local features of cast iron give some idea of the uses to which the fecund Victorian imagination put this malleable material. It provided forms of complexity and visual interest which would not have been possible had more costly stone or bronze (or wrought iron) been necessary. The point has been raised that a fountain, traditionally bronze or stone, being cast in iron and painted, is not being "truthful" (an important 19th century tenet); but it is simply one of the pleasant inconsistencies that makes 19th century works enjoyable, revealing the complexity of the period. And it could be argued that cast iron, a manifestation of the industrial advances of the 19th century, *was* in fact being true at least to the developments and needs of the time.

281. Cast iron fence and gate, dated 1858, Thomas G. Abell plot, Forest Hill Cemetery.

283. *Terra cotta fountain, made for the Crystal Palace Exposition of 1851 by a Berlin company.*

282. *Mark Fountain in eastern part of Barker Common (photo 1992).*

284. *Cast iron fence post, Forest Hill Cemetery.*

285. *Cast iron fence post in Ghirardelli Square, San Francisco.*

286. *Cast iron hitching post, one of a pair, formerly at 68 Center St.*

"Better and cheaper" methods of building houses were not just a 19th century quest. We have already seen two outstanding 20th century efforts: the pre-cut house, as developed by Aladdin in 1906; and concrete block dwellings. The latter movement, as well as two mid- and later 20th century methods, can be explored here.

Fowler's concrete houses of the 1850s were poured-in-place mass concrete. By the 1870s experiments in casting individual blocks, to emulate stone construction, were widely attempted; but it took improved methods of manufacturing Portland cement by 1900, and the invention of a machine to produce concrete blocks easily (patented by Harmon S. Palmer in 1900) that the "modern" concrete block was born. Its success was instantaneous. By 1905 there were over 1,000 firms in the United States making concrete blocks; the dramatic price increase of lumber during the previous half-dozen years made them an especially attractive building option.

One of its main appeals was that individuals, not just companies, could make the blocks, using machines sold by any number of firms. The Sears ad of 1908 notes that "farmers and small land owners who have gravel pits or sand banks on their property, are the ones who can reap the greatest benefits" in making blocks themselves. The hollow core models (developed 1906) made it possible for one person to handle concrete blocks easily, and many people actually built their own homes. The variety of surface textures possible, and even specialized equipment for making concrete columns, balusters, railings, and the like (depicted in the 1908 Sears catalog on p. 581) meant that sophisticated-looking buildings could be erected at a fraction of the cost for real cut stone.

There are several good concrete block houses in Fredonia, notably those at 33 Curtis Pl. (1908), 37 Newton St. (1910), 49 Maple Ave. (c. 1910—see Fig. 202), and the double house at 46–48 Maple Ave.[64] Countless houses and other buildings with concrete block foundations, usually in the ever-popular (and standard issue for Sears) rock face design, can be found in Fredonia too. Their popularity remained strong until about 1930, though some work in it has continued to this very day.[65]

Domestic needs during World War II brought about a great number of companies which manufactured prefabricated housing. At the end of 1946 there were at least 280 such companies (though within a year that number had dropped to less than 100). One of the companies that *began* in the post-war housing boom, and continued the prefabricated system, was The Lustron Corporation of Columbus, Ohio. Founded in 1946, the idea was to build highly efficient two-bedroom factory built houses of steel (the exterior and interior surfaces of enameled panels over a steel framework), which would need little maintenance, and never need painting.

Despite massive infusions of government aid, the company did not prosper, and between 1948 and 1950 produced less than 3,000 houses. Even though consumer satisfaction was high and the buildings received praise from the architectural press, many economic and business factors led to its demise. Despite this Fredonia has its own Lustron House, and other examples can be found in Westfield and Chautauqua Institution. The Lustron House at 10 Holmes Place is "Model 02," the "Westchester," with two bedrooms; it bears the serial number 01998. The original colors were pale gray for the exterior 2' square panels, cream for trim, and dark green for the roof. Trucked to the site in pieces, the house was erected on a 32x36' concrete slab foundation. Over the years the recessed entry porch has been filled in, an addition put on the north end, and the exterior painted brown; but unlike most Lustron houses this one has a Lustron two-car garage, surely a rarity for the day.

The demise of the all-steel "modern" house was in part due to the unfamiliar new construction technology. Our third illustration shows a subsequent development which *did* catch on, as it used familiar balloon frame construction: modular houses. Built in widths up to 14' in a factory, with the economy and efficiency that this entails, a house is usually composed of two such units put together at the site. Here we see the front half being lifted up to be placed on the foundation further back on the lot. Because it is of standard wood frame construction, local assembly—and later repairs or additions — are easy. Seeing it today on the street one would never guess it is a "factory built house"— as, in fact, are a surprising number of homes being erected in Fredonia today.[66]

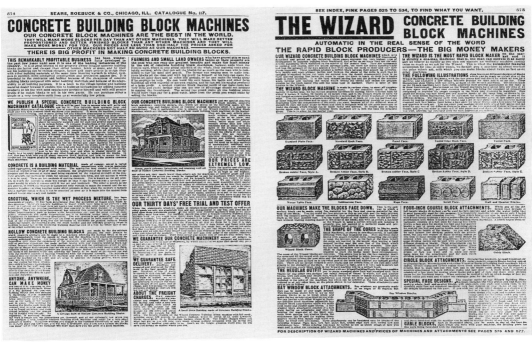

287. *Sears, Roebuck & Co. 1908 catalog, pp. 574–75.*

288. *Lustron House at 10 Holmes Place.*

289. *Modular house at 81 Newton St.*

We have seen that much of the pleasure of living in Fredonia is from the streets lined with handsome trees; but there are other factors in the composition of the village, as it relates to open spaces, which should also be touched on.

By the 1860s Barker Common was quite formally laid out. The west side had a fountain in the center, and a bandstand to one side. The painting of 1862 (title page) confirms that for well over a century it has been a pleasant, well-tended park.

More informal than this was the plan (and planting) of Forest Hill Cemetery. Such informally designed, mid-19th century garden cemeteries contained flowering trees, rustic benches, and winding paths and roads, to make visits to the cemetery more restful and enjoyable. In fact, garden cemeteries, such as Mt. Auburn in Cambridge, Mass., became so popular as places of public resort that regulations had to be issued against picnicking and shooting the birds. While Forest Hill Cemetery is not now frequented as much as garden cemeteries were in the 19th century, it still provides a pleasant wooded green area in the center of town which many enjoy for bird-watching. And, since informal public parks (such as Central Park in New York, begun 1858) were inspired directly from the popularity of garden cemeteries, Forest Hill has extra significance, having been laid out as early as 1855.

Individual owners a century ago embellished their own lawns too which, before the subdividing of some of the more ample lots, were quite spacious, and artfully planted. Even today, the neat alignment of houses along streets gives a pleasant sense of order and regularity to the village.

Further into the country, the clustering of houses and barns in regular and geometrical fashion created attractive groups to come upon after acres of orchards, vineyards or fields. The Daniel Fairbanks House (Fig. 106) has already been illustrated by an 1881 view showing the arrangement of such a farm. Another group, at 435 East Main Street, is a further example. This was built by Sayles Aldrich, apparently in the late 1880s. The farm consisted of the main house, carriage house and barn, and a subsidiary building (demolished c. 1980) which was built as the packing house for the vineyard. When this ensemble was published in the June 15, 1895 *Grape Belt* as a "Model Fruit Farm," of the 20 acres, 14 were in grapes and a few were in orchards. The house ("in modern style, with verandas on three sides") was much admired, as was the barn ("handsomely finished with a cupola"). But the article also indicates that considerable attention was paid in the late 19th century to the grounds and their plantings, just as today: the authors were "enthusiastic in admiring the fine residence on either side [of East Main St.], the roomy yards, set off with ornamental trees and shrubs, and fragrant with the perfume of the first spring flowers."

290. Sayles Aldrich farm, 435 East Main St.

291. Barker Common (with fountain and bandstand) and Methodist Church, c. 1870.

292. General view, Forest Hill Cemetery.

1. See "Introduction," in [Daniel D. Reiff and Ellen J. Schwartz], *Georgetown Architecture* ("Historic American Buildings Survey Selections No. 10;" Washington, D. C.: U. S. Commission of Fine Arts and the Historic American Buildings Survey, 1970), pp. vii–xxxvii.

2. For some of the history of the Urban Renewal program, and its impact on neighboring Dunkirk, N. Y., where over 235 buildings were swept away between 1972 and 1978—which provided an interesting comparative backdrop for activities in Fredonia—see my "Preface," with 20 before-and-after views of this architectural carnage in J. A. Chewning, *Dunkirk, New York: Its Architecture and Urban Development* (Dunkirk, N. Y.: Access to the Arts, Inc., 1992), pp. 11–25.

3. For information on the establishment of the Fredonia Normal School, the 1867–68 building, and its replacement (1901–03), in their educational context, see the 1964 doctoral dissertation by John Ford Ohles (SUNY Buffalo School of Education) "The Historical Development of State University of New York College at Fredonia as Representative of the Evolution of Teacher Education in the State University of New York," esp. pp. 118–20, 124–28, 132, 142–43, 173–78, 213, and 218–19. For a telephoto detail of Old Main's pediment and its sculpture, see [Daniel D. Reiff], *A Book of Reminders* (Fredonia Preservation Society, 1992), Fig. 22.

4. An overview of the preservation campaign to save and restore this building can be had by scanning the selected clippings listed in the "For Further Reference" section. Additional illustrations of the building (telephoto details of brickwork and other features) are reproduced in *A Book of Reminders* (1992), Figs. 13, 30–32, and p. [iii].

5. Of course during this period a number of houses of little architectural interest (though who knows their possible historic significance) were demolished, for example on Canadaway St. (1977), at 63 Day St.—a small house that blew up in a gas explosion (1992), and 81 Cleveland Ave. (1993).

6. For a fuller discussion (with illustrations), see my articles on painting and siding in the *Evening Observer* of April 1989 or May 1995 listed in the "Reference" section at the back of the book.

7. Eight letters by Aaron L. Putnam (1804–80) or his wife Dolly, written between April 5, 1835 and Feb. 13, 1839, are preserved in the Darwin R. Barker Historical Museum, Fredonia, and provide a wealth of interesting local detail for this period. My thanks to Ann Fahnestock for bringing them to my attention. Aaron L. Putnam's son Aaron O. Putnam (1836–96) became a well-to-do local businessman.

8. This slip is preserved in a copy of William Pain's book *The Carpenter's and Joiner's Repository* (London, 1792) owned by Thomas Jones, in the collection of the Barker Historical Museum.

9. For an interesting account of Dr. Squire White in the medical context, see Doug Shepard, "The Good Doctor White," *Barker Historical Newsletter* , Fall, 1996, pp. 2–5.

10. The old rear view photo shows that the corners were articulated with *quoining*, a high-style feature usually found in Georgian, not Federal-style, buildings—though they are indeed treated with a Federal-style slenderness here. But they were included probably for functional, structural, reasons: the walls are built up of irregular, thin pieces of stone, and for sturdy, and sharp, corners, quoins of cut stone blocks are required.

11. An oval attic window with delicate metal cameing complete with cast rosettes for junctures of the metal bars today can be found at 50 Forest Place. The house was modernized in Italianate style in the mid-19th century, but the front porch (facing Hart St.) and the door/window above it are clearly Federal in origin. For a detail of the facade showing the porch and window, see *A Book of Reminders* (1992), Fig. 2.

12. According to Douglas Shepard, the architect for the Smith-White House was C. K. Porter, who also designed the first Normal School building (1867–68).

13. The doorway at 100 Eagle St. is illustrated in *A Book of Reminders* (1992), Fig. 12.

14. Although converted to student housing about a dozen years ago, the interiors have survived remarkably well. The elaborate plaster medallions, overdoor panels, and cornice moldings are intact (though the cornice band has come away in two portions in the rear parlor); the rear large chamber has now been divided in two, but the grained doors, moldings, and china closet remain, though the painting is now a bit banged up. The exterior is currently (August, 1997) being vinyl sided, but the width of the original clapboards has been maintained, and window frames are clad, not removed. The main visual difference is that the frieze ventilators are covered over.

15. For further information on 74 E. Main St., see Fredonia Preservation Society *Historic Preservation Series* newsletter VI, 2 (1993), which includes 7 photos or prints of the house, inside and out.

16. For two histories of the Baptist Church, see the "For Additional Reading." The building's foundations (below the brickwork) were repaired in the 1980s, at which time the cement finish was removed, revealing the attractive stonework. The brick was also cleaned at this time. The modern office and education wing at the rear was added in 1963.

17. The shop at 71–73 W. Main was remodeled and resided about 1985, at which time the windows on both floors were altered, and the louvered lunette in the pediment removed.

18. Research by Douglas Shepard reveals that "although John Jones does not seem to have actually moved [to Fredonia] before 1836, there is a reminiscence by Major Charles Kennedy (*Fredonia Censor* Aug. 8, 1909) in which he says he remembered Trinity being built [1834–35], and that Capt. Jonathan Sprague was superintendent and John Jones was the architect and builder. Sprague was indeed on the building committee from 1828, and the committee to superintend the construction consisted of Sprague, D. W. Douglass and Chauncy Tucker." For a thorough history of Trinity Episcopal Church, see the "For Additional Reading."

19. The front rooms in the Baker House are not large. For how a more grandly proportioned, and more "high style" Gothic Revival interior would look, see the proposed design by Downing (1850) reproduced in *Architecture in Fredonia* (1972), Fig. 68. For a telephoto detail of the facade bargeboards and window, see *A Book of Reminders* (1992), Fig. 7.

20. Although the house appears to be "solid brick," it is actually of balloon frame construction with a brick veneer—just as most brick houses today are constructed. See the article describing this in the *Censor* of Sept. 11, 1867. The Barker Museum has a set of hand-written (but unsigned) specifications which seem to be for this house.

21. For a telephoto detail of the brackets, and a window "lintel," see *A Book of Reminders* (1992), Fig. 17.

22. For a thorough account, see Kathryn S. Silliman, "The McKinstry House," FPS *HPS* , IX, I (1996), 4 pp., illus. with 7 photos.

23. For detail photos of the two cupolas, see *A Book of Reminders* (1992), Figs. 28 and 29.

24. Artistically, bay windows provided Picturesque animation to an otherwise plain exterior wall, and interior spatial variety as well. But they also admitted more sunlight—a desideratum of many Victorian designers. As Hussey explains, "The bay-window in the parlor is a very pleasant addition" which will permit "plenty of sunshine in ..., thereby assuring a dry, light, healthy atmosphere" (text for Plate 3, n. p.).

25. According to Douglas Shepard, Pratt's father was an architect and builder—perhaps a clue to his interest in this "radical" form of architectural design. For additional data on Pratt and his octagon, see Kathryn S. Silliman, "The Octagon House," FPS *HPS* , II, 2 (1989). The plan is depicted in *Architecture in Fredonia* (1972), Fig. 91.

26. For an illustration of the Corcoran Art Gallery, see *Architecture in Fredonia* (1972), Fig. 96.

27. The woodwork of the Curtis-Taylor House was completed by Robert Wolfers in 1869. The interior is described in a *Censor* article of March 16, 1870. For a telephoto detail of the facade tower, see *A Book of Reminders* (1992), Fig. 26.

28. For a fuller account of Putnam's life, career, and his house, see my illustrated articles "Aaron O. Putnam and Early Life in Fredonia," *Evening Observer*, March 10, 1982, p. 8 and "The Aaron O. Putnam Residence in Fredonia,", *EO*, March 11, 1982, p. 13. For a telephoto detail of the remarkable northwest chimney, see *A Book of Reminders* (1992), Fig. 27; for a detail of the front porch gable, see Fig. 4.

29. Originally the Canadaway Creek mills all ran on water power only; but later—as the tall chimneys denote—steam power was more and more used to supplement, and finally replace water power.

30. For a view of the other side of the Clark-Johnson House, see *Architecture in Fredonia* (1972), Fig. 124. A telephoto detail of the facade bargeboards is in *A Book of Reminders* (1992), Fig. 9.

31. For a telephoto detail of the south gable, see *A Book of Reminders* (1992), Fig. 23.

32. Another handsome carriage house, behind an Italianate dwelling, is at 18 Leverett St. Others are depicted in *Architecture in Fredonia* (1972)—but not this edition—in Fig. 31 (Squire White's vernacular barn), and Fig. 64 (two simple ones between Trinity Church and the adjacent Italianate house).

33. My thanks to Paul A. Bowers for digitally processing this photograph and removing two automobiles parked squarely in front of the carriage house.

34. Despite this date, both buildings were up late in 1895 (*Censor*, Dec. 25, 1895). The cost was $11,500.

For additional information on Forest Hill Cemetery, including a detail of its ground plan, and data on its antecedent Pioneer Cemetery, see Douglas Shepard, "Fredonia's Burial Grounds and How They Grew," FPS *HPS* VIII, 1 (1995). See also the brochure [Holly Hewitt], *A Walking Tour of Forest Hill Cemetery Fredonia, N. Y.*, published by the Barker Historical Museum (n. d.), which has a brief history of the cemetery, and describes eight of the noted graves. An overall plan, and old view of the Chapel wing, are reproduced.

Some time around 1980 the open porch depicted in Fig. 182 was filled in with Permastone on the exterior and made into a fireproof vault inside. Though the Chapel wing (now used as the Cemetery office) has a dropped ceiling (probably 1950s), a number of the acoustical panels came off in Sept., 1994 and the original ceiling treatment of varnished wood became visible. A molded cornice, with a frieze band of square panels, surrounds the room, and the ceiling itself is composed of large rectangular panels (giving a somewhat "beamed" appearance) ceiled with matched boarding. A circular feature at the middle undoubtedly marks the location of a now-lost chandelier.

35. Two notices in the *Censor* (courtesy Ann Fahnestock) date this remodeling, and comment upon it. The first item from Aug. 15, 1900 mentions that the Curtis house "is torn up and over-run with carpenters and plasterers, but the Curtises will have a beautiful home when it is finished." The item from May 29, 1901 is worth quoting at length:

"Capt. Curtis Did it.—How some animals shed their skin and get a new one on without exposing their inwards is one of nature's mysteries, and Capt. E. A. Curtis did about as wonderful a thing in demolishing his old house and building a new one in the same place, without disturbing his family. There may be some of the old house left in the new structure but it is not apparent. For all practical purposes he has an elegant new home, and in many respects it is the finest dwelling in Fredonia. There is no such handsome stair case, or polished oak finishing, in any other house that we have seen. The exterior also reflects great credit on Capt. Curtis as a skillful architect."

36. For a telephoto detail of one of its Ionic capitals, see *A Book of Reminders* (1992), front cover.

37. For a 1967 sketch which shows the interior prior to the ceiling being lowered (but with some proposed—but not executed—curved counters for tellers), see *Architecture in Fredonia* (1972), Fig. 160.

38. Gustav Stickley's design for "A Pleasant and Homelike Cottage Designed for a Small Family," the apparent archetype for this mode, first appeared in *The Craftsman* for Feb. 1905, and was reprinted by Stickley in his book of house designs and plans *Craftsman Homes* published in 1909, pp. 76–77. This volume has been reprinted by Dover Books (1979).

39. The house is illustrated in *Architecture in Fredonia* (1972), Fig. 167.

40. As the photo of the group shows, both 197 and 195 had surfaces enriched, in the Craftsman mode, with shingles—those of 197 laid in courses of alternating widths to add extra visual variety; those of 195, cladding the entire bungalow, more traditional dark brown vernacular-style shingling. Around 1995 both houses were refaced in horizontal siding.

41. Fenton Hall at Fredonia State was erected opposite Mason Hall in 1953. As originally designed it was to have a gabled roof (like Mason Hall), which would have augmented its Colonial appearance. See *Architecture in Fredonia* (1972), Fig. 183.

42. For more information on the Ralph B. Jones House, and a photo of it, see *Architecture in Fredonia* (1972), p. 94 and Fig. 188.

43. It no longer appears "International Modern" however, as it was clad in vinyl siding about 1994.

44. The building was repointed about 1990 at which time the mortar joints were widened and a light-colored mortar employed—so that now the building has a much different appearance than as originally constructed (and as depicted in the 1972 photograph).

45. According to contemporary information, the designers, engineers, and contractors for the main buildings of the Fredonia campus were as follows: Architects: I. M. Pei & Partners—Henry N. Cobb, partner in charge (design); Werner Wandelmaier, associate partner (management); Theodore J. Musho, senior associate (design); Robert Bates, resident architect. Engineers: Garfinkel & Marenberg (structural); Segner & Dalton (mechanical). Landscape consultants: Office of Dan Kiley, Joseph R. Gangemi. Acoustical consultants: Bolt, Beranek & Newman Inc. General contractors: John W. Cowper Co., Inc. (library, lecture hall center, administration building); Paul Tishman Co. (fine arts center); C. E. Knowles (site work).

46. The prominent hill north of the Arts Center was created in 1971 by dumping excavated earth from the foundations of Thompson Hall here rather than carting it away.

47. Before the Fredonia Campus was completed in 1971 other buildings or complexes by the Pei firm were eliciting national acclaim: The Christian Science Center in Boston (1968–73), the Christian Science Church Complex in Washington, D. C. (1970–72), and the Johnson Museum of Art at Cornell (1970–73). One of his finest works had its genesis during these same years, the East Building of the National Gallery in Washington, D. C., whose plans date from 1969–70 (constructed 1971–76).

Since completing the Fredonia campus the Pei firm has become even more widely known through its success with the National Gallery addition (which opened in 1978), the John F. Kennedy Library in Boston (1979), the addition to the Museum of Fine Arts, Boston (1980) and, most famous of all, the "glass pyramid" and renovation to the Louvre in Paris (1984–94). The firm is now called Pei Cobb Freed & Partners.

48. For example, the doors to all the buildings have been replaced, but retain generally the

original look and the dark metal frames. The dormitory complexes needed brick repair and replacement for cornices and parapets. Rockefeller Arts Center has had, probably, the most alterations—but they are not evident to all but the expert eye. About 1981 handicapped access ramps were added to the front and courtyard; in 1986 another was added to the rear. In both cases, concrete with similar patterning was employed. The concrete paving of the interior plaza was replaced in 1993. In 1994 a new ventilating system for the studios was installed, resulting in prominent ductwork and ventilators on the roof. In 1996 all the windows were replaced (in King Concert hall as well as the studio, classroom and office portions) using thermopane glazing. The frames and mullions are now, therefore, a bit heavier, but the overall design appearance is about the same.

49. We are so used to 20th century remodeling that strips off and eradicates all the distinctive architectural features of a house in "modernizing" it—leaving a meaningless husk of its former being—that the successful and striking remodeling of the 19th century provides a cogent lesson in both architectural self-confidence, and esthetic theory.

50. For an example from Vaux, see *Architecture in Fredonia* (1972), Fig. 239.

51. For a telephoto detail of one of the Ionic capitals (and its entablature), see *A Book of Reminders* (1992), Fig. 33.

52. Twenty-five years later, this view from the driveway to 244 Central Ave. is much the same. Several of the large maples on the strip between the street and the sidewalk are gone, now replaced by younger trees; but all the others remain, including the majestic maple at the far right, enlarged even further by a quarter century of growth.

53. The brick paving of Day St. is clearly shown in *Architecture in Fredonia* (1972), Fig. 181. For a real idea of what the brick streets of Fredonia were like, one must visit those surrounding Washington Park in Dunkirk, or pay a visit to Jamestown, where a great many brick streets are still extant.

54. Macadam roads had the subgrade slightly arched, or cambered; the next two layers (each 4" thick) were of broken stones of 3" size maximum; and the final 2" layer was of the finer 1" broken stone. Hard stone, such as granite, was best, as the pieces retained their sharp edges which helped in their compacting and interlocking.

55. For a photograph taken Sept. 28, 1892 of workmen laying bricks on a street in Dunkirk, see *Architecture in Fredonia* (1972), Fig. 214.

56. Although this carriage block (and the stone sidewalk in the photo) is no longer extant, a larger one, decorated on the front with a spoked wheel design, is still in place at 81 E. Main St.

57. The post is no longer in situ, having been found one morning broken off (probably from being hit by a vehicle) c. 1991; but it is still preserved by the house's current owner, D & F Telephone.

For a pair of stone hitching posts (and accompanying carriage blocks) depicted in an 1881 print, see *Architecture in Fredonia* (1972), Fig. 216. Extant ones can be found in Laona, however: single stone hitching posts are at 151 and 9660 Porter Ave., and a pair at 9674.

58. Cobblestones were also employed in the foundations and porch supports for 51 Seymour St.; a retaining wall (see *Architecture in Fredonia* [1972] Fig. 241) next to the sidewalk at 157 E. Main St. (house demolished 1992) uses stones of varying sizes but laid up in a cobblestone-like manner, as do the piers flanking the entrance to Lowell Place.

59. In Chicago balloon frame construction caught on at once: the population of Chicago grew from 8,000 in 1844 to 84,000 in 1855, and it was housed quickly thanks to the ease and rapidity of balloon frame construction. But it was slow to be accepted everywhere. The first depiction of it in a pattern book appears to be William E. Bell's *Carpentry Made Easy; or, the Science and Art of Framing....* (Philadelphia, 1858), in which balloon framing is only one of many methods depicted. In the 1870s it was still considered just one option available.

60. Welded (or soldered) together, sheet metal also was perfect for elaborate but light-weight cornices, such as depicted in Fig. 278, here in conjunction with cast iron cresting. It was also adapted for many other modern uses. The cleverly designed "Emerson Ejecting Ventilator"—a house and attic ventilating system based on scientific principles—touted by A. J. Downing in 1850 (*Architecture of Country Houses* , Fig. 87), could be made of galvanized iron (or zinc or tin). A splendid example still survives in Fredonia at 27–29 Lambert Ave. See Daniel D. Reiff, "New Technology over a Century Ago,", *EO* May 15, 1991, p. 3. See also *A Book of Reminders* (1992), p. [i].

61. When the ruins of the Masonic Building were being torn down in March, 1973 I purchased three of the cast iron lintels from the demolition contractor; one of them I subsequently donated to the Barker Historical Museum. The leaf-patterned "drops" at each end of the lintel were attached by rivets or bolts; as the photo shows, over time some of these rusted loose. The opening for the window is just 3' 3" wide, and one of the sizes available for Lintel No. 45 from Buffalo Eagle Iron Works was this dimension (at a cost of $4.50 each in their 1859 catalog). When the "Murphy Block" was restored in 1986, fiberglass casts of one of the drops I had salvaged were used to restore missing elements.

The only commercial building with cast iron ground floor treatment intact (and with sumptuous cast iron lintels on the two floors above) is at 34 W. Main St.

62. Other illustrations of architectural uses of cast iron can be seen in Figs. 126, 138, 148, 152, and 158. See also *Architecture in Fredonia* (1972), Figs. 144–45, and 147–48 for varied uses of cast iron in a Dunkirk commercial building; and for cast iron urns depicted on a front lawn in the 19th century, Fig. 216.

63. This hitching post and its mate are no longer extant; but one of similar design is still found on White St. next to the White Inn. Two others like this are near the front of 289 Central Ave., moved there in 1993 from an adjacent property. One of them (possibly both) as well as the carriage block came originally, c. 1965, from 154 Center St.

64. Although concrete block houses are often generically called "Sears Houses," since Sears was a great popularizer of concrete block machines, and are indeed often based on plans from Sears, many designs were prepared locally, or obtained from other mail-order house or plan companies. For example, 37 Newton St. (see *Architecture in Fredonia* (1972), Fig. 171) follows exactly plans from The Chicago House Wrecking Co. Other concrete block buildings in Fredonia are at 85 and 91 Cushing St., 20 Orchard St., and at 174 and 179 Eagle St.

One of the most remarkable concrete block buildings locally is the Adams Memorial Church (now Adams Art Gallery) in Dunkirk of 1934. Rock-faced walls, smooth corner quoins, pediments, parapets, balustrades, arched window caps, and four large Greek Ionic columns are all of concrete.

65. After 1930 concrete blocks diminished in popularity as the national industry switched to lighter-weight cinder blocks, and rock faced was dropped in favor of smooth faced finishes—still in use today.

A recent (1995) example of using concrete block with rock-faced treatment can be found at 10651 Brigham Rd., where the house was jacked up and a new foundation built. Local Amish craftsmen provided the blocks, and did the masonry work.

66. A more recent example of a Fredonia modular home is at 314 E. Main St., erected in 1995.

There are a number of useful works on local history which those wishing to learn more about Fredonia may want to consult. The five volumes of essays by Elizabeth L. Crocker, *Yesterdays ... In and Around Pomfret, N. Y.* (1960–1964) are especially helpful; briefer, but also very readable, are the booklets *Frontier Fredonia, to 1825* (1959) and *Historic Fredonia 1825–1875* (1960), student publications done under the direction of Prof. William Chazanof. The published histories of the Baptist and Episcopal churches are useful also for local history. These are the [S. S. Crissey], *Centennial History of the Fredonia Baptist Church, 1808–1908* (1909?), and C. Allyn Russell, *A History of the Fredonia Baptist Church* (1955), both of which have numerous illustrations; and Merwin A. Garland, *The History of Trinity Episcopal Church, Fredonia, New York 1822–1967* (1968), a large book—it has 136 pages of footnotes—with nine pages of plates. In older sources, the centennial histories published at the turn of the century are full of useful information.

Readers who wish to explore buildings by style more fully now have a wealth of guides to choose from. Marcus Whiffen's *American Architecture since 1780: A Guide to the Styles* (1969; revised edition, 1992), is very good, and has a bibliography to direct one to specific books and articles on any style. Two subsequent handbook-type "guides to the styles" can be mentioned: John J.-G. Blumenson's *Identifying American Architecture: A Pictorial Guide to Styles and Terms, 1600–1945* (1977; rev. ed. 1981), and John C. Poppeliers et al., *What Style is It? A Guide to American Architecture* (1983; 2nd ed. 1984) are each slender volumes of about 115 pages. An encyclopedic guide over 500 pages long with hundreds of photos of every conceivable variant of the major house styles, plus maps, charts, and a thorough bibliography, is Virginia and Lee McAlester, *A Field Guide to American Houses* (1984)—which even includes a Fredonia house!

For American architectural history, three books can be suggested. Both Leland M. Roth, *A Concise History of American Architecture* (1979), and Marcus Whiffen and Frederick Koeper, *American Architecture 1607–1976* (1981; 2nd ed. 1983) are excellent, well-illustrated surveys. A study which focuses more on cultural aspects—and includes furniture and interiors as well—is Alan Gowans, *Images of American Living: Four Centuries of Architecture and Furniture as Cultural Expression* (1st. ed. 1964). All three have helpful bibliographies.

For a further look at local architecture two useful (but very different) books are J. A. Chewning, *Dunkirk, New York, its Architecture and Urban Development* (1992); and Jewel Helen Conover, *Nineteenth-Century Houses in Western New York* (1966)—actually it deals only with Chautauqua County—which includes illustrations of 15 Fredonia houses.

During the period 1972 to 1997 a great many articles regarding Fredonia's historic architecture, as well as articles on historical and other matters relating to specific buildings, have appeared in the Dunkirk *Evening Observer*. Other newspapers, and regional magazines, also on occasion have had relevant material. In addition, brochures and reports on various topics, occasional publications of the Barker Historical Museum, and newsletters of the Fredonia Preservation Society contain a wealth of interesting material on our local architecture, and its context. Not only do these articles and other items contain much useful data, but they often have photos of special interest as well.

Below I have arranged, by topic, a chronological listing of a selection of the articles and other publications or reports (a few from pre-1972 are also included). A review of them highlights some of the architectural and preservation issues in Fredonia during the last 25 years; they are also an excellent starting point for further research. Note that items in one category may have relevance to others as well.

Throughout, *Evening Observer* has been abbreviated as *EO*, *Sunday Observer* as *SO*, and Fredonia Preservation Society *Historic Preservation Series* as FPS *HPS*, but other publications have been given their full titles.

Houses Illustrated in Book

Phil McGan, "Historical Risley Home in Fredonia is Renovated, Restored, by New Owners," *EO*, Jan 28, 1971, P. 16 (5 photos). [63 Risley St.]

Daniel D. Reiff, "Architecture in Fredonia, New York 1811–1972," (Summary of main categories in *Architecture in Fredonia*.) Fredonia: Michael C. Rockefeller Arts Center Gallery, [1974]. 15 pp. with 3 illus.

Louise Ratkoski, "Charm of Grant-Richmond Home Will be Retained by New Owner," *EO*, Jan. 9, 1974, p. 10. [74 E. Main St.]

Holly Hewitt, "Tunnel in Central Avenue Building Stirs Speculation," *EO*, Oct. 28, 1978, p. 3 (1 photo). [20 Central Ave.]

"Fire Heavily Damages College-owned Building," *EO*, April 9, 1979 (2 photos). [178 Central Ave.]

[Holly Hewitt], *A Walking Tour Of Forest Hill Cemetery Fredonia, N. Y.* Fredonia, N. Y.: Barker Historical Museum, n. d. (6 panel brochure, 1 photo, 1 plan).

Doug Fenton, "Same Architect Designed Fredonia Village Hall as did Fenner Fire Station," *EO*, Jan. 18, 1980 (2 photos) [article about E. A. Curtis—though Harry Beebe was in fact designer of Fire Station]

Sean Kirst, "Mark Twain Speculated Heavily, and Lost Much Money," *EO*, March 31, 1981 (4 photos). [20 Central Ave.]

Daniel D. Reiff. "The Aaron O. Putnam House: A Victorian Showplace in Fredonia, New York." Society of Architectural Historians/Western New York Chapter *Little Journal*, 6, 1 (Feb. 1982), pp. 21–29, including 8 photos. [134 Temple St.]

"Putnam Home Featured in Regional Journal," *EO*, March 2, 1982, p. 5, (1 photo). [134 Temple St.]

Daniel D. Reiff, "Aaron O. Putnam and Early Life in Fredonia," *EO*, March 10, 1982, p. 8 (4 photos). [134 Temple St.]

Daniel D. Reiff, "The Aaron O. Putnam Residence in Fredonia," *EO*, March 11, 1982, p. 13 (5 photos). [134 Temple St.]

"New College Admissions House is More Accessible to Public on Central Avenue," *EO*, Nov. 8, 1984, (2 photos). [178 Central Ave.]

Paula Voell, "How Fredonia Saved Fenner House," *Buffalo News*, March 3, 1985, Sec. E, p. 1 (4 photos). [178 Central Ave.]

"Alumni House Opens on Avenue," and "New Headquarters has Museum, Precious Artifacts," *Statement*, 3, 4 (June 1985), p. 1 (3 photos). [172 Central Ave.]

The President's Home: 194 Central Avenue, 8 page brochure, illus. with 10 photos and 2 drawings; published by the State University of New York College at Fredonia, [1987]

M. Louise Ratkoski, "A Distinguished Fredonia Home Ages Gracefully," *EO*, Feb. 27, 1987, p. 10 (6 photos). [194 Central Ave.]

"Poster Shows Fredonia Architecture", *EO*, Sept. 1, 1987 (1 photo).

Yvonne Wilensky, "Do You Know This House?" FPS, *HPS* I, 1, 1988 (2 pp.; 1 drawing). [171 Eagle St.]

Norma Braude, "Fire Damages Rear Portion of Historic Home," *Buffalo News*, Feb. 6, 1989. [4587 W. Main Rd.]

Kathryn S. Silliman, "The Octagon House," FPS *HPS* II, 2, 1989 (3 pp.; 4 drawings). [99 Chestnut St.]

Louise Ratkoski, "Liener Home has 1880s Charm, Today's Comforts," *EO* Supplement, May 5, 1989, pp. 1, 12 & 13 (8 photos). [174 E. Main St.]

Robert Macre, "Varied Reactions on Pit Found at Carriage House in Fredonia," *EO*, June 9, 1989, (2 photos). [42 Central Ave.]

Louise Ratkoski, "W.C.A. Home Facelift an Eyecatcher," *EO*, Sept. 19, 1989, p. 1 (1 photo). [134 Temple St.]

Daniel D. Reiff, "Greek Revival Details of Elijah Risley House," *EO*, May 13, 1991, p. 3 (2 photos, 1 drawing). [89 Risley St.]

"Fredonia Preservation Society's Heritage House Tour," *EO*, Nov. 30, 1992, p. 10. [194 Central Ave.; 4587 W. Main Rd.; 89 Risley St.; 79 East Main St.; 29 Newton St.]

Kathryn S. Silliman, "The Three Faces of 74 East Main Street," FPS *HPS*, VI, 2, 1993 (4 pp.; 2 drawings, 5 photos).

Todd Pignataro, "Koch Family Home in Fredonia 'Radiates Warmth'," *SO* June 4, 1995 (1 photo). [63 Central Ave.]

Steve Palisin, "WCA Home a Showpiece on Temple Street," *SO* June 25, 1995 (1 photo). [134 Temple St.]

Steve Palisin, "Forest Hill Cemetery Gate Houses are Nearly 100 Years Old," *SO*, July 23, 1995 (1 photo).

Todd Pignataro, "Risley Mansion Remains a Home for Fredonia Family," *SO*, Oct. 8, 1995 (1 photo). [63 Risley St.]

"Fredonia Houses Featured in National Magazine," *SO*, Oct. 8., 1995, Sec. E. p. 4 (3 photos). [199 Water St., 37 Newton St., 38 Leverett St.]

Steve Palisin, "Pratt House's Restoration only Halfway Complete," *SO*, Oct. 29, 1995, Sec. F, pp. 1 and 2 (1 photo). [99 Chestnut St.]

Steve Palisin, "Italian Villa Home in Fredonia could be Only One of its Kind," *SO*, Dec. 17, 1995, (1 photo). [67 E. Main St.]

Steve Palisin, "Risley Home one of Two Mansions on Fredonia's Risley Street," *SO*, Oct. 13, 1996, Sec. B, p. 10 (1 photo). [63 Risley St.]

Douglas H. Shepard, "More Information Offered on Risley Street Home," *SO*, Oct. 20, 1996, Sec. D, p. 3 (People's Column). [63 Risley St.]

Pamela Doto, "Historic Home Lured Manhattan Couple to Fredonia," SO, Dec. 8, 1996 (1 photo). [150 Central Ave.]

Doug Coy, "College's Fenner House Has Rich History in Fredonia," *SO*, March 30, 1997, Sec. D, p. 1 (1 photo). [178 Central Ave.]

Douglas H. Shepard, "Fredonia Baptist Church Clock has Unique History," *EO*, June 3, 1997, p. 4 (People's Column).

"Forest Hill Cemetery Gatehouse Slated for Rehabilitation Project," *EO*, Aug. 9, 1997, p. 3 (1 photo).

"Restoration of Cemetery Gate Lodge Progressing," *EO*, Sept. 30, 1997, p.3 (1 photo).

Daniel D. Reiff, "The Octogon Mode," *Chautauqua Mirror* (Sept.–Oct. 1997), pp. 28–29, 31–32, (4 photos, 1 plan; expanded version of entry in this book). [99 Chestnut St.]

DOWNTOWN FREDONIA BUILDINGS

Phil McGan, "Flames Engulf Fredonia Business Block; Officials Estimate Loss Near $Million," *EO*, Feb. 28, 1973, pp. 1 and 16 (9 photos). [14 W. Main St.]

Phil McGan, "Some Businesses Lost, Others ready to Open after Fredonia Fire," *EO*, March 1, 1973.

Phil McGan, and Ron Murphy, "No Federal Aid Available for Fire-Damaged Fredonia Property," *EO*, March 2, 1973 (3 photos).

"Demolition of the Fire-Ravaged Buildings," *EO*, March 5, 1973, p. 5 (1 photo).

"UDC Has Proposal for Rebuilding Fire-Destroyed Section of Fredonia," *EO*, June 11, 1973 (1 plan).

Hank McKee, "Downtown Area of Fredonia Proposed as Historic District; Survey Completed," *EO*, March 4, 1975, p. 12 (1 photo).

"Proposed Municipal Complex," *EO*, May 15, 1975, p. 24 (1 plan). [for site between Water, Canadaway, and W. Main Streets]

Hank McKee, "How Long can Fredonia Fire Hall Function?" *EO*, Jan. 13, 1977, p. 16 (4 photos).

"Fredonia Commons Historic District," *Federal Register*, 42, 16 (January 25, 1977), p. 4552.

Hank McKee, "Removal of Overhanging Signs Among Ideas Being Studied for Downtown Area," *EO*, Feb. 16, 1977, p. 5.

[Donna Carlson], "Economic Depression Produces Post Office 'Harvest' Mural," *EO*, Nov. 8, 1977 (1 photo).

Jerry Reilly, "Blaze Rips Through Section of Downtown Fredonia; Damage Estimate close to $500,000," *EO*, Nov. 17, 1978, p. 1 (1 photo; four others elsewhere in issue). [25, 27, 29 and 31 E. Main St.]

"Fire Ruins 4 Businesses in Fredonia," *Buffalo News*, Nov. 18, 1978 (1 photo).

"Buildings Surrounding Barker Common Also Are Included in Historic District," *EO*, Nov. 30, 1978, p. 12.

Jerry Reilly, "Another Building in Downtown Fredonia Destroyed by Flames," *EO*, Dec. 20, 1978, pp. 1, 2, and 8 (4 photos). [36 W. Main St.]

Doug Fenton, "Several Alternatives Listed for Burned Out Section in Fredonia," *EO*, Dec. 20, 1978.

"Roof Goes Up," *EO*, Jan. 18, 1979 (1 photo). [29 and 31 E. Main St.]

Elizabeth L. Crocker, "Early Main Street Stores in Fredonia," *EO*, April 27, 1979, p. 14.

Elizabeth L. Crocker, "Hotels Marked Key Site in Fredonia," *EO*, May 2, 1979. [discusses site of Russo Building; and also Fredonia Academy]

"Historic Presentation" [re Fredonia Commons Historic District], *EO*, June 12, 1979, p. 5 (1 photo).

Doug Fenton, "Renovating Former Fredonia Fire Hall is Test Project for Historical Preservation," *EO*, Dec. 18, 1979 (1 photo).

Doug Fenton, "Historic White Inn will have New Owners," *EO*, June 11, 1980.

Doug Fenton, "Architectural Theme Discussed by CAC," *EO*, April 7, 1981, p. 5.

Doug Fenton, "[Downtown] Fredonia Architectural Theme is Victorian," *EO*, June 2, 1981, p. 5.

Doug Fenton, "Local Officials Give Solid Support to Erie Savings' Fredonia Proposal," *EO*, June 19, 1981.

[Daniel D. Reiff], *The White Inn* (6 page brochure with 8 photos, 1 drawing, 1 map), 1982; color edition of same, 1984.

Ann M. Fahnestock, "Fredonia's Newly Decorated IOOF Building Part of Fredonia's Historic American Block," *EO*, Nov. 2, 1983 (2 photos).

Hazel Nixon, "The White Inn," *Erie & Chautauqua Magazine*, Spring, 1984, pp. 74–75 (1 drawing, 4 photos).

John Moore, "White Inn Gets a New Look," *Jamestown Post-Journal* "Tempo Magazine," May 19, 1984, pp. 1, 8 and 9 (8 photos).

Doug Fenton, "Architect and Barker Library Board have Valid Reasons for Painting Addition," *EO*, May 31, 1984.

Paula Voell, "Fredonia's White Inn," *Buffalo News*, July 22, 1984, Sec. E, P. 1 (3 photos).

Donna Hoke, "Fredonia's Historic White Inn has Come a Long Way," *The Leader*, March 3, 1986, p. 7 (2 photos).

"Downtown Fredonia Revitalization," *EO*, May 14, 1986, p. 10 (1 photo from May 15, 1948).

Robert Macre, "Addition Planned at St. Joseph's Church," *EO*, April 12, 1989, p. 3.

Kathryn S. Silliman, "The Fredonia Post Office Mural," FPS *HPS*, VI, 1, 1993 (4 pp; 5 photos).

Steve Palisin, "New Lightposts to be Part of Renovation in Fredonia," *EO*, Aug. 17, 1994, p. 5.

Kristen Everett, "Magnificent White Inn has Proud History," *EO*, Sept. 8, 1994, p. 6 (1 photo).

"Hardware Store," *EO*, Oct. 20, 1994, [1 photo, c. 1910, W. Main St.]

Steve Palisin, "Public Hearing on Proposed Route 20 Reconstruction Scheduled Wednesday," *EO*, Nov. 8, 1994.

"Facade Improvement Discussion set for Wednesday in Village Hall," *EO*, Nov. 28, 1994, p. 6 (2 photos).

Steve Palisin, "Village Businessmen Attend Presentation on Improving Facades," *EO*, Dec. 3, 1994.

Steve Palisin, "Free Facade Consultations are Available to Village Merchants," *EO*, April 11, 1995, p. 5.

"Downtown Fredonia Photos Displayed at Chamber of Commerce Offices," *EO*, May 25, 1995 (1 photo).

Steve Palisin, "Fredonia Seeks its Place in History" [regarding E. and W. Main Historic District Survey], *EO*, June 1, 1995, pp. 1 and 2 (1 photo).

Steve Palisin, "M & T Bank Building Reflects French Style," *SO*, Aug. 27, 1995 (1 photo).

Steve Palisin, "Medical Group Unveils New Office Building [Design]," *SO*, Dec. 3, 1995, Sec. B, p. 8 (1 photo).

Steve Palisin, "Committee is Working to Expand Fredonia's Historic District," *EO*, Dec. 26, 1995, p. 3.

Jen Osborne, "Crusaders Converge in Fredonia—Forming Woman's Christian Temperance Union," *Chautauqua Sampler*, March 1997, pp. 1 and 8 (3 photos). [Baptist Church]

Steve Palisin, "Home in the Grange," *SO*, March 24, 1996, Sec. C, p. 1 (4 photos).

Daniel D. Reiff, "Architectural Details of Fredonia's M&T Bank are Fascinating," *EO*, May 21, 1997, p. 8 (3 photos).

HAMILTON-LESTER HOUSE, AND McCLEUR MILL (FIRE HALL SITE)

(Most of the following clippings are from a more comprehensive collection of 78 items regarding this controversy which I compiled between 1975 and 1979; a copy of the complete file was donated to the Barker Historical Museum.)

Elizabeth L. Crocker, "Old (Still Standing) Lester Mansion in Fredonia First to be Illuminated by Gas and Lafayette was a Witness," *EO*, May 12, 1975, p. 17. (2 photos).

"The Germania Hotel?" *EO*, June 19, 1975, p. 13 (1 photo). [70-72 W. Main St.]

"The Germania—Twice," *EO*, June 24, 1975 (People's Column).

Hank McKee, "Village Board Unanimously Favors Fire Hall Site Despite Late Historical Considerations," *EO*, Feb. 3, 1976, p. 8.

Hank McKee, "Demolition of Property for New Fire Hall Could Begin in January," *EO*, Sept. 28, 1976.

Hank McKee, "Architect Hired for Fredonia Fire Hall Project; Floor Plan has been Revealed," *EO*, Aug. 31, 1976, p. 10 (1 plan).

"Albany Architect Tours Buildings in Fredonia," *EO*, Oct. 12, 1976.

Elizabeth L. Crocker, "Historically-Important Fredonia Counts an Authentic Mill Among its Many Interesting Old Structures," *EO*, Nov. 1, 1976, p. 21 (2 photos).

Hank McKee, "Committee to Study Historical Value of Buildings at Proposed Fire Hall Site," *EO*, Nov. 5, 1976.

Elizabeth L. Crocker, "Current Fredonia Fire Hall Site Discussion Involves Old Lester Mansion on Main Street," *EO*, Nov. 11, 1976, p. 13 (2 photos).

Hank McKee, "Committee Meets Wednesday to Start Discussion on Fire Hall and Buildings," *EO*, Nov 15, 1976, p. 12.

Hank McKee, "Historian Dr. Reiff Urges Fredonia to Undertake Renovation of Downtown," *EO*, Nov. 16, 1976.

Hank McKee, "HUD Official Confirms Earlier Report Stating Buildings are Blighted," *EO*, Nov. 17, 1976.

Hank McKee, "Moving Lester Building (Colonial Jack's) May Solve Fredonia Fire Hall Controversy," *EO*, Nov. 18, 1976, p. 5.

Daniel D. Reiff, "Old, New can Live Together," *EO*, Dec. 3, 1974 (People's Column).

"Historic Committee Will Meet," *EO*, Dec. 6, 1976, p. 9.

Hank McKee, "Lower Portion of Mill is Expected to Remain," *EO*, Dec. 7, 1976.

Hank McKee, "Historic Group, Village Officials in Verbal Swipes about Saving Buildings," *EO*, Dec. 14, 1976, p. 16.

Hank McKee, "State Official Issues Report on Historic Buildings in Fredonia," *EO*, Dec. 21, 1976, p. 7.

Hank McKee, "'Specialist' Says Historical Buildings are Structurally Sound and Repairable," *EO*, Dec. 24, 1976, p. 10.

Ron Gustafson and Hank McKee, "Funds Rejected for Fredonia Fire Hall," *EO*, Jan. 4, 1977.

Hank McKee, "Historical Buildings, Central Location for Fire Hall, are on Collision Course," *EO*, Jan. 13, 1977.

Hank McKee, "Fredonia Trustees Approve Demolition of All Buildings at Fire Hall Location," *EO*, Jan. 25, 1977, p. 9.

"Historic Committee Calls Action by Village Board 'Shortsighted'," *EO*, Jan. 26 , 1977.

"Historic Committee says Village Had Other Options on Fire Hall," *EO*, Jan. 27, 1977, p. 10.

"Demolition at Fire Hall Site May Start Soon," *EO*, Feb. 14, 1977.

Hank McKee, "Preliminary Injunction Issued to Halt Demolition at New Fire Hall Location," *EO*, Feb. 17, 1977, p. 16.

Hank McKee, "Fire Hall Site: Court Order Route Last Chance to Halt Demolition," *EO*, Feb. 18, 1977, p. 7.

Hank McKee, "Fredonia Confident Courts Will Rule in Its Favor on Demolition At Fire Hall Site," *EO*, Feb. 21, 1977.

Neil Chaffie, "Fredonia Due in Court Today to seek Razing of 3 Buildings," Buffalo *Courier-Express*, Feb. 22, 1977, (1 photo).

"Jurisdiction Question Snags 'Historic Building' Court Case," *EO*, Feb. 22, 1977 (1 photo).

"Walls Come Tumbling Down," *EO*, Feb. 22, 1977, (1 photo). [70–72 W. Main St.]

Hank McKee, "Wrecker Moves in on 'Historic' Structures When Injunction Fails," *EO*, Feb. 23, 1977, p. 5 (4 photos).

"Reiff says Efforts to Preserve Buildings Began over Year Ago," *EO*, Feb. 24, 1977.

"Discussions Continue Between Historic Group, Village Officials," *EO*, March 2, 1977, p. 11.

Don MacLeod, "Historical Fredonian Site Demolished," *The Leader*, March 3, 1977, p. 2 (1 photo).

"Survey Still Possible for the Old Mill," *EO*, March 22, 1977.

Hank McKee, "Agreement is Reached on Fredonia's 'Old Mill'," *EO*, April 19, 1977, p. 5.

Hank McKee, "Thorough Documentation is Planned for Old Mill," *EO*, April 21, 1977, p. 10 (1 photo).

Hank McKee, "Partial Funding OKd for Fredonia Fire Hall," *EO*, June 4, 1977.

"Archeological Study Begins at Old Mill," *EO*, June 24, 1977, p. 10.

"Federal Money Can't Be Used for Partial Fire Hall Construction," *EO*, June 28, 1977.

Hank McKee, "Archeologists Uncover Raceway at Old Mill," *EO*, June 28, 1977, p. 4.

"Raceway Excavation," *EO*, June 29, 1977 (1 photo).

Hank McKee, "Old Mill is Coming Down for Fire Hall Construction," *EO*, Oct. 20, 1977.

"Demolition Begun," *EO*, Oct. 21, 1977, p. 11 (1 photo).

"Old Mill Site Nearly Cleared for Firehall," *Buffalo Evening News*, Oct. 24, 1977.

Ashton Nichols, "Buildings Razed, Consciousness Raised," *Preservation News* (Washington, D. C.), October 1977, pp. 1 and 2 (1 photo).

"A Horse Drawn Cart" [at Sackett Screen Co., 1905] *EO*, April 14, 1979, p. 3 (1 photo).

VILLAGE HALL AND OPERA HOUSE

(Most of the following clipping, report and brochure citations are from a more comprehensive collection of 515 items regarding the saving and renovation of the building which I compiled between 1978 and 1995; a copy of the complete file was donated to the Barker Historical Museum. Below are some of the highlights.)

Elizabeth L. Crocker, "History of the Fredonia Opera House, a Prominent Part of the Village Hall," *EO*, Feb. 22, 1979.

Doug Fenton, "Fredonia Village Board, with 3–1 Vote, will Proceed with Restoration of Tower," *EO*, Dec. 10, 1982, p. 4.

Daniel D. Reiff, "Additional Perspective Given on Fredonia Village Hall Tower," *EO*, Dec. 17, 1982, p. 4 (2 photos).

Doug Fenton, "Study Committee to Recommend Vacating Fredonia Village Hall within a Few Years," *EO*, Feb. 25, 1983, p. 5.

Doug Fenton, "Options Outlined [by Dr. Reiff] for Future of Fredonia Village Hall Structure," *EO*, April 13, 1983, p. 7.

Joseph A. Siracuse, P. E., *Roof Structure Condition Survey Village Hall—Fredonia, N. Y.* April, 1983, 6 pp.

"Consultant Says Repairs Should Begin Now on Fredonia's Village Hall," *EO*, May 13, 1983, p. 4.

Doug Mohart, "Board Takes no Action on Seeking Funds for Village Hall Renovation," *EO*, June 30, 1983, p. 4.

Lilia W. Taddio, "Restore Village Hall," *EO*, July 21, 1983 (People's Column).

Doug Fenton, "Pomfret Town Board Rejects Joint Municipal Building Plan," *EO*, Aug. 30, 1983, p. 4.

Jack L. Cogdill, "Save the Hall," *The Leader*, Sept. 19, 1983, p. 17.

Philip Morris, "Save Fredonia Village Hall," *Artifacts*, Oct. 1993 (Editorial).

Daniel D. Reiff, "The Unseen Richness of the Village Hall in Fredonia," *EO*, Oct. 6, 1983, p. 18 (9 photos).

"The Mayor and his Committee—Their Stories Differ," [re Fredonia Village Hall], *The Leader* (Extra), Oct. 24, 1983, pp. 1–4 (2 photos of Village Hall).

Doug Fenton, "489 Sign Petitions to Keep Village Hall," *EO*, Nov. 15, 1983.

Shelly Miller, "Future of Village Hall to be Decided by Trustees," *Spectator*, Nov. 22, 1983, pp. 6-7 (1 drawing).

James M. Sedota, *Memorandum: Village Hall* [Estimated Costs of New Building and of Renovation of Current Building], Dec. 8, 1983, 8 pp.

Doug Fenton, "Village Hall Renovation Ideas Discussed at Joint Meeting," *EO*, Jan. 13, 1984, p. 4.

Doug Fenton, "Estimates Given for Full Restoration of Fredonia Village Hall Range to $1 Million," *EO*, Feb. 14, 1984, p. 4.

Doug Fenton, "Safety Repairs Authorized for Fredonia's Village Hall," *EO*, Feb. 24, 1984.

Elizabeth L. Crocker, "Early History of Fredonia Village Hall and Its Predecessor [on site], Fredonia Academy," *EO*, Feb. 24, 1984.

Jack Cogdill, *The Village Hall Opera House* [Estimated costs for essential basic improvements], Feb. 1984, 5 pp.

Doug Fenton, "Large Crowd Attends Meeting on Fredonia Village Hall Work," *EO*, April 6, 1984, p. 4.

Doug Fenton, "Village Carpenter has Doubts About Renovating Village Hall," *EO*, April 25, 1984 (3 photos).

Doug Fenton, "Reiff Points to Village Administrator's Report Regarding Village Hall Restoration," *EO*, May 1, 1984, p. 4.

Lisa Eikenburg, "Pros and Cons Offered on Village Hall," *EO*, May 16, 1984, p. 4 (1 photo).

Doug Fenton, "Fredonia Board Has Meeting on Future of the Village Hall," *EO*, May 18, 1984.

Doug Fenton, "Preservation of Fredonia Village Hall Strongly Urged in Discussion by Reiff," *EO*, June 1, 1984.

Doug Fenton, "Structural Condition Analysis of Village Hall is Approved," *EO* June 8, 1984, p. 5.

Daniel Y. Bauer, "History of the Fredonia Opera House," *EO*, Aug. 3, 1984, p. 10 (5 photos).

Doug Fenton, "Structural Report Given on Fredonia Village Hall," *EO*, Aug. 3, 1984.

Doug Fenton, "CAC Hears Views on Village Hall," *EO*, Aug. 7, 1984.

Joseph A. Siracuse, P. E., Consulting Engineer. *Structural Appraisal of Fredonia Village Hall.* Revised Aug. 29, 1984. 16 pp. with 14 pages of plans and tables.

"Tower Work Begins," *EO*, Sept. 6, 1984 (1 photo).

Doug Fenton, "Grant is Approved for Architectural Fees for Fredonia Village Hall Study," *EO*, Sept. 21, 1984, p. 5.

Doug Fenton, "Lancaster Officials Tell about Hall Preservation," *EO*, Nov. 30, 1984.

"Preservation Society Membership Reaches 350," *EO*, Dec. 17, 1984, p. 4.

Lisa Eikenburg, "Fredonia Village Hall Options are Studied," *EO*, Feb. 1, 1985.

Daniel D. Reiff, "Additional Figures" [on Village Hall Renovation], *EO*, Feb. 11, 1985 (People's Column).

Doug Fenton, "Fredonia Board Unanimously Favors Village Hall Restoration," *EO*, Feb. 12, 1985, pp. 1 and 4.

John Moore, "Ohio Company [Gaede Serne Zofin Architects Inc.] Hired by Fredonia [for Village Hall Renovation]," *EO*, June 11, 1985, p. 5.

John Moore, "Fredonia Village Board Takes Big Step Toward Village Hall Restoration," *EO*, July 23, 1985, p. 5.

"Petitions for Fredonia Vote are Being Filed," *EO*, Aug. 19, 1985, p. 4.

John Moore, "Sept. 10 Set as Date for Village Hall Referendum," *EO*, Aug. 23, 1985.

John Moore, "Restoring Fredonia Village Hall is Least Costly Way to Solve Problem—Officials," *EO*, Sept. 6, 1985, pp. 1 and 4.

John Moore, "Fredonians Strongly Approve Bonding Referendum [1132 to 469]," *EO*, Sept. 11, 1985, p. 1.

John Moore, "Brick Cleaning Begins at Fredonia Village Hall," *EO*, Sept. 26, 1985, p. 5.

John Moore, "Fredonia Village Hall Exterior Work Could Be Done in 10 Weeks," *EO*, Oct. 1, 1985, p. 4 (2 photos).

John Moore, "Repointing Work Starts on Fredonia Village Hall," *EO*, Oct. 23, 1985, p. 3.

John Moore, "First Phase of Repairs Finished at Village Hall," *EO*, Dec. 13, 1985.

John Moore, "Figures Listed for Village Hall Restoration Could Be Reduced," *EO,* April 18, 1986, p. 5.

Lisa Eikenburg, "Preservation Society and Fredonia Sign Agreement," *EO*, May 7, 1986, p. 5.

"Restoration of Fredonia Opera House is Discussed," *EO*, Feb. 16, 1987, P. 7.

Robert Macre, "Funds Are Needed to Restore Fredonia Opera House," *EO*, Feb. 20, 1987, p. 5 (1 photo).

Robert Macre, "Preservation Society Conducts Fredonia Opera House Program," *EO*, March 30, 1987 (1 photo).

The Restoration of the Fredonia Opera House: Case Statement 1987, 6 page brochure published by the Fredonia Preservation Society (2 photos, 1 drawing).

"Fredonia Opera House Fund Campaign Begins," *EO*, April 23, 1987, p. 5.

"Fredonia Opera House Drive Hits 37 Percent," *EO*, June 4, 1987, p. 7.

Fredonia Opera House: 1987 Restoration Campaign, 12 p. brochure with 11 photos, 2 drawings, and 2 plans.

Robert Macre, "Fredonia's Application for Funding Village Hall Project is Under Review," *EO*, June 5, 1987, p. 6.

"Village Hall Masks," *EO*, Aug 12, 1987, p. 11 (2 photos).

Robert Macre, "Fredonia Village Board Okays Bid for Exterior Restoration," *EO*, Aug. 25, 1987, p. 5.

Robert Macre, "Fredonia Opera House Fund More than Half Way to Financial Goal," *EO*, Oct. 20, 1987, p. 5.

Robert Macre, "Fredonia Again Bypassed for Preservation Grant," *EO*, Dec. 9, 1987, p. 8.

Robert Macre, "Fredonia Came Close for Grant for Restoration of Village Hall," *EO*, Jan. 5, 1988, p. 3.

Robert Macre, "Fredonia Village Hall Prepares for a Renaissance," *EO*, May 13, 1988, p. 14 (3 photos, 1 plan).

"First Phase of Work At Opera House Begins," *EO*, May 27, 1988, p. 5.

"Opera House Renovations," *EO*, June 14, 1988, p. 3 (1 photo).

Peter Simon, "Fredonia Group's Efforts Pay Off as Opera House Restoration Begins," *Buffalo News*, Aug. 1, 1988 (2 photos).

"Fredonia Preservation Society Receives Grant for Opera House Work," *EO*, Aug. 8, 1988, p. 6.

Robert Macre, "[Village Hall] Restoration Moves Up on its Goal," *EO*, Oct. 1, 1988, p. 16 (3 photos, 4 plans).

Robert Macre, "Fredonia Village Hall Restoration History," *EO*, Feb. 16, 1989, p. 7.

"Fredonia Village Hall Reopens Tuesday," *EO*, Feb. 20, 1989, p. 3 (3 photos).

Robert Macre, "Fredonia Receives [$262,000] State Grant for Opera House," *EO*, March 21, 1989, p. 5.

Robert Macre, "Fraternity Members Help in Restoration of Opera House," *EO*, April 10, 1989, p. 6 (3 photos).

M. Louise Ratkoski, "Chair Endowments Will Enhance History of Fredonia Opera House," *EO*, Oct. 16, 1989 p. 12 (2 photos).

John Vaughan, "Fredonia Village Hall: History and Comparisons," FPS *HPS*, III, 1, 1990 (3 pp.; 2 photos).

John Vaughan, "Fredonia Village Hall and the Architecture of the 19th Century," FPS *HPS*, III, 3, 1990 (4 pp.; 4 photos).

Robert Macre, "Fredonia Village Hall Rededicated," *EO*, Jan. 29, 1990 (2 photos).

"Historic Day," [Laying of Fredonia Village Hall Cornerstone, June 11, 1890], *EO*, March 15, 1990, p. 20 (1 photo).

[Daniel D. Reiff, Douglas H. Shepard, and Winifred O. Shepard], *Fredonia Opera House Historic Structure Report*, 1990 (121 pp. with 40 photos and 1 drawing).

Robert W. Plyler, "Restoring Fredonia Opera House," *Jamestown Post-Journal*, May 5, 1990, "Tempo" Sec., pp. 1 and 13 (4 photos).

"Opera House Historic Structures Report is Approved in Albany," *EO*, June 7, 1990, p. 5.

Kyle Kubera, "Fredonia Opera House Work Proceeding but Slows Down," *EO*, Dec. 24, 1990, p. 6 (1 photo).

"Opera House Chairs," *EO*, Feb. 28, 1991, p. 6 (1 photo).

"Opera House Centennial Celebration was Conducted," *EO*, April 24, 1991, p. 1 (1 photo).

Angela Wayne Randazzo, "Opera House, Being Restored, Has Colorful History," *EO*, April 18, 1991, p. 7 (2 photos),

Kyle Kubera, "Fredonia Board Approves Funding for Opera House Work," *EO*, Jan. 14, 1992, p. 3.

"Major Gifts Received for Opera House," *EO*, Feb. 20, 1993, p. 6.

"Last Major Elements Planned for Fredonia's Opera House," *EO*, May 10, 1993, p. 6 (1 photo).

Kyle Kubera, "Steel Beams Installed to Support Opera House Theatrical Equipment," *EO*, Nov. 17, 1993, p. 5 (1 photo).

"Fredonia Preservation Society Hires Consultant [David Munnell] for Opera House Operations," *EO*, Sept. 23, 1994, p. 9.

Susan Chiappone, "Fredonia Opera House Nearly Ready for Opening," *EO*, Oct. 22, 1994, pp. 1 and 2 (2 photos).

Fredonia Opera House: A Renaissance Unveiled, EO, Nov. 4, 1994, special tabloid issue, 20 pp. (19 photos, 1 drawing).

Peter Simon, "After 8 Years, Opera House Set to Reopen," *Buffalo News*, Sec. B, pp. 1 and 4 (3 photos).

"Fredonia Opera House: A Gem for Entire Area," *EO*, Nov. 11, 1994 (Editorial).

Jim Boltz, "Remember Those with Far-Reaching Vision," *EO*, Nov. 12, 1994 (People's Column).

Susan Chiappone, "Fredonia Opera House Sparkles on Opening Night," *EO*, Nov. 14, 1994, pp. 1 and 10 (2 photos).

Fredonia Opera House: First Grand Opening 1891, Grand Re-opening 1994 Fredonia, N. Y.: Fredonia Preservation Society, 1994 (22 p. booklet with 19 photos).

Steve Palisin, "Fredonia Opera House Receives State Historic Preservation Award," *EO*, March 28, 1995, p. 1.

Steve Palisin, "State Preservation Award Presented to Village Officials," *EO*, May 5, 1995, p. 3 (1 photo).

Douglas Shepard, "An 'Operatic' Encore" [the Fredonia Opera House and its local predecessors], *Chautauqua Mirror* (March 1997), pp. 14–19, (4 photos).

"Pewter Plate Award Given to Fredonia Opera House," *EO*, June 17, 1997, Sec. B, p. 6 (1 photo).

"1891 Opera House History Collection on Display," *EO*, July 17, 1997 (1 photo).

BARKER COMMON AND MARK FOUNTAINS

"Barker Common in Historic Register," *EO*, Nov. 28, 1978.

Doug Shepard, "Fredonia's Barker Common Has Had Fountains since 1858," *EO*, May 12, 1989, p. 5.

Robert Macre, "Fredonia's Search for Repairs to Fountain Leads to Atlanta, Ga.," *EO*, Sept. 5, 1990.

Elizabeth Crocker, "Historian Provides Interesting Information on Fredonia Fountains," *EO*, Sept. 11, 1990.

Kyle Kubera, "First Meeting of Barker Common Fountain Committee is Tuesday," *EO*, March 22, 1991, p. 5.

Kyle Kubera, "Special Fund is Approved to Repair Fountains in Barker Common," *EO*, April 23, 1991, p. 5.

"Work Begins on Restoring Fountains," *EO*, May 23, 1991, p. 6.

"Restoration Work," *EO*, May 24, 1991, p. 1 (1 photo).

Kyle Kubera, "Fountains are Restored in Barker Common in Fredonia," and "History of Barker Common," *EO*, Aug. 22, 1991, p. 6 (1 photo).

"Skills Needed for Fountain Restoration," *EO*, Aug. 27, 1991, Sec. C, p. 11 (2 photos).

Kyle Kubera, "Urn is Stolen from Fredonia Fountain," *EO*, Nov. 26, 1991.

"Second Urn Broken Off in Fredonia," *EO*, Nov. 30, 1991.

Kyle Kubera, "Reward Fund hits $550 for Damage at Fountain," *EO*, Dec. 5, 1991.

Kyle Kubera, "Fredonia gets Grant for Barker Common Survey," *EO*, Dec. 6, 1991.

Kyle Kubera, "Committee to Develop Plan for Barker Common," *EO* Feb. 17, 1992, p. 3.

Kyle Kubera, "Urns Replaced in Fredonia Fountain," *EO*, June 4, 1992.

Landscape & Prospect [Syracuse, N. Y.]. *Barker Commons Renovation Plan* (Prepared for the Village of Fredonia, Fall, 1992). 19 pp. with 32 pp. of plans, charts, and supplemental data.

Kyle Kubera, "Detailed Plan Presented to Upgrade Barker Common," *EO*, Feb. 9, 1993, p. 3.

"Standout Sculptures: 80 From Area being Researched," *Jamestown Post-Journal*, Nov. 27, 1994, Sec. E, p. 1 [western Mark Fountain, and the WCTU fountain, both illustrated in color].

Old Main

Daniel D. Reiff, "Architectural Significance [of Old Main]," *EO*, May 16, 1973, p. 7 (People's Column).

Hank McKee, "Many Comments Made about 'Old Main' But the State Will Retain Ownership," *EO*, Feb. 6, 1974, p. 10.

Daniel D. Reiff, "Recycle Old Main," *EO*, Feb. 5, 1975, p. 7 (People's Column).

Deb Devlin, "F.S.U.C. Bids Farewell to Landmark," *The Leader*, Feb. 27, 1975, pp. 1, 3, 10, and 17 (3 photos).

"Floor Plan [of redesigned Old Main]," *EO*, May 7, 1975, p. 18 (1 plan).

Hank McKee, "Much of Old Main to be Razed under New Proposal by Sysol," *EO* Dec. 4, 1976 (1 photo).

Hank McKee, "Sysol Seeks HUD Help to Renovate Old Main," *EO*, March 2, 1977, p. 5.

Jim Fox, "UDC Contract Signed for $2.5 Million Old Main Housing for Elderly in Fredonia," *EO*, June 16, 1977.

"Old Main Has a Future," *EO*, June 17, 1977, p. 6 (Editorial).

"Old Main Apartments Could Be Ready by Late Summer 1978," *EO*, July 13, 1977.

"Old Main Renovation to Begin Soon as Final Transfer Papers are Made," *EO*, Dec. 17, 1977.

Gary Margiotta, "Feasibility Study Says 'Old Main' Auditorium Could Be Senior Center," *EO*, Feb. 17, 1978.

Gary Margiotta, "Many Senior Citizens' Services could be Performed in Center at 'Old Main'," *EO*, Feb. 20, 1978.

"Old Main Auditorium's Only Chance is as Senior Center," *EO*, March 2, 1978.

Doug Fenton, "Fredonia Village Board Gives Unanimous OK for Bond Sale to Start Old Main Project," *EO*, Nov. 28, 1978, pp. 1 and 9.

Doug Fenton, "Final Papers Approved, Work Starts Soon on Old Main Housing," *EO*, Feb. 6, 1979.

"Renovations Begin at Old Main in Fredonia," *EO*, March 17, 1979, p. 5 (3 photos).

Tom Jones, "Old Main: A Look at Its History and Its Future," *The Leader*, April 23, 1979, p. 2 (1 photo).

Doug Fenton, "Old Main, Saved from Demolition Ball, Has an Interesting History," *EO*, May 10, 1979, p. 12 (1 photo).

Doug Fenton, "Renovation of Former Old Main Building into Senior Citizen Housing is 35 Percent Done," *EO*, May 11, 1979 (1 photo).

"Old Main at the Heart of the Village," *EO*, Aug. 28, 1979 (6 photos).

Judy Lynn Lazerson, "Old Main Revived with New Look and Purpose," *The Leader*, Oct. 8, 1979, p. 3 (1 photo).

"Target Date for Completion of One Temple Square is Jan. 15," *EO*, Dec. 26, 1979, p. 5.

Cornerstone: The Fredonia Story, (8 page brochure, illus. with 9 photos and 2 line drawings, on the Fredonia Academy and Old Main) Fredonia, N.Y.: State University of New York College at Fredonia, [1986].

Holly Hewitt, "Genealogy of Fredonia's 'Sunset Hill'. Former Home of Judge Lambert," *EO*, April 11, 1975 (1 photo).

Ron Gustafson, "Fire Damages Fredonia Apartment Complex," *EO*, June 9, 1977, p. 1 (2 photos). [57-63 Temple St.]

Hank McKee, "Fire-Damaged Structure built in 1853 as 'Oriental Water Cure Building'," *EO*, June 9, 1977, p. 10.

Louise Ratkoski, "Like her Music, Jessie Hillman's Home Inspired Culture," *EO*, March 2, 1978, p. 10 (6 photos). [99 Central Ave.]

"'Lasting Impressions' Photo Exhibit Museum's Gift to Village of Fredonia," *EO*, July 26, 1979 (1 photo). [45-53 W. Main St.]

Sean Kirst, "Mark Twain's 'Honeymoon' With Fredonia Didn't Last," *EO*, March 30, 1981, p. 16 (4 photos). [36 Central Ave.]

Agnes Palazzetti, "Catalog 'History': Fredonia Professor to Study Area's Mail Order Houses," *Buffalo News*, Sept. 9, 1984, Sec. E, pp. 1 and 10 (5 photos). [193 Central Ave.]

"'The Wiley Cottage' is Tour Attraction," *EO*, July 18, 1985, p. 13 (1 photo from c. 1867). [28 Hamlet St.]

"Many Local Homes Came from Mail-Order Catalog," *EO*, Aug. 27, 1985, (1 photo). [130 Lambert Ave.]

Douglas Shepard, *The Barker Library and Museum: A History* (Fredonia, N. Y.: n.d.) (includes some details about early buildings and their interiors.)

[Daniel D. Reiff] *Homes of Historic Fredonia* poster, with 21 color photos. Fredonia, N. Y.: Fredonia Preservation Society, Inc., 1987; reprinted, 1993.

Kathryn S. Silliman, "Not Faster than a Walk," FPS *HPS*, II, 3, 1989 [on 19th c. exterior decorative details], (4 pp., 12 line details, 3 illus.)

Pam Milleville, "Literary Legend has Roots in Fredonia," (Mark Twain and 36 Central Ave.), *Leader*, Nov. 27, 1989.

Douglas Shepard, "The Lost Buildings of Fredonia," Part I, FPS *HPS*, IV, 2, 1991 (4 pp.; 2 illus.) [Houses moved from their original sites] [39 Spring St., 35 Curtis Pl.]

Douglas Shepard, "The Lost Buildings of Fredonia," Part II, FPS *HPS*, IV, 4, 1991 (3 pp.; 3 illus.) [24 White St., 120 Eagle St., 7 Lambert Ave.]

Daniel D. Reiff, "New Technology—over a Century Ago," *EO*, May 15, 1991, p. 3 (2 photos, 1 drawing). [27-29 Lambert Ave.]

Daniel D. Reiff, "House in Laona Shows Creative Architecture," *EO*, May 17, 1991, p. 3 (2 photos, 1 drawing). [Enoch Curtis]

[Daniel D. Reiff]. *A Book of Reminders...* (Calendar-book including 3 pp. intro., and 40 photos of details of Fredonia architecture) 28 pp. Fredonia, N. Y.: Fredonia Preservation Society, Inc., [1992].

Kathryn S. Silliman, "Sunset Hill," FPS *HPS*, V, 1, 1992 (4 pp.; 2 illus., 3 photos). [17 Central Ave.]

Kathryn S. Silliman, "From Ugly Duckling to Swan," FPS *HPS*, V, 3, 1992 (4 pp.; 8 photos). [73 Eagle St.]

Louise Ratkoski, "Keepsake Postcard Stirs Memories of Columbia Hotel and Historic Site," *EO*, Feb. 23, 1993 (1 photo).

Douglas Shepard, "Christmas Eve in Branksome Hall," *Barker Historical Newsletter*, Winter 1994, pp. 3–8 (includes some details about interior of 52 E. Main St. c. 1840)

Kathryn S. Silliman, "A Paean to Porches," FPS *HPS*, VIII, 2, 1995 (4 pp.; 7 photos). [210 Chestnut St., 211 Chestnut St., 1034 Chestnut Rd., 60 Forest Pl.]

Kathryn S. Silliman, "The McKinstry House," FPS *HPS*, IX, 1, 1996 (4 pp.; 7 photos). [87 Central Ave.]

Kathryn S. Silliman, "Crowning Glories," FPS *HPS*, IX, 2, 1996 [cupolas, turrets and towers] (4 pp.; 10 photos). [4587 W. Main Rd., 225 E. Main St., 99 Chestnut St., 67 E. Main St., 47 Eagle St., 42 Central Ave., 44 Temple St., 71 Central Ave., 54 Risley St.]

Todd Pignataro, "No Matter What the Street Name, This House is a Rock," *SO*, Jan 14, 1996 (1 photo). [81 E. Main St.]

Steve Palisin, "Cushing Street Home Noted for Historical Significance," *SO*, March 31, 1996 (1 photo). [36 Cushing St.]

Joan Josephson, "Victory for Victorian Homes," *SO*, June 2, 1996, Sec. D, p. 1 (4 photos). [73 Eagle St.]

"American Legion Post 59," *EO*, Oct. 13, 1996 (Special Legion Supplement), p. 3 (1 photo, 1950s). [156 E. Main St.]

[Daniel D. Reiff], "Walking Tour of Downtown Fredonia," Fredonia Preservation Society, Feb. 1997, (1 p. text, 1 p. map).

[Daniel D. Reiff], "Walking Tour: Houses of Fredonia" [Central Ave.], Fredonia Preservation Society, Feb. 1997 (1 p. text, 1 p. map).

[Daniel D. Reiff], "Walking Tour: Houses of Fredonia" [Temple St., Risley St., and Forest Pl.], Fredonia Preservation Society, Feb. 1997 (1 p. text, 1 p. map).

Doug Fenton, "Home Sweet Home: Preservation Society Plans Historic House and Garden Tour," *SO*, June 1, 1997, pp. D1 and 4 (9 photos).

Doug Fenton, "McKinstry House Important Part of Fredonia History," *SO*, June 15, 1997, p. D1 (1 photo). [97 Central Ave.]

Doug Fenton, "Newton Street House Part of Historic Homes, Gardens Tour," *SO*, July 27, 1997, p. D1 (1 photo), [29 Newton St.]

OTHER ITEMS OF LOCAL ARCHITECTURAL RELEVANCE

Daniel D. Reiff, "Dunkirk Architecture: Urban Renewal vs. Historic Preservation," *EO*, Nov. 23, 1973, p. 11 (2 photos).

Daniel D. Reiff, "Architectural Controls," *EO*, Nov. 27, 1973, p. 8 (People's Column).

"Architecture Vulnerable, Dr. Reiff Proclaims," *EO*, Sept. 13, 1975, p. 3.

"More Jewel Conover Materials are Deposited in Reed Library." *EO*, Oct. 22, 1976, p. 12.

Elizabeth L. Crocker, "How Natural Gas Was Found in Fredonia," *EO*, Feb. 22, 1977, p. 14 (1 photo).

Nelson Palmer, "New Architectural Awareness Growing," *Artifacts*, May, 1977, p. 1.

"Fredonia Renovation Committee Lauded by Chamber Directors," *EO*, May 17, 1977, p. 16.

Gary Margiotta, "New Sidewalks, Lighting to Brighten Downtown Fredonia; Merchants Reluctant to Change Overhanging Signs," *EO*, Dec. 10, 1977, p. 7.

Ellen Owen, "Recent Uncovering of East Main Street Trolley Lines Stirred Many Memories," *EO*, July 7, 1978, p. 8 (3 photos).

"Historic Preservation in Chautauqua County," *EO*, Dec. 20, 1978, p. 17.

Elizabeth L. Crocker, *ed. Fredonia, New York Sesquicentennial: Souvenir Historical Book 1829–1979*. Fredonia, N. Y.: Pioneer Press, 1979. 80 pp. including 64 illus.

"County, Pomfret Historian [Elizabeth Crocker] to be an Honored Guest at Banquet," *EO*, April 19, 1979, p. 10 (1 photo).

"National Trust Works to Save Historic Places," *EO*, May 15, 1979, p. 14 (1 photo, of Barker Common).

"Fredonia Architecture is Topic for Study in New FSUC Course," *EO*, Dec. 28, 1979, p. 7.

"[Video] Program on Early County Architecture Completed," *EO*, Oct. 31, 1980 (1 photo).

"Fredonia Architecture Course to Be Offered at Fredonia State," *EO*, Jan. 14, 1981 (2 photos).

"'Adaptive Reuse' Topic for Friends of Barker Library," *EO*, Feb. 26, 1981, p. 10.

"Chautauqua County Photos in Albany Mall," *EO*, Aug. 28, 1984, p. 10 (6 photos). [Mark Fountain, Fredonia State Campus, William Risley House]

"Profiles of Leaders in State and Local History: Elizabeth Crocker, Chautauqua County Historian," *New York State History Network*, Sept. 1984, pp. 2 and 5 (1 photo).

"Fredonia Architecture Topic for Dr. Reiff at National Conference," *EO*, April 12, 1985, p. 5.

John Moore, "Indian Artifacts Found at 'Dig'," *EO*, July 31, 1985 (2 photos).

"Fredonia Architecture Topic for FSUC Course," *EO*, Aug. 23, 1985, p. 5 (1 photo).

"Fredonia Architecture Course to be Offered at Fredonia State," *EO*, Aug. 21, 1986, p. 4 (2 photos).

"'Pomfret's Creek Communities' Exhibit Opens Thursday at Barker Library Museum," *EO*, May 20, 1987, p. 10 (1 photo).

"Walking Tour Sponsored by Preservation Society," *EO*, Sept. 9, 1987, p. 9 (1 photo).

Douglas H. Shepard, "Zattu Cushing's Revenge and How the County Fair Landed in N. Chautauqua," *EO*, Dec. 18, 1987, p. 6.

Sheila Borgstrom, "Local Canning Industry: Booming Business had Humble Beginnings," *EO*, Aug. 4, 1988, p. 7 (1 photo).

Sheila Borgstrom, "Local Canning Industry: Few Companies Remain to Tell History," *EO*, Aug. 5, 1988, p. 5 (2 photos).

Daniel D. Reiff, "Home Painting or Siding—the Right Way," *EO*, April 19, 1989, p. 11 (2 photos). [193 Central Ave.]

Daniel D. Reiff, "Home Painting or Siding—the Right Way," *EO*, April 20, 1989, p. 11 (3 photos). [30 Central Ave.]

Douglas H. Shepard, *Fredonia By Gaslight*, Fredonia, N. Y.: Historical Museum of the Darwin R. Barker Library, "Occasional Pamphlet Series" No. 1, 1989. 28 pp., incl. 5 illus.

Robert Macre, "Proposed Developer Challenged on Report by Fredonia Residents," *EO*, Nov. 16, 1989, p. 6.

Robert Macre, "Possible Moratorium, Master Plan are Discussed in Fredonia," *EO*, Dec. 15, 1989.

Robert Macre, "Future Growth of Fredonia is Discussed at Meeting," *EO*, Dec. 19, 1989, p. 5 (1 photo).

Robert Macre, "Concerns Regarding Growth in Fredonia are Taken to the CAC," *EO*, Jan. 9, 1990, p. 5.

Robert Macre, "Proposal Would Update Fredonia's Master Plan," *EO*, Jan. 9, 1990, p. 3.

Robert Macre, "Planning Board Approves Preliminary Plans for Construction of Townhomes," *EO*, Jan. 18, 1990.

Robert Macre, "In Fredonia and Pomfret, Street Names Bear Witness to Local History," *EO*, Feb. 20, 1990.

Robert Macre, "Environmental Impact Study Sought for Fredonia Townhome Development," *EO*, Feb. 22, 1990.

Daniel D. Reiff, "Responsible Renovation: Respecting the Integrity of the Older Home," *Erie & Chautauqua Magazine*, v. 8, no. 1 (1990), pp. 166, 168, 170 (5 photos). [30 Central Ave.]

Robert Macre, "Fredonia Architecture Discussed by Dr. Reiff at Meeting of CAC," *EO*, March 6, 1990, p. 3.

Donna N. Carlson, *1891: A Brief Historical Account of Life & Times 100 Years Ago*, Dunkirk and Fredonia, N.Y.: Lake Shore Savings & Loan Association, 1991. 12 page booklet, with 7 photos.

Kathryn S. Silliman, "A Burst of Color," FPS *HPS*, IV, 1, 1991 (3 pp.; 3 photos) [on changing styles in color of exterior house paint]. [155 Temple St., 29 Newton St., 134 Temple St.]

Kathryn S. Silliman, "Bandstands: A Cultural Symbol," FPS *HPS*, IV, 3, 1991 (2 pp.; 3 illus.)

Louise Ratkoski, "Squire White, Hezekiah Barker descendant Visits Fredonia to Research Family Roots," *EO*, May 9, 1991, p. 15 (1 photo).

Kyle Kubera, "Tornado Strikes Fredonia; Damage is Estimated between $2–3 Million," *EO*, July 13, 1992, pp. 1, 6, and 11 (11 photos).

Kyle Kubera, "State of Emergency Will be Lifted in Fredonia," *EO*, July 14, 1992, pp. 1 and 5 (4 photos).

Kyle Kubera, "Tornado Rips Through Fredonia," *EO*, "Special Edition," July 17, 1992, 8 pp. tabloid (12 photos, 1 map).

"Tornado in Fredonia," *EO*, Dec. 31, 1992, Sec. B., p. 5 (1 photo).

Kathryn S. Silliman, "Fredonia Brickwork," FPS *HPS*, VI, 3, 1993 (2 pp.; 12 drawings).

[Shirley Albaugh], "Circle of Trees Still Standing," *EO*, Mar. 5, 1993, p. 8 (1 photo).

"Postcards Recall an Earlier Fredonia," *EO*, March 29, 1993, Sec. B, p. 5 (12 photos).

Kyle Kubera, "Curtis Place Residents Want Street to Stay Brick," *EO*, May 25, 1993, p. 3.

Daniel D. Reiff, "Brick Streets Add Beauty to Neighborhood," *EO*, June 1, 1993, p. 4 (People's Column).

Patricia McQuiston, "Brick Streets Add Beauty, Historic Value to Fredonia," *EO*, June 8, 1994 (People's Column).

"Laying a Brick Street," *EO*, June 10, 1993, Sec. B., p. 16 (1 photo).

Kyle Kubera, "Leverett St. Residents Want Brick Pavement Retained," *EO*, June 15, 1993, p. 3.

Kyle Kubera, "Young People Make Futile Attempt to Keep Fredonia Street Brick," *EO*, Aug. 6, 1993 [Gillis Street].

Bill Barth, "If it Ain't Broke, Don't Fix Brick Leverett Street," *EO*, July 21, 1994 (People's Column).

Steve Palisin, "Plans for Leverett Street Paved Over in Fredonia," *EO*, Aug. 5, 1994, p. 3.

Douglas Shepard, "Fredonia's Burial Grounds and How they Grew," FPS *HPS*, VIII, 1, 1995 (4 pp.; 2 plans, 3 photos). [Pioneer Cemetery and Forest Hill Cemetery]

Steve Palisin, "'Visit Historic Fredonia' Brochure is in the Works," *EO*, Feb. 4, 1995.

Daniel D. Reiff, "Painting Your Home—The Right Way," *SO*, May 7, 1995, Sec. F, pp. 1 and 6 (4 photos). [160 Temple St., 44 Maple Ave.]

Daniel D. Reiff, "Artificial Siding has Real Appeal for the Homeowner," *SO*, May 21, 1995, p. 7 (4 photos). [233 Temple St., 30 Central Ave.]

Douglas H. Shepard, "First Buildings Lighted by Gas were in Fredonia," *EO*, May 24, 1995 (People's Column).

Steve Palisin, "Fredonia Seeks its Place in History," *EO*, June 1, 1995, pp. 1 and 2 (1 photo).

Steve Palisin, "New Brochure Promotes Historic Fredonia," *EO*, June 12, 1995, p. 3 (1 photo).

[Daniel D. Reiff] *Visit Historic Fredonia*. Six panel brochure with 10 photos and 1 map. (Village of Fredonia, 1995).

Daniel D. Reiff, "Identifying Mail-Order & Catalog Houses," *Old-House Journal*, Sept.–Oct. 1995, pp. 30–37 (27 photos). [37 Newton St., 38 Leverett St., 199 Water St.]

Steve Palisin, "Fredonia Ad-Hoc Committee Will Look at Zoning Update," *EO*, Jan. 17, 1996, p. 3.

Steve Palisin, "Village Residents Voice Concerns About Changing Housing Pattern," *EO*, Sept. 25, 1996, p. 3.

Douglas Shepard, "The Good Doctor White," *Barker Historical Newsletter*, Fall, 1996, pp. 2–5.

Kathryn S. Silliman, "Fredonia—A Century Ago," FPS *HPS*, X, 1 (1997) (6 pp., 3 photos).

"Dr. Reiff to Present Lecture on Architecture of Fredonia," *EO*, Feb. 10, 1997 (1 photo).

FPS Board of Trustees, "Revised Fredonia Zoning Code will Provide Huge Help," *SO*, Feb. 16, 1997, Sec. C, p. 3 (People's Column).

Maggie Duffy, "Fredonia Limiting Building Expansion," *EO*, Feb. 22, 1997, pp. 1 and 2.

Norma Braude, "Fredonia: Moratorium on Housing Conversions OK'd," *Buffalo News*, Feb. 25, 1997.

Douglas Shepard, "Sensational Fredonia," *Barker Historical Newsletter*, Spring, 1997, pp. 2–8 (details about location of early structures, 1807–15).

CAMPUS ARCHITECTURE

"$27 Million Fredonia State Building Program Unveiled," *EO*, March 20, 1964, pp. 1, 12, 13 (3 photos, 1 plan).

The Academic Center, State University College at Fredonia, New York (Fredonia, N. Y.: SUNY College at Fredonia Public Relations Office, [1969]). 28 pp. brochure with 19 photos, 17 floor plans, 1 section, and 1 site plan.

State University College at Fredonia Michael C. Rockefeller Arts Center (Albany, N. Y.: State University Construction Fund, [1969?]). 4 page brochure with 3 photos and 4 plans.

James Bailey, "Academic Center at Fredonia," *The Architectural Forum*, May, 1969, pp. 37–47 (15 photos, 1 plan, 4 diagrams).

Doug Fenton, "Dedication of Field House on Saturday to Highlight Fredonia St. Homecoming," *EO*, Sept. 30, 1983.

"Reed Library Addition Will Be Finished in 1992," *Statement*, Dec. 1989, p. 1 (1 photo, of groundbreaking).

"Library Work Progressing," *EO*, Feb. 8. 1990, p. 6 (1 photo).

"Library Work Continues," *EO*, July 30, 1990, p. 5 (1 photo) .

Michele Dubert, "Collapsed Crane will Delay College Project," *EO*, Aug. 31, 1990, pp. 1 and 3 (4 photos).

"Still Ahead of Schedule," *EO*, Sept. 5, 1990 (1 photo).

"Library Work Continues," *EO*, Sept. 21, 1990 (1 photo).

"Reed Library Addition Wins Design Award," *EO*, April 14, 1992 (1 photo).

"Renovation Work Continues on Original Reed Library," *EO*, Aug. 25, 1992 (1 photo).

Joy Stein, "Library Renovations Will Be Completed for Next Semester," *The Leader*, May 3, 1993, p. 8 (1 photo).

Daniel A. Reed Library. Fredonia, N. Y.: State University of New York College at Fredonia, 1994. (8 page brochure with 10 photos and 1 drawing).

"Reed Library Addition Architects Win Award," *EO*, Oct. 22, 1995.

ACKNOWLEDGMENTS

The original edition of this book required the helpful cooperation of many, in addition to those already cited in the Preface. At the Barker Historical Museum Miss Louise Belden and Mrs. Lawrence Urbscheit assisted me in tracking down old photographs and other data, as did librarian Louise V. Nowak at the Dunkirk Free Library. Marilyn Bomasuto typed the final draft of the original manuscript. Many people in Fredonia and Dunkirk—owners and former owners of houses, current occupants, and others—provided much useful information; writing this book would not have been possible without their help and cooperation. I repeat the 1972 list below; if I have inadvertently omitted any, my apologies, and thanks:

Mrs. Cosma Albana
Mr. Thomas A. Ambrose
The Reverend and Mrs. Roland L. Archer
Mrs. and Mrs. Francis Ardillo
Mr. and Mrs. Hack Arroe
Mrs. William B. Aular
Miss Louise F. Belden
Mr. and Mrs. Donald C. Brandt
The Reverend David J. Broad
Mr. Douglas Carter
Mr. Vincent DeJoe
Mr. Samuel L. Drayo
Mr. and Mrs. Robert F. Fortney
Mr. and Mrs. Harold L. Furness
The Reverend M. A. Garland
Mr. John Glenzer
Mr. and Mrs. Douglas F. Golder
Mrs. Daniel Graziano
Mr. and Mrs. Lewis H. Green
Mr. Joseph Gugino
Mrs. Lynn Hawkins
The Reverend Harold Hubert
Mrs. Ralph B. Jones
Mr. and Mrs. William Larson
Dr. and Mrs. Anthony Leone

Mrs. Sidney Limekiller
Mr. and Mrs. Therold Lindquist
Mr. and Mrs. Amerigo Lucci
Mrs. George Luke
Mr. Theodore Lutz
Mr. and Mrs. James P. Mahoney
Mr. and Mrs. James Mooney
Mr. and Mrs. Albert Morrison
Mr. and Mrs. Mason R. Nash
Mr. John F. Nolan
Mr. and Mrs. Nelson J. Palmer
Dr. and Mrs. Ronald A. Passafaro
Mrs. Harry Peters
Mr. and Mrs. Robert Quayle
Mr. B. Robert Rand
Mrs. Florence Rich
Mrs. Jean Richmond
Dr. and Mrs. J. Carter Rowland
Mr. and Mrs. Richard Russell
Mr. and Mrs. Edward J. Sweet
Mr. and Mrs. George Tadt
Mrs. Arthur D. Toomey
Mr. Joseph N. van der Voort
Mr. George Weaver

For the 1997 revised edition (in addition to those mentioned in the Preface) I must add the names of several more local residents who helped in one way or another:

Anthony O. and Amy Bartholomew
Paul A. Bowers
Jean B. Harper
Priscilla Koch
Concetta Lanza
Wally Latimer

John Lowther
Marilyn Maytum
Julius and Laura Paul
L. Walter and Jean Schultze
Carol Case Siracuse
Jack and Marcy Sternisha

My special thanks to the Board of Trustees of the Fredonia Preservation Society, Inc., whose interest, and confidence, in this project made its republication possible; and to Elaine LaMattina and Linda Cowan of White Pine Press for all their help in the production of this book. Last but not least, a heartfelt thank you to Joanne Foeller who word-processed the various Byzantine drafts of this study with great accuracy, and good humor.

Most of the photographs—and the copy work from catalogs, books, and vintage photos—used in this study were taken by myself between 1970 and 1997. My sincere thanks to all those who lent material, and permitted my photographing within their homes or businesses. Most of the pattern books and catalogs used are reprints or originals from my own collection. The issues of *The American Architect and Building News* I consulted are in the Buffalo and Erie County Public Library. Below are given the sources of illustrations not specifically identified in captions. Some of the photos I printed from copy negatives produced from my color slides; for these negatives my thanks to Ronald Warren, Deborah Lanni, and Robert Siedentop. And thanks as well to Colin Plaister of SUNY Fredonia's Information Technology Services for making a black-and-white darkroom available for my use in printing the many new photos which improve this edition.

The Architecture of Henry Hobson Richardson in North Easton Massachusetts (1969)—181
Archives and Special Collections, Reed Library—258
Charles H. Atherton—38
Mr. and Mrs. William B. Auler—95
Barker Historical Museum—18, 35, 42, 43, 46, 48, 51, 59, 82, 83, 92, 126, 127, 138, 140, 141, 143, 145, 147, 162, 260, 273
Elizabeth L. Crocker—39, 55, 91
Dunkirk Free Library—52
Fredonia Baptist Church—156
Mr. and Mrs. Harold L. Furness—121, 123, 124
Mr. and Mrs. Douglas F. Golder—102
Mrs. Albert Morrison—79
Mrs. Harry Peters—164, 165
Photographer/source unknown—242, 285
Shepp's World's Fair Photographed (1893)—193
Mr. and Mrs. John Sternisha—131
Bruno Taut, *Modern Architecture* (1929)—230
Trinity Episcopal Church—87

Front cover: *Top*, Elijah Risley, Jr. Mansion (1844-45) by John Jones; *bottom*, SUNY Fredonia Campus (1967–71) by I. M. Pei and Partners (photos by Daniel D. Reiff)

Stanley-Whitman House (Farmington): 117
Stapf Building (Dunkirk): 24
Standard Homes Co.: 110
State University College: 31, 120
Steele Hall: 124
Gustav Stickley: 104
Alford Stoddard: 44
D.F. Straight Building: 9
Stratford-on-Avon (England): 112
George Edmund Street: 78
William Strickland: 25, 38, 48
Strong Place Baptist Church (Brooklyn): 80, 81
Stuart and Revett: 15
Louis Sullivan: 18, 98, 100
Henry F. Sysol, Jr.: 2

Tadt's Old Mill: 77
Frank Tarbox: 70
H.L. Taylor: 66, 100
Taylor House: 48
G.W. Teft: 76
Barbara Lewis Thompson: iv
Trinity Episcopal Church: 22, 23, 28, 50, 51
St. George Tucker House (Williamsburg): 110
Rev. Thomas P. Tyler: 50

United Methodist Church, See: Methodist Church
Urban Renewal: 1
United States Post Office: 108, 109
United States Treasury Building: 40, 41

Mies van der Rohe: 114, 122
J. Nelson van der Voort, Jr.:108
Vassall-Longfellow House (Massachusetts): 97
Calvert Vaux: 17, 54, 55, 66, 67, 128
Villa Rotunda (Vicenza): 14

Village Hall: 5, 6, 7, 28, 29, 50, 134
Mrs. Lydia Vinton: 70

E.F. Warren House: 58, 59, 60
Judge Warren: 56
Ronald Warren: v
Dr. John A. Waterhouse: 70, 82
Waterhouse House: 83, 84
Webb & Knapp: 120
Westover Plantation (Virginia): 109
Marcus Whiffen: iv
D.A. White: 38
Squire White: 27, 32, 33
White Inn: 2, 24
G.H. White Planing Mill: 76, 77
G.W. Wiley: 76
Richard Williams: 32
Williams Center: 120, 123, 124
Ward Willits House (Chicago): 17
Wilson & Colburn Ice House: 76
Edward Woleben: 36
Richard Woleben: 36, 37
Woleben Block: 38
Robert Wolfers: 23, 70, 146 n.27
Robert Wolfers House: 54, 55
Women's Christian Association: 74
Women's Christian Association House: 75
Ronald Wooden: 2
William M. Woollett: 128
Christopher Wren: 14
Frank Lloyd Wright: 17, 18, 100, 114, 116, 118, 126
Jesse G. Wright: iv
Sir Jeffrey Wyatville: 52, 53

William Zeckendorf: 120

ADDRESS INDEX

The page numbers directly after the street name lead to references to the street in general terms; the indented numbers refer to specific houses and the pages on which the commentary may be found.

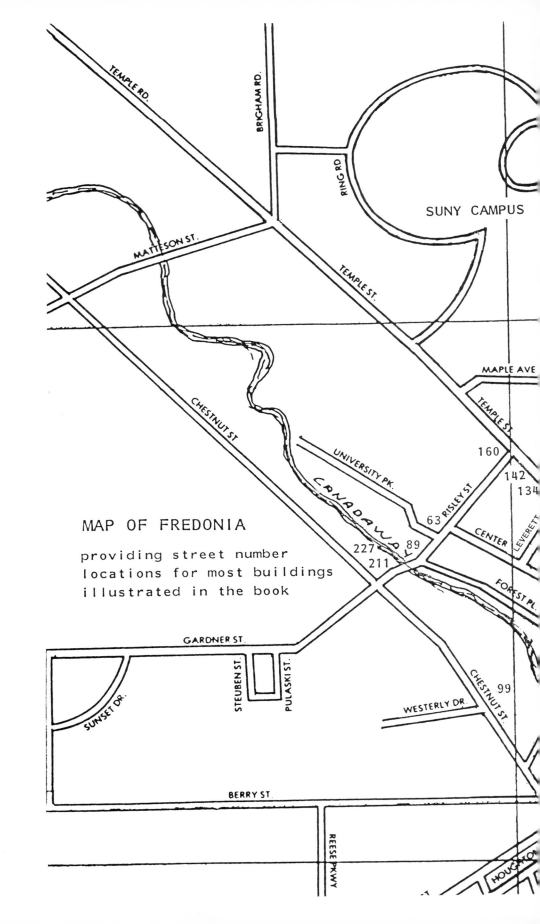

MAP OF FREDONIA

providing street number
locations for most buildings
illustrated in the book

Daniel D. Reiff, Professor of Art History at the State University of New York College at Fredonia, graduated from Phillips Academy, received his B.A., M.A., and Ph.D. degrees from Harvard University, and did graduate work at the Université de Liège, Belgium. He has taught at Baylor University, and in 1969–70 was Acting Assistant Secretary of the U.S. Commission of Fine Arts, Washington.

Professor Reiff has conducted architectural research and surveys for many years, including projects for the Historic American Buildings Survey in Georgetown (Washington, D.C.) and in Cambridge, Massachusetts. The two Georgetown surveys which he co-authored were published in the series "Selections from HABS."

Since joining the Fredonia faculty in 1970 he has been active in architectural surveys and historic preservation in Fredonia as well as Chautauqua County. During the summers of 1975 and 1976 he was Project Director and Editor for five county-wide architectural surveys conducted by graduate students under the sponsorship of the county arts council. He was a co-founder of the Fredonia Preservation Society in 1984 (and became its President in 1995). In 1986 he received an Architectural Heritage Honor Award from the Preservation League of New York State for his work.

Professor Reiff has published widely in the field of American architecture. His books include *Washington Architecture 1791–1861: Problems in Development* (1971); *Architecture in Fredonia 1811–1972: Sources, Context, Development* (1972); and *Small Georgian Houses in England and Virginia: Origins and Development Through the 1750s* (1986). This book, published by the University of Delaware Press, received their 1983 award for "the best book-length manuscript on Early American culture prior to 1840." His articles have appeared in the *Journal of the Society of Architectural Historians*, *Journal of Architectural Education*, *Nineteenth Century*, *Historic Preservation*, and others. He contributed five articles to the *Macmillan Encyclopedia of Architects* (four volumes, 1982). A recent book-length study, "Houses from Books: The Influence of Treatises, Pattern Books, and Catalogs in America, 1738–1950" is being reviewed for publication.

His professional memberships include the College Art Association, Society of Architectural Historians, Victorian Society in America, SPNEA, Preservation League of N. Y. State, and The National Trust for Historic Preservation. He lives in Fredonia with his wife Janet, and two sons, Nicholas and Michael, in a vernacular Queen Anne style house of c. 1903.